IMAGES
of America

EARLY YUMA

On the Cover: Frame structures quickly became kindling in the sizzling heat of Yuma. There to combat the flames were Yuma's early firemen and the city's cherished hose carts. In 1899, businessman E. F. Sanguinetti purchased a small hose cart to protect his store. Playfully in line with its diminutive size, Sanguinetti assembled a junior fire department. The fire boys of the Sanguinetti Fire Department, beaming in the spotlight, became the stars of Yuma's early town pride parades.

IMAGES
of America

EARLY YUMA

Robert Nelson

Arizona Historical Foundation

ARCADIA
PUBLISHING

ISBN 978-0-7385-4857-9

Published by Arcadia Publishing
Charleston, South Carolina

Printed in the United States of America

Library of Congress Catalog Card Number: 2006926129

For all general information contact Arcadia Publishing at:
Telephone 843-853-2070
Fax 843-853-0044
E-mail sales@arcadiapublishing.com
For customer service and orders:
Toll-Free 1-888-313-2665

Visit us on the Internet at www.arcadiapublishing.com

Dedicated to Uncle John and all others,
Quechan to Mormon, who dared to go first.

Contents

ACKNOWLEDGMENTS

This book would not have been possible without the guidance of Carol Brooks, archivist at the Arizona Historical Society's Sanguinetti House Museum in Yuma, who for months dealt with myriad irritating requests from the author with skill and good humor. The research and writings of Rosalie Crowe, Sidney Brinckerhoff, Frank Love, and Yuma's chief newspaperman for more than 30 years, John Dorrington, were also critical, as were more than 100 academic and popular works from the last century and a half. Finally, this book wouldn't exist if not for Prof. Jack August, the executive director of the Arizona Historical Foundation, who not only assisted this project but forged a relationship between the foundation and Arcadia Publishing during the making of this book that will benefit history and historians in Arizona for decades to come.

INTRODUCTION

And thus began another day of intolerable glare and heat. Conversation lagged; no topic seemed to have any interest except the thermometer, which hung in the coolest place on the boat; and one day when Major Worth looked at it and pronounced it one hundred and twenty-two in the shade, a grim despair seized upon me, and I wondered how much more heat human beings could endure.

—Martha Summerhayes,
writing of her steamboat trip up the Colorado River to Fort Yuma in August of 1874

Even Yuma's first residents, the Quechan, vacationed in the mountains during summer. The Quechan would plant and harvest their crops during the cool months, then caravan west to the San Diego Mountains to avoid the oppressive summers at the confluence of the Colorado and Gila rivers.

Prior to the damming of the Colorado and Gila, which meet within a stone's throw of Yuma, the valley's intense heat was also combined with humidity and apocalyptic swarms of mosquitoes. Before the dams, the Colorado River often overran and always swelled from snowmelt in the vast Rocky Mountains.

This, after all, is the violent river that forged the Grand Canyon, the river so mighty it hauled much of the great void. When the rivers receded during summer, miles of boggy bank line, a gumbo of fine silt, served as incubator for mosquitoes and steam engine to the otherwise dry Sonoran air. No matter how tough the race, no matter how well the people adapted, the summers here were just plain miserable. But that steaming deposited silt, soil ground from the eons of sediment laid, stratified and uplifted over the American West, was rich like few others on earth.

Spaniards first passed through the area in 1540, following in the footsteps of prehistoric Paytan Indians who discovered that the geological chokepoint just beneath the confluence of the rivers was the easiest place at which to access and ford the notoriously fickle current. The Quechan first made contact with the Spaniards in 1603. Near the beginning of the 18th century, Spaniards again in search of Cibola, the mythical Seven Cities of Gold that conquistadors somehow didn't realize were mythical, began moving through the area. Other Spaniards such as Fr. Eusebio Francisco Kino, the fearless and beloved padre explorer who crossed the Colorado River several times beginning in 1700, were searching for souls to save as well as trade routes between New Spain and the California coast.

Men of God from Spain, who respected the native people of the river—Quechan, Cocopah, Mohave—were welcomed and often adored. Those who came to subjugate, though, arrived with one foot already in the grave. As outsiders began lingering amid their fields, and building ferries at the strategic crossing, the Quechan began staying permanently to protect their lands.

During the mid-18th century, as American colonists in the East became frustrated with British colonial rule, the Quechan came under increased subjugation by Spanish political and military men wanting Mission La Purisma Conception to be more a strategic post than a House of God.

In 1781, Quechan rebels rose up and routed out the Spaniards. The crossing would remain strongly in Quechan hands long after the Mexican War of Independence from Spain in 1821. As they stayed longer, the Quechan began building more substantial homes of poles, mud, thatch, and arrowweed that would serve as the basic architecture for Native Americans, Spaniards, Mexicans, and, finally, Anglos until the beginning of the 20th century.

Kit Carson passed through the here in 1829 with trappers and again in 1846 to guide Col. Stephen Kearny and a band of soldiers trying to secure former Mexican lands between Santa Fe and San Diego. Most every explorer took various roads generally parallel to what is now called the Gila Trail. Col. Philip St. George Cooke followed with the Mormon Battalion along this path, creating the first transcontinental road across the southwest. Forty-niners crossed heading west on Cooke's Road for the gold fields of the Sierra Nevada. Filibusters, or scalp hunters, crossed heading south for mercenary riches in Mexico, and miners passed in search of riches like those found by Jacob Snively 20 miles up the Gila from Yuma in 1857. American soldiers crossed heading to the forts of Arizona. The Butterfield Stage began passing through beginning in 1858. Union troops from California crossed here to chase the Confederates back to the old South. The great steamboats of the Colorado Steam Navigation Company dropped anchor in Yuma with people and goods that had traveled 2,500 miles from San Francisco. From here, giant 20-mule freight wagons rumbled out to the gold mines throughout the region. The Southern Pacific train bridge, as well as the great highway linking the Southern United States, crossed the area.

Like earlier Yumans, modern residents cross the river on their way west to the cool mountain air or the refreshing sea breezes surrounding Mission San Diego de Alcala.

The reason then that a thriving city exists here is simple: every kind of human coming from every direction for all kinds of reasons has used this spot as their crossing point of the American Nile.

There is money to be made at the crossroads, as long as one can survive at the crossroads. But once the U.S. Army set up shop for good at Fort Yuma in 1852, it became clear to ambitious pioneers that a good living could be made here selling goods to travelers and soldiers. And with military protection, these businesspeople might just live long enough to enjoy the fruits of their labor.

Charles Poston and Herman Ehrenberg established the first incarnation of Yuma, Colorado City, near the fort in 1854. In 1858, Colorado City was renamed Arizona City. In 1873, the name was changed to Yuma, after the Yuma Indians.

Whatever its name, the spot built a hellish reputation. "It was said to be the very hottest place that ever existed," wrote Summerhayes. To Yuma's early businessmen and promoters, people like Jose Maria Redondo, David Neahr, and E. F. Sanguinetti, the relentless bad press got very old. These settlers saw the potential of their "Gateway City" with the fine farmlands and winters, the healthful sunshine and air, and the powerhouse trade center.

These early settlers lived and thrived where others feared to die. They turned adversity into advantage and, with grand civic plans and momentous efforts to channel river water into irrigation water, set the stage for the booming city that now stretches far into what once was desert and farmland.

This then is a photographic tribute to those indomitable early pioneers of this feared landscape. They lived in a tougher time, and they were considered the toughest of their time. As such, the people of Early Yuma were truly a breed of their own.

One

First Residents

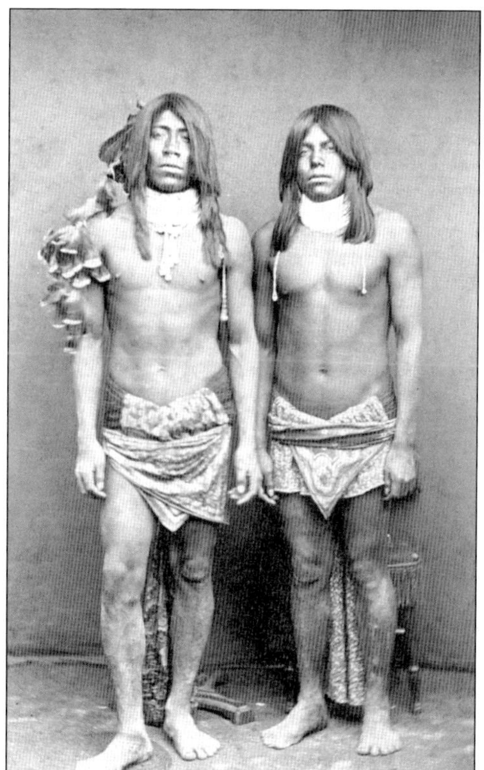

The Quechan were a favorite subject of Elias A. Bonine, a photographer from Pasadena who made a living selling hundreds of images of Quechan and other Colorado River tribes. Although the Quechan were generally peaceful people, they were at the same time, as implied in this image, ferocious warriors. In 1781, sick of increasing subjugation by the Spanish, the Quechan rebelled, killing 55 people and taking another 76 captive. They took control of the river crossing, making it increasingly difficult for Spain to get supplies to its colonies in California. In time, the Spanish influence faded in the region.

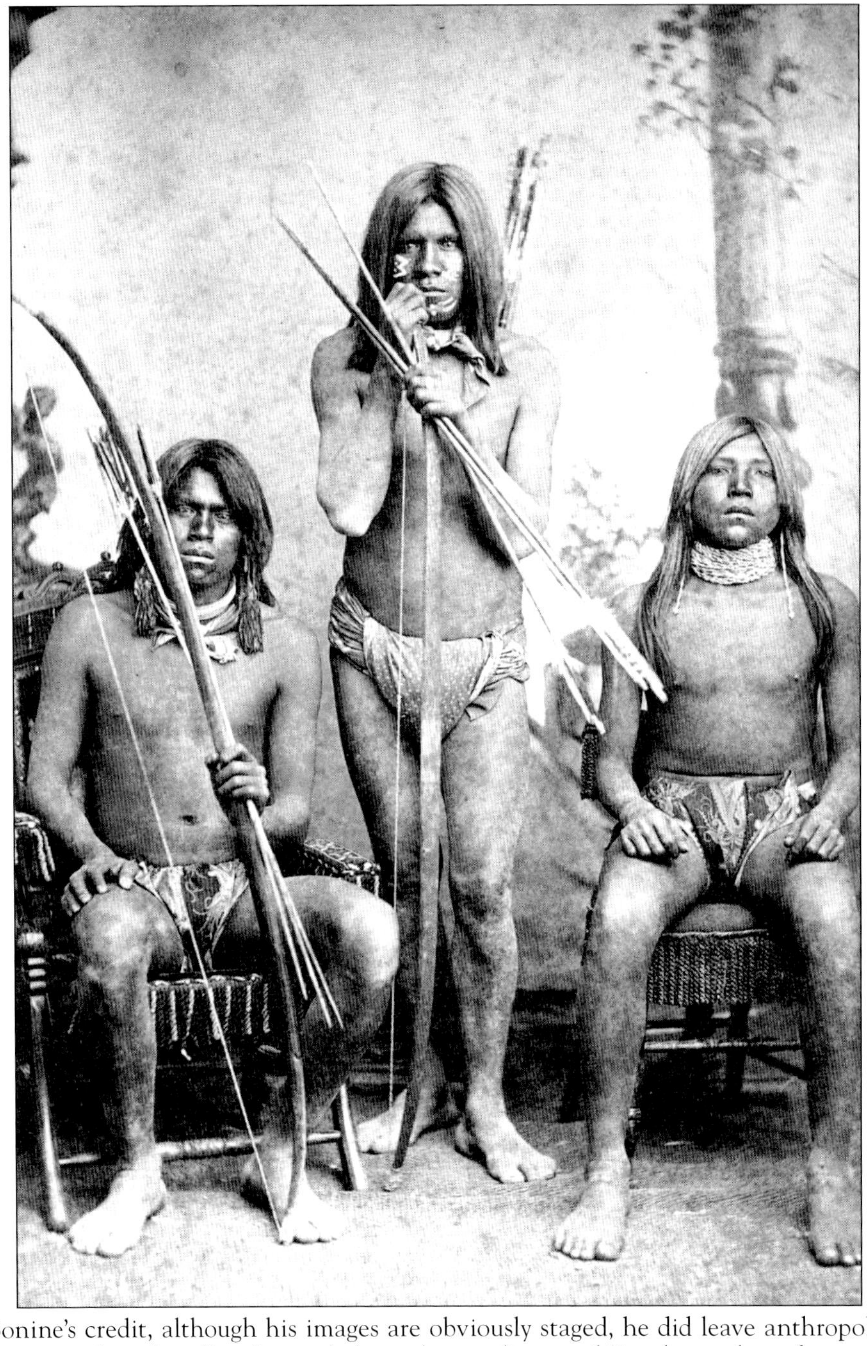

To Bonine's credit, although his images are obviously staged, he did leave anthropologists, historians, and modern Quechan tribal members a glimpse of Quechan culture frozen around 1875. About half the tribe's food came from farming the rich silt deposits near the river, where they raised wheat, beans, corn, squash, and melons. Women and children of the tribe gathered the bean pods of the mesquite and screw bean trees, which provided the base foodstuff for the tribe once the beans were ground into meal and formed into cakes. When it was time for war, the Quechan men adorned themselves to create fear in their enemy. As one U.S. Army officer said in the 1880s, the Quechan "decorate themselves most splendidly for war."

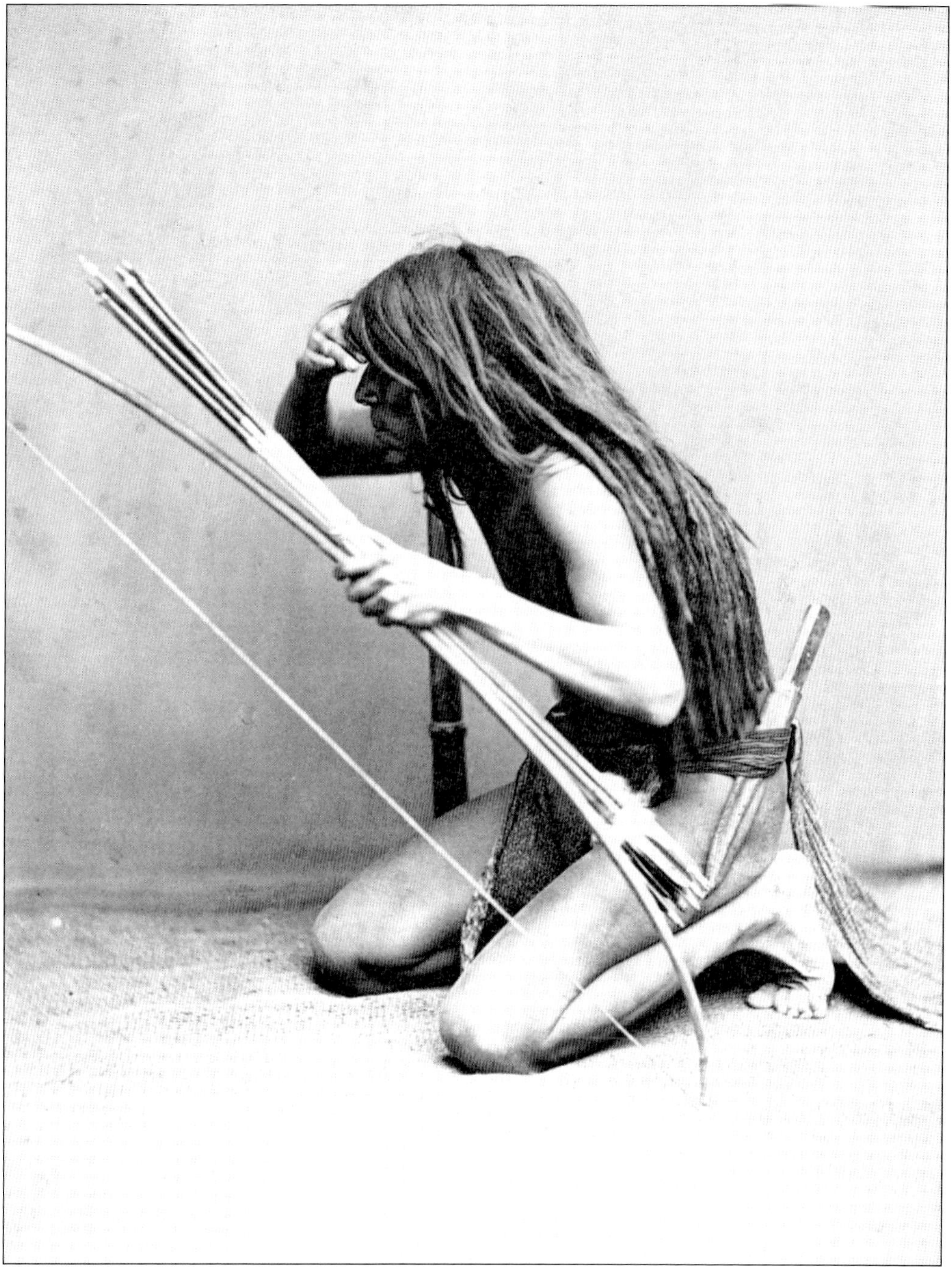

The Quechan men were considered fine hunters. For this image, Bonine, who set up an office in Yuma in 1881, staged a photograph in which a Quechan man demonstrates how he stalks his prey. While mesquite beans and crops from the river bottoms provided most of the foodstuff, the meat brought home by the hunters made up the prized meals. The hunters typically went out in search of rabbit, deer, and birds. At the time of this photograph, Bonine's images went for as little as $3 a dozen. As of 2006, some of Bonine's more striking images of Yuma Indians were selling for more than $1,000.

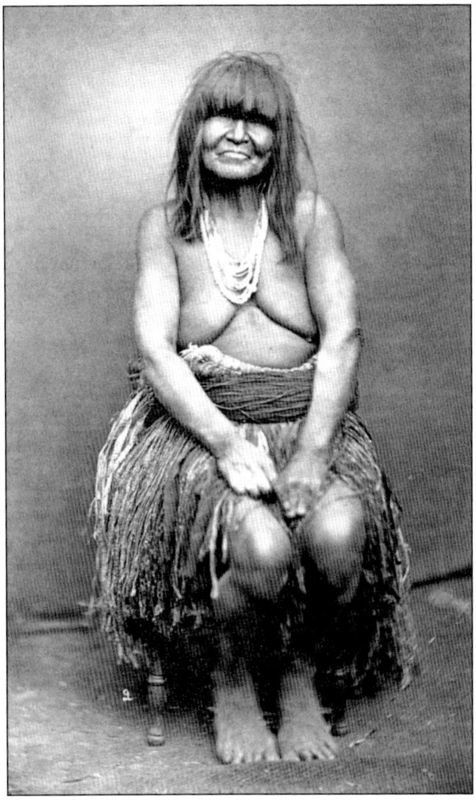

To deal with the summer heat, the Quechan women went torsos exposed, a style of dress that Spanish, Mexican, and Anglo women condemned in public but often praised in private as the only sensible way to dress in a Yuma summer. And those good Christian women shocked by such nudity in public were often the same women, bound in Victorian corsets and heavy full-length wool dresses, who were so often seen at Yuma events fainting in public.

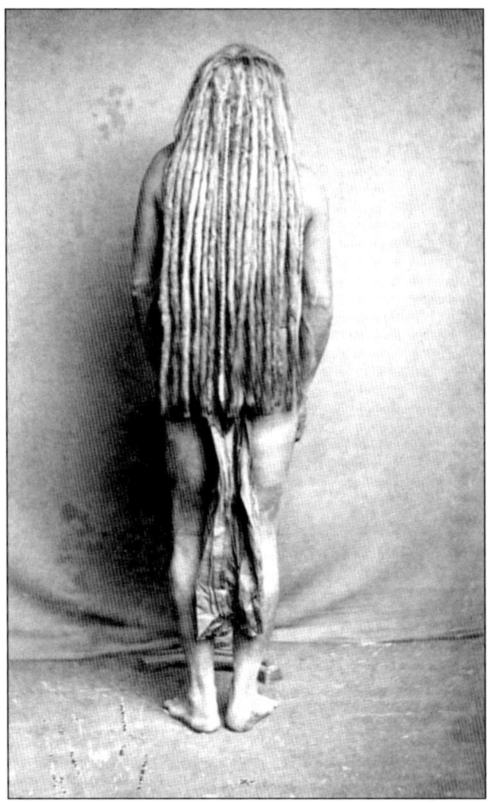

This time-consuming hairstyle was accomplished by wrapping the hair around long sticks and caking each strand with mud. Once the mud dried, the sticks were withdrawn to create long tubes of hair.

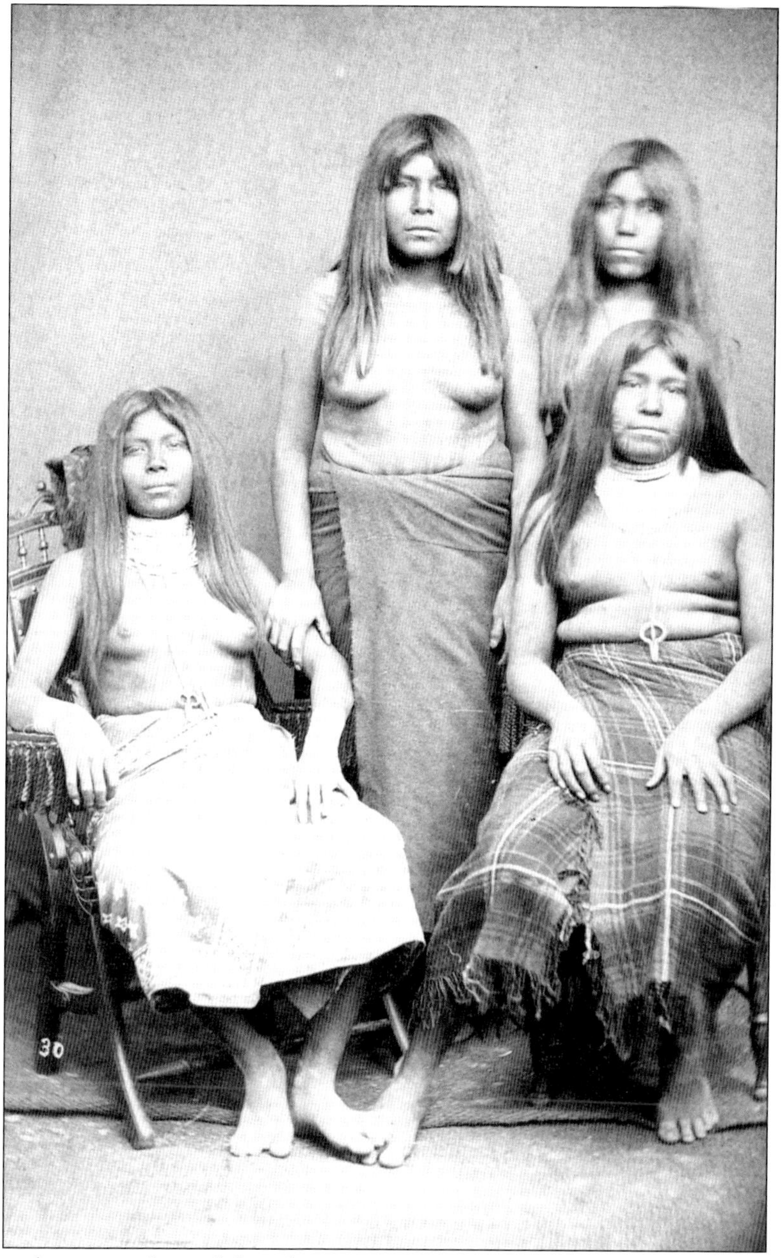

These four girls wear traditional Quechan aprons while the two (likely) older girls in front also wear traditional necklaces. Both girls in front also are wearing Jew's harps (now, more often termed "juice harps"), the cheap and very portable European instrument that the Quechan women enjoyed as jewelry. Those who know the story of the Oatman massacre will recognize the face tattoo on the girl at front right. The blue lines running down from the chin with triangles on both cheeks signify that she is married. The markings are nearly identical to those tattooed on the face of Olive Oatman, the famed lone survivor of the Oatman massacre along the Gila Trail who lived one year with the Yavapai and later the Mohave, a Yuma tribe with traditions similar to the Quechan. After she was ransomed at Fort Yuma in 1856, Oatman vehemently denied that she had been willingly married by tribal custom.

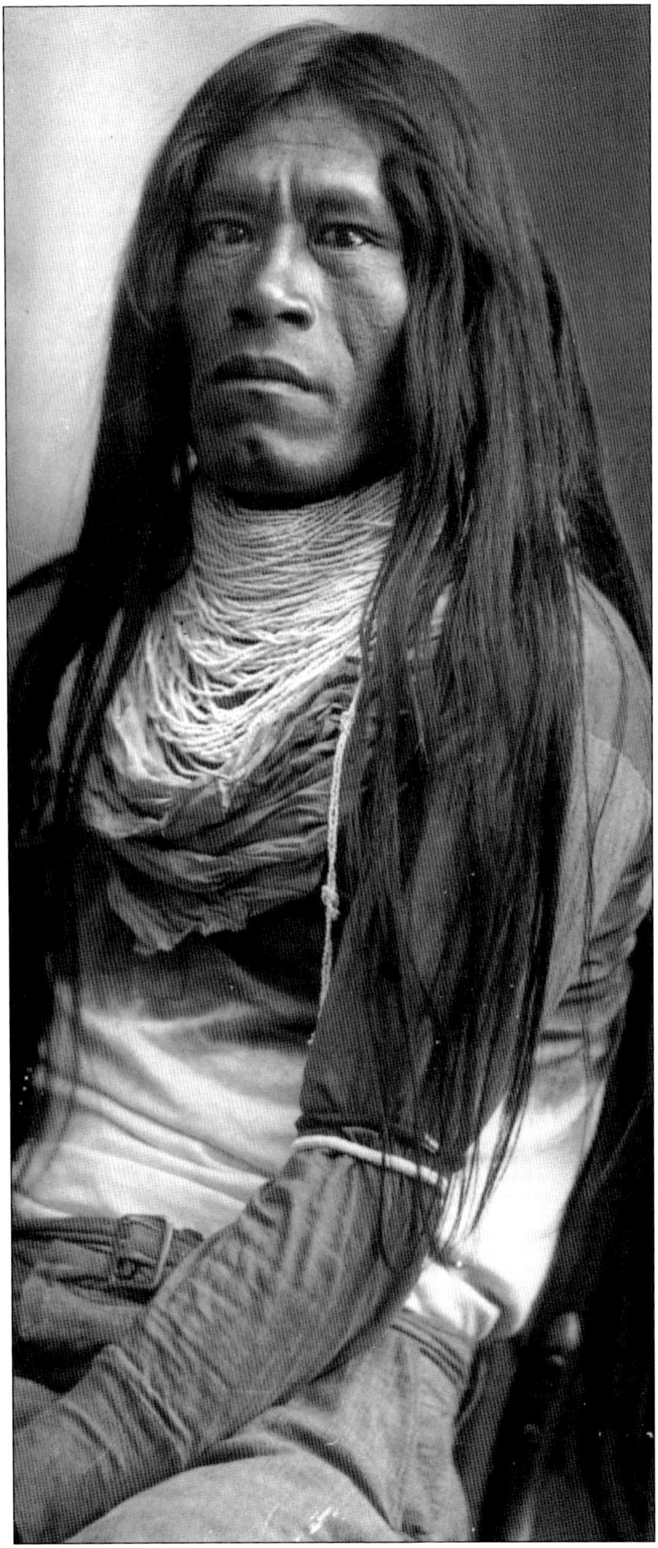

By the time this photograph was taken in 1912, Cocopah Jim was famous for his scouting skills and his immense knowledge of the Colorado River. The Cocopah navigated the river on tule rafts, using poles to work their way down to the mouth of the Colorado River to harvest wild wheat. Like the Quechan, the Cocopah would often travel in the summer to visit Kumeyaay friends and family in the high country to the west. The present Cocopah Reservation was created 13 miles south of Yuma in 1917. From the 1880s on, representatives of the tribes and concerned Yuma citizens, led by the editor of the *Arizona Sentinel*, petitioned the U.S. government to honor the promises made to the tribes. Still, more often than not, the Quechan and Cocopah people were left by the federal government to languish.

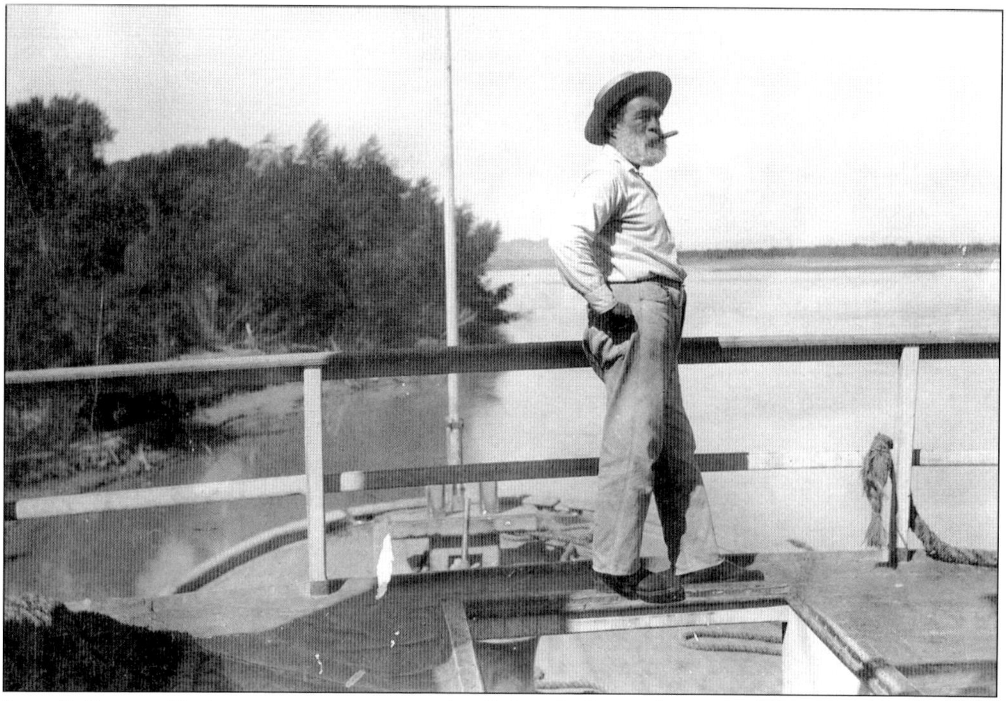

Isaac Polhamus likely spent more time on the Colorado River than any other man, first working for George Johnson as captain of the *Colorado*, then buying Johnson's company and renaming it the Colorado Steam Navigation Company. His famed business controlled transportation on the Colorado until the dams ended the era of the steamer.

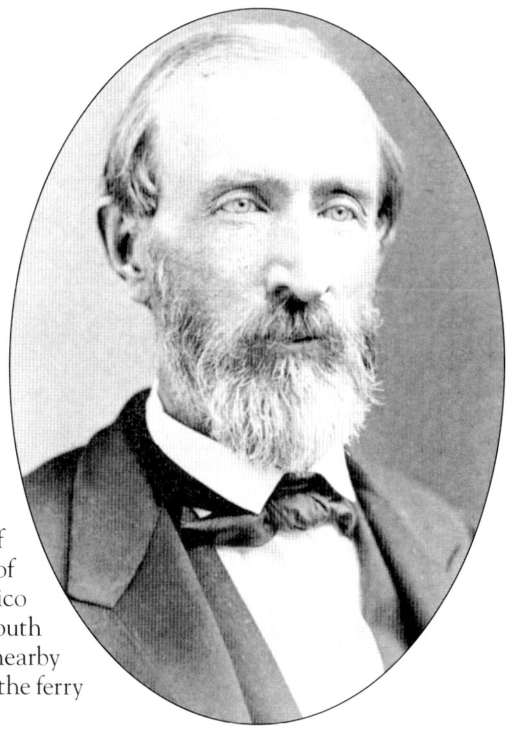

L. J. F. Jaeger was one of the first permanent residents of what would become Yuma, arriving from San Francisco after he and a group of entrepreneurs there heard of the large influx of people moving through the area from New Mexico and Mexico. Jaeger set up a ferry nine miles south of present Yuma, building the flatboats out of nearby cottonwood trees. Later, Jaeger began operating the ferry near Fort Yuma.

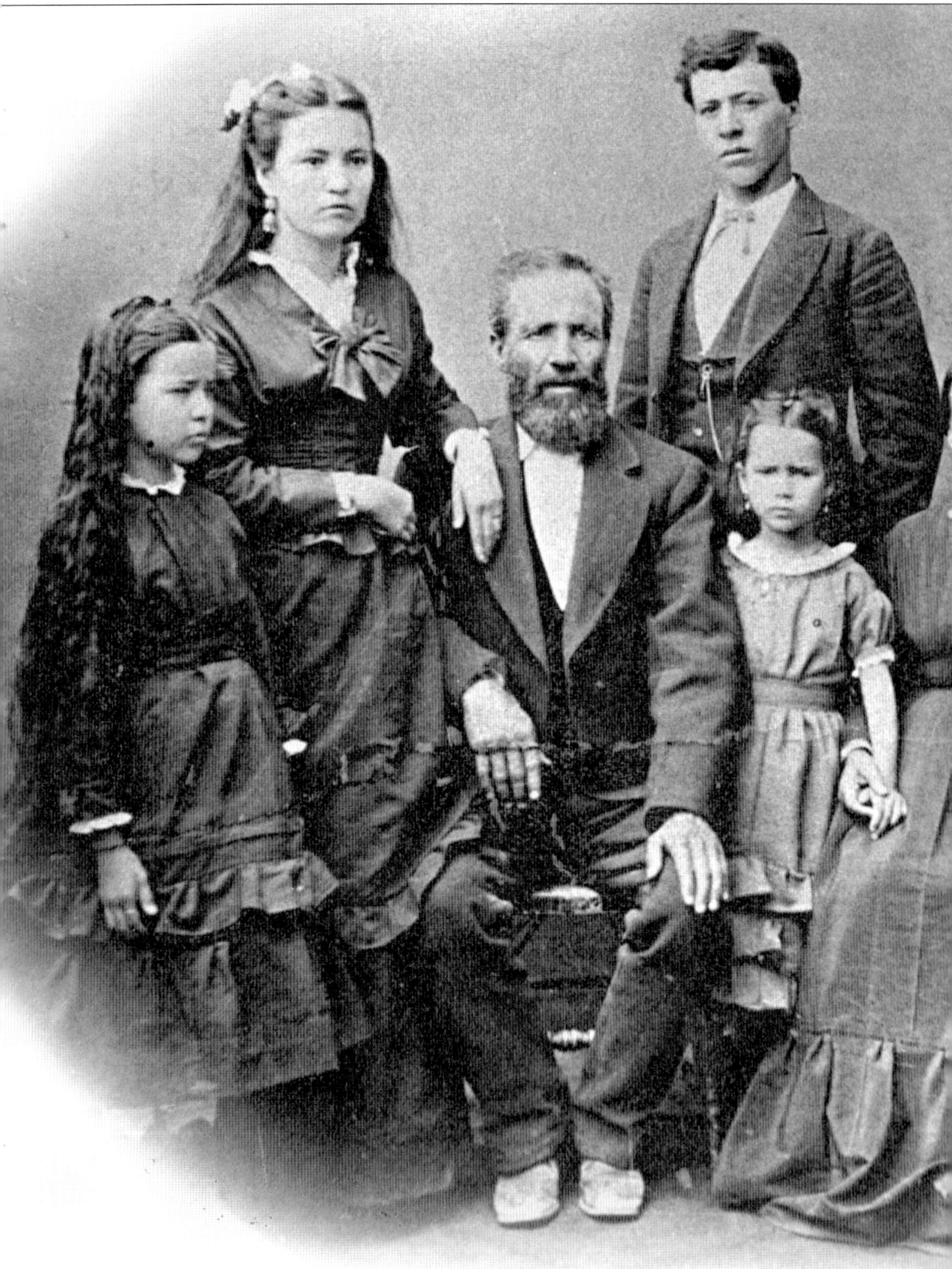

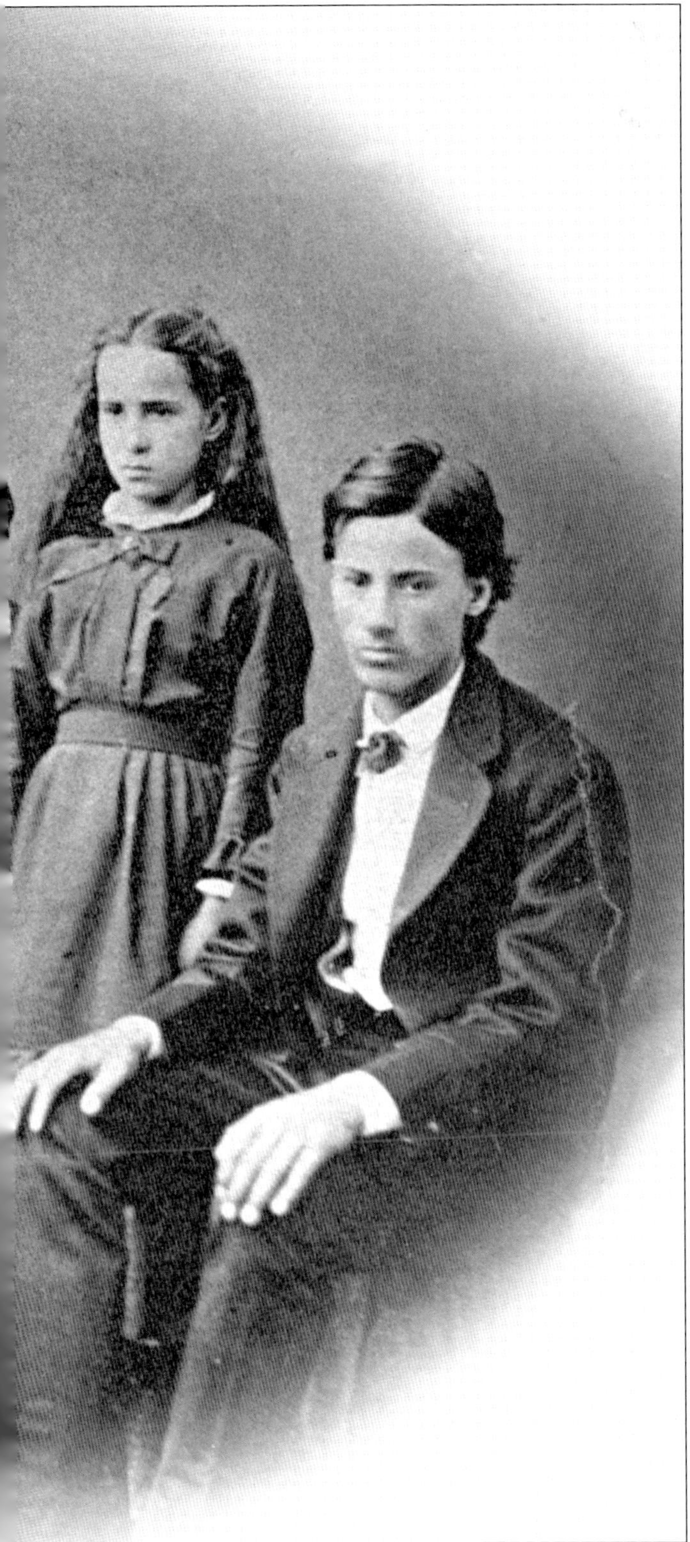

Jose Maria Redondo (seated with the beard) is considered not only the patriarch of one of Yuma's most respected families but patriarch of the city as well. In the mid-1860s, Redondo dammed the Gila River about 15 miles east of its confluence with the Colorado River and built 27 miles of irrigation canals. Along these canals, he established La Hacienda de San Ysidro, a 3,000-acre ranch with 2,500 head of cattle and a farm producing barley, oats, wheat, alfalfa, corn, and bran. While Redondo's brother operated the ranch, Jose went looking for markets. While serving in the Territorial Legislature of Arizona, Redondo is credited with wrestling away the $25,000 territorial prison from the new settlement of Phoenix.

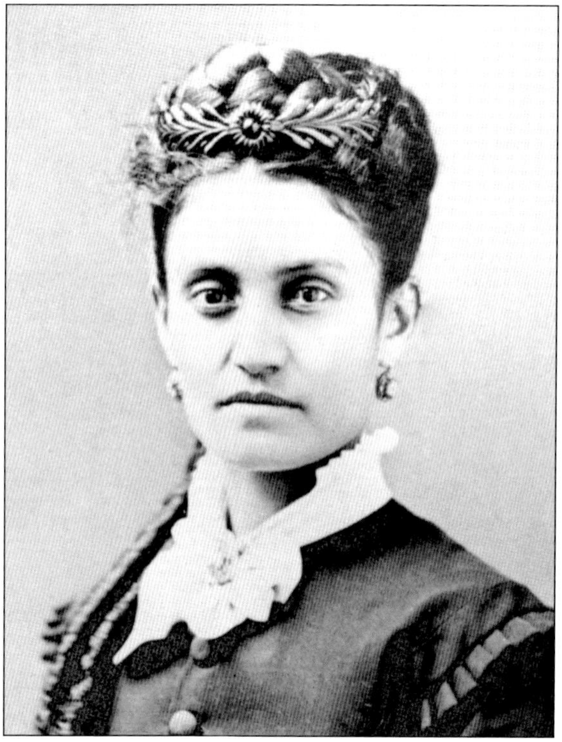

Born in Altar, Sonora, Sacramento Sambrano Polhamus, wife of Isaac Polhamus, had one of many early marriages between Mexican and Americans in the Southwest that promoted a racial harmony in the region unseen in other parts of the country. It is said Isaac never learned to speak Spanish and Sacramento never learned to speak English, which, they playfully claimed, was the secret to their happy marriage.

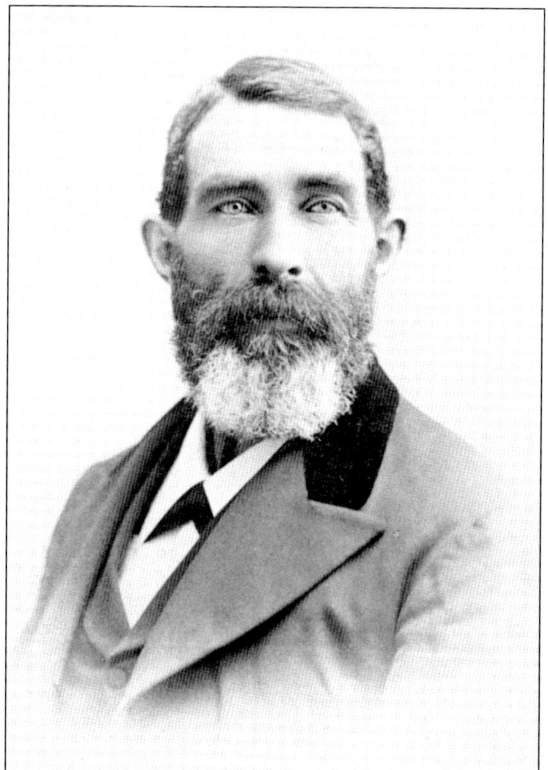

Like many of the steamboat captains on the Colorado, young Isaac Polhamus gained experience with boats along the California coast. Prior to working on the Sacramento River beginning in 1849, Polhamus, a New York native, had worked on the Hudson River with his father.

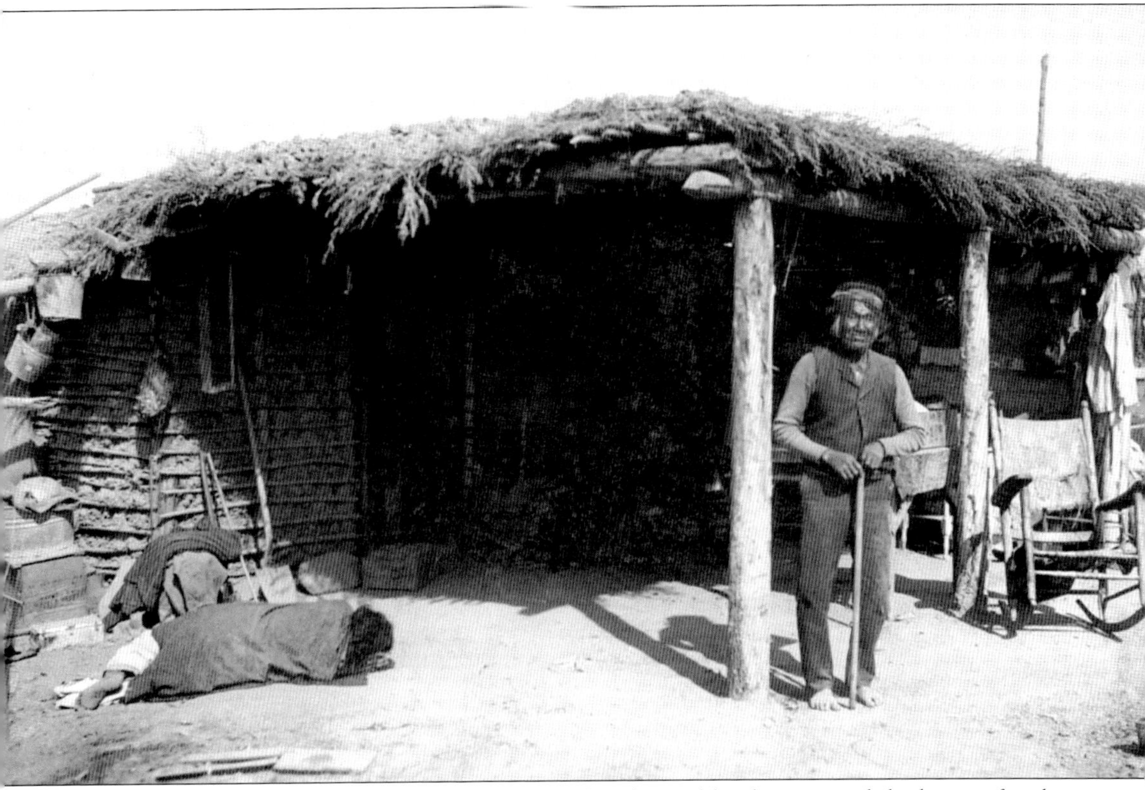

It is difficult to tell the difference between a Quechan home like this one and the home of early Anglo settlers. It was simply a type of architecture that worked best in the Arizona climate from available materials—true form follows function. Later, white pioneers tended to adopt the thick adobe structures of the Mexicans for their homes. Those who replicated too closely the structures of their eastern homes tended to suffer. The Quechan home was essentially a breezeway. The thick adobe walls of the Mexican design held the heat of the day for night and the cool of the night for day. In this image, likely taken in winter, an old man poses for the photograph as a woman lies in the sun near the home's ramada.

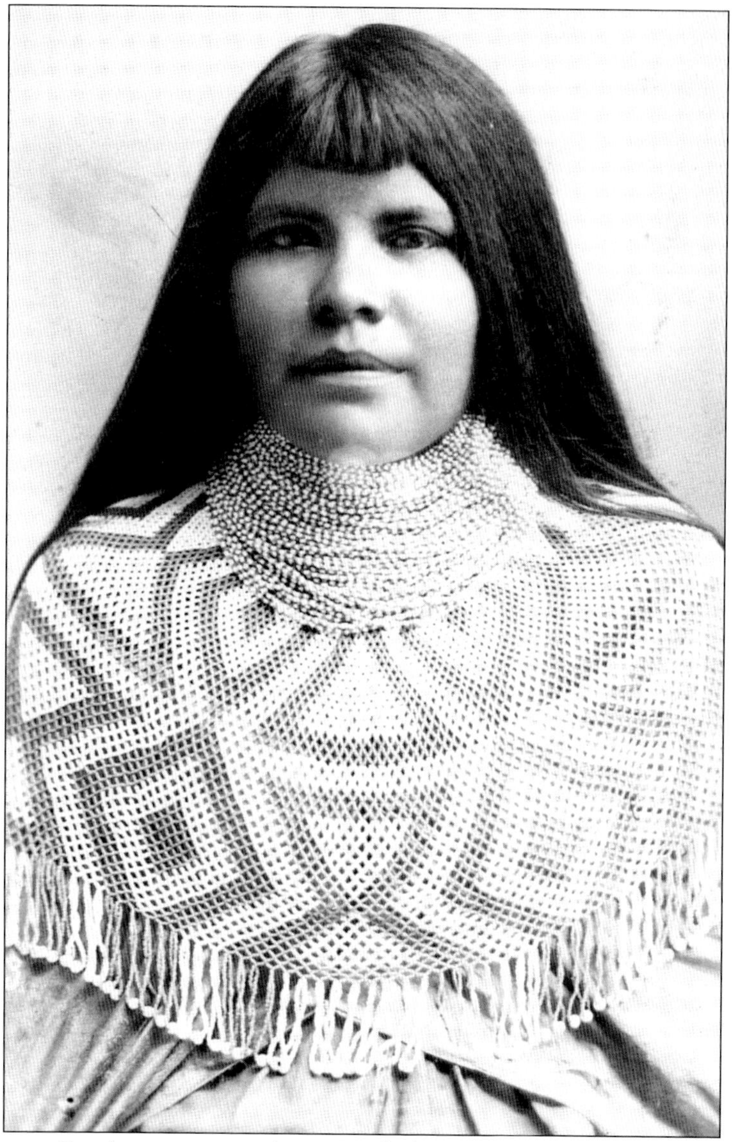

For special events, Quechan women made intricately designed shawls, necklaces, and other finery. As the previous images suggest and Anglo women soon learned, this was not appropriate summer attire. Martha Summerhayes wrote of her journey to Yuma by boat in 1874:

> The heat in the Gulf of California was intense. Our trunks were brought up from the vessel's hold, and we took out summer clothing. But how inadequate and inappropriate it was for that climate!
>
> Our faces burned and blistered; even the parting on the head burned, under the awnings which were kept spread. The ice-supply decreased alarmingly, the meats turned green, and when the steward went down into the refrigerator, which was somewhere below the quarter-deck, to get provisions for the day, every woman held a bottle of salts to her nose, and the officers fled to the forward part of the ship.
>
> The odor which ascended from that refrigerator was indescribable: it lingered and would not go. It followed us to the table, and when we tasted the food we tasted the odor.

Two

GETTING HERE, GOING THERE

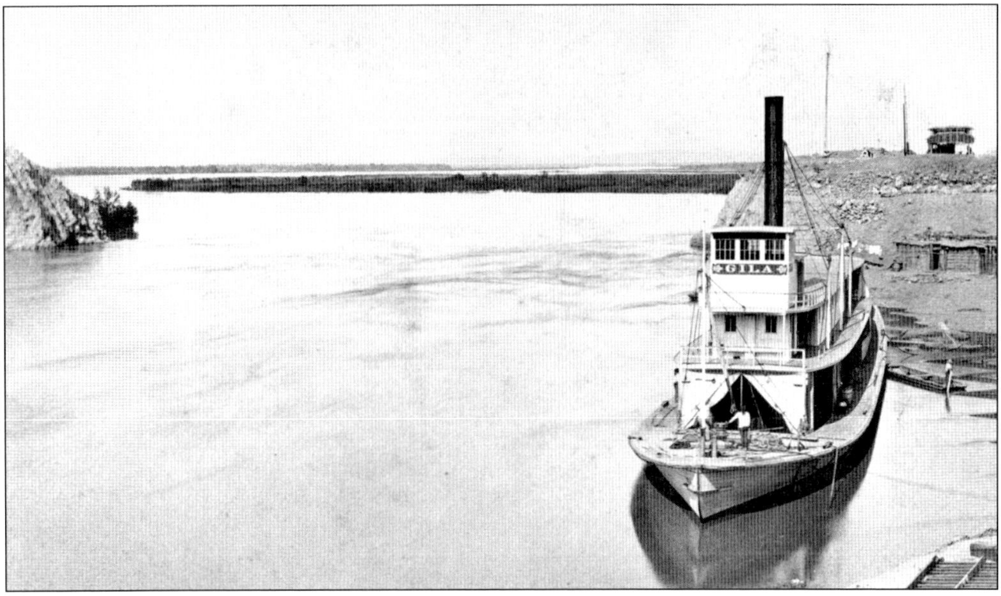

The U.S. Army first established a fort in the Yuma river bottoms in 1850 to protect the ferries before moving it to a small elevation above the river in 1851. But both land routes from San Diego and schooners around Baja failed in their attempts to supply the fort, which was abandoned the same year when provisions ran nearly dry. What did work, though, was to bring supplies around the Baja point and up to Port Isabel. From there, river steamers, built to traverse shallow waters, could make the trip safely to the fort. The fort was reactivated in 1852, and the massive quartermaster shop was born in 1864. For the next half century, the steamboats ruled the river and supplied much of the early building blocks of the territory. In 1852, Captains George Johnson, B. M. Hartshorne, and A. H. Wilcox organized a company under the name "George A. Johnson & Co." They believed they could successfully transport freight and people from San Francisco to stops all along the Colorado River in Arizona. The steamers also made stops in La Paz, Mazatlan, and Guaymas. In the time of the riverboat steamer, the fortunes of southwestern Arizona was linked more to Sonora than to the rest of the United States.

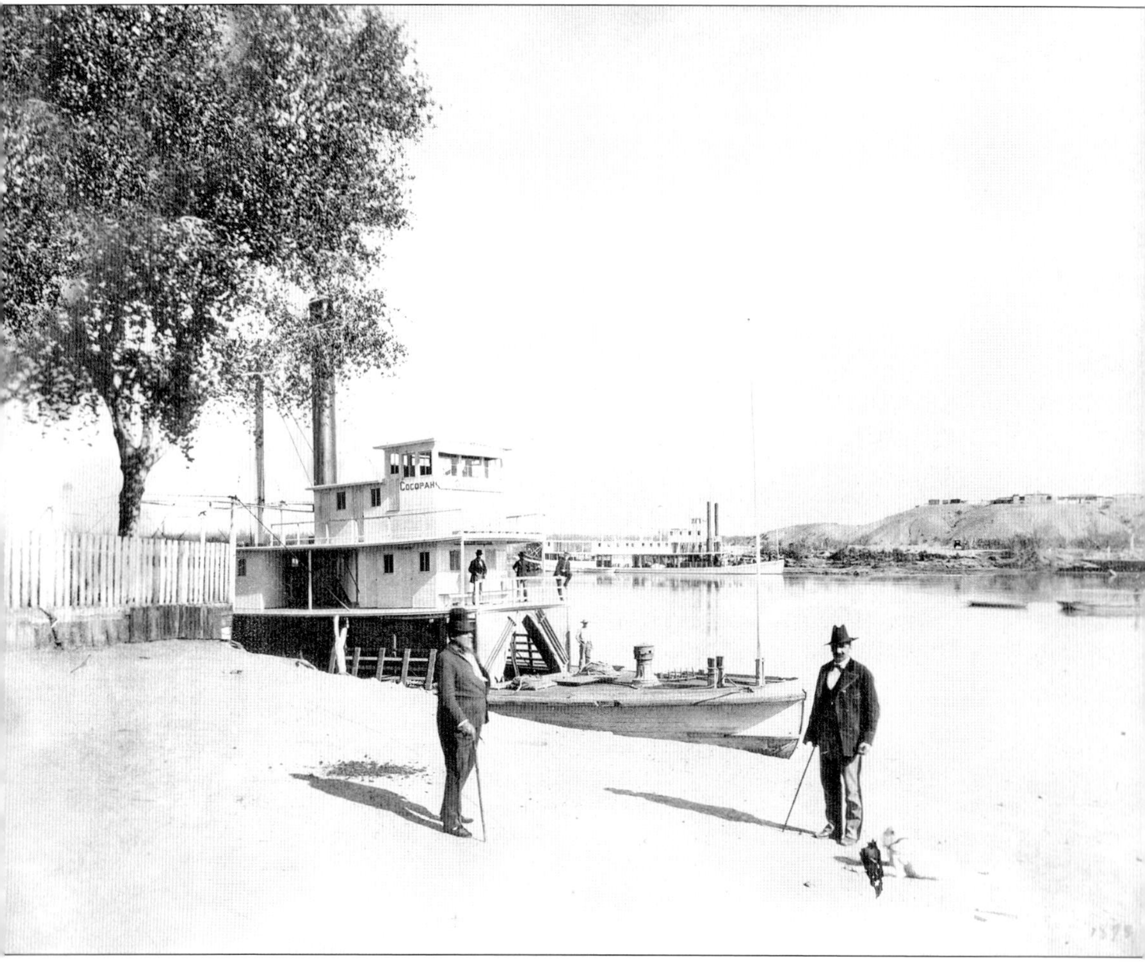

Without the steamboats, Arizona's development prior to the coming of the railroad would not have been possible. For example, in 1875 alone, more than 4,500 tons of freight were brought to Arizona from San Francisco through Yuma on the steamers. That year, according to the book *As It Is: Or, The Coming Country*, the steamers took from Arizona at Yuma nearly 1,000 tons of mineral ore, 60 tons of wool, 6,170 tons of hides, and 1,400 tons of pelts. It is little wonder that a city sprung up at this critical point of trade.

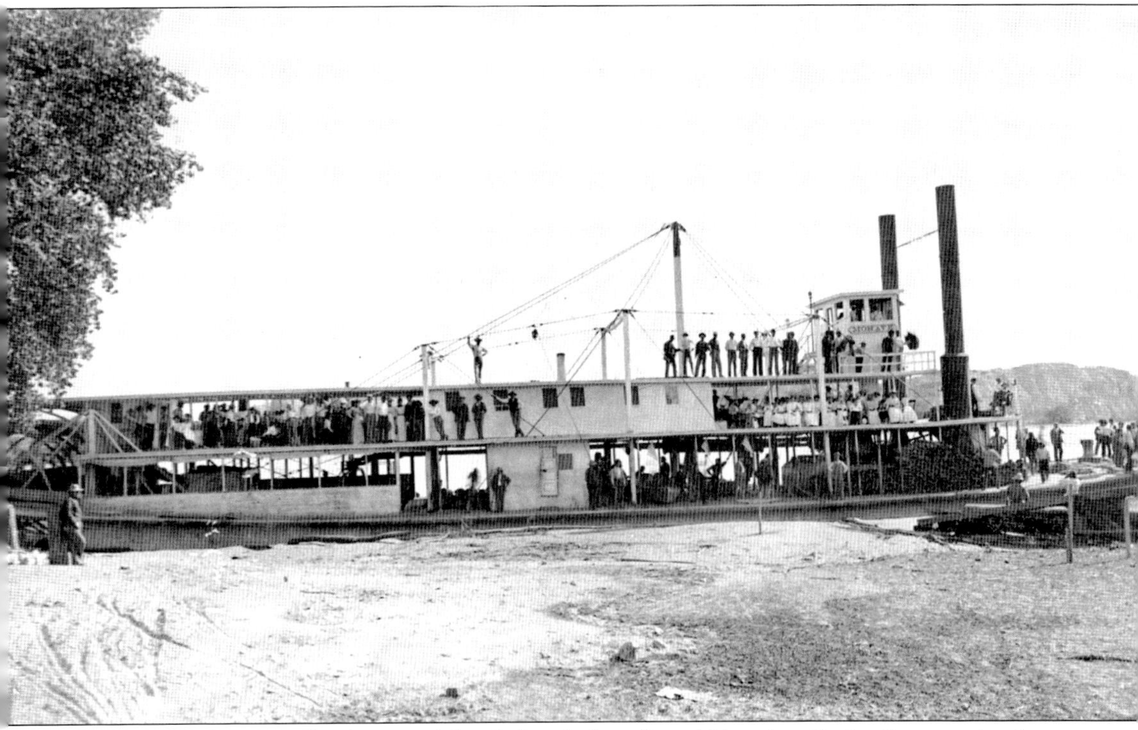

The grand *Mohave II*, "the Queen of the Colorado Line," could be identified miles away by the dual smokestacks of the boat's powerful steam engines. From this angle, there is a sense of the massive storage space of the *Mohave II*. Notice, too, that the river steamer carries most of its cargo above the water line. A traditional boat, with a traditional cargo-carrying hull, would quickly snag in the shallow and ever-shifting Colorado River.

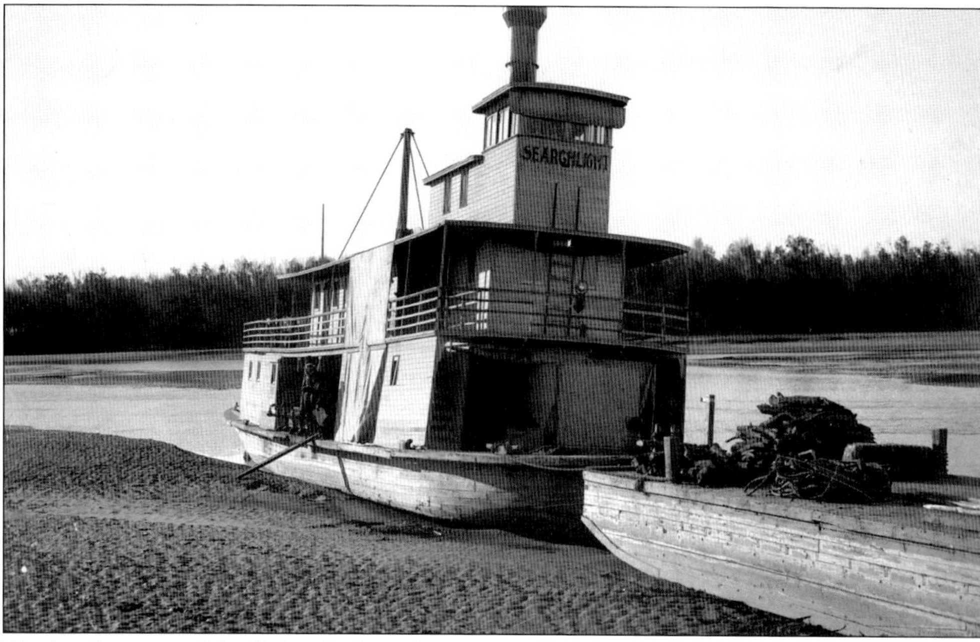

The headquarters of the Colorado Steam Navigation Company was one of the lifeblood businesses of the young village of Yuma. Indeed, the fate of the young territory depended on this port. In *As It Is: Or, The Coming Country*, in a collection of observations about the state of the territory in 1874, 1875, and 1876, the author writes of the Colorado Steam Navigation Company, "This company has occupied a position, in supplying the necessities of the Territory, which could not have been filled in any other manner."

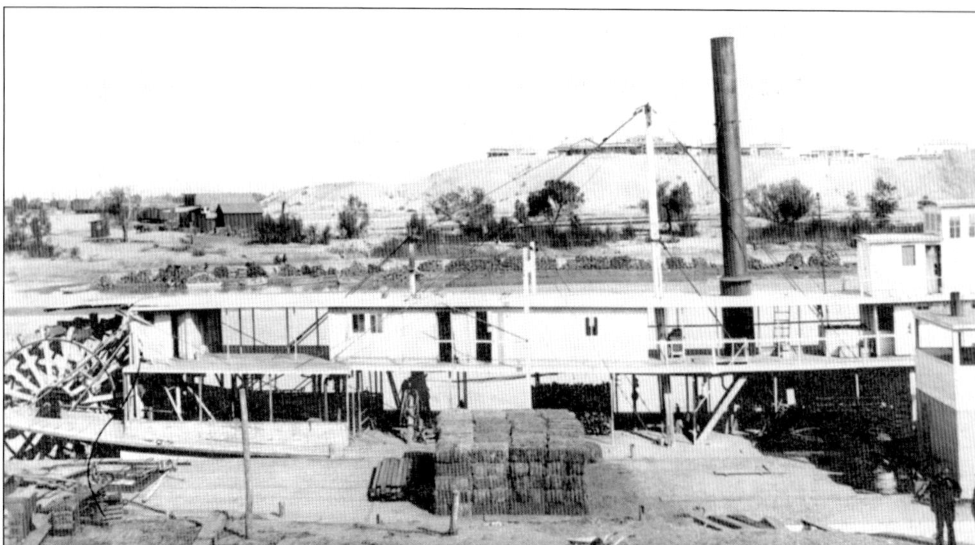

The steamer *Cochan* waits for a load of hay to feed the horses of the northern mining towns. From *As It Is: Or, The Coming Country*, in 1876, "One of the ocean steamers leaves San Francisco every twenty days, running to the head of the Gulf of California, a distance from San Francisco of 1,900 miles. At the head of the gulf the passengers and freight are transshipped to four river steamers, and taken thence up the Colorado River to Yuma."

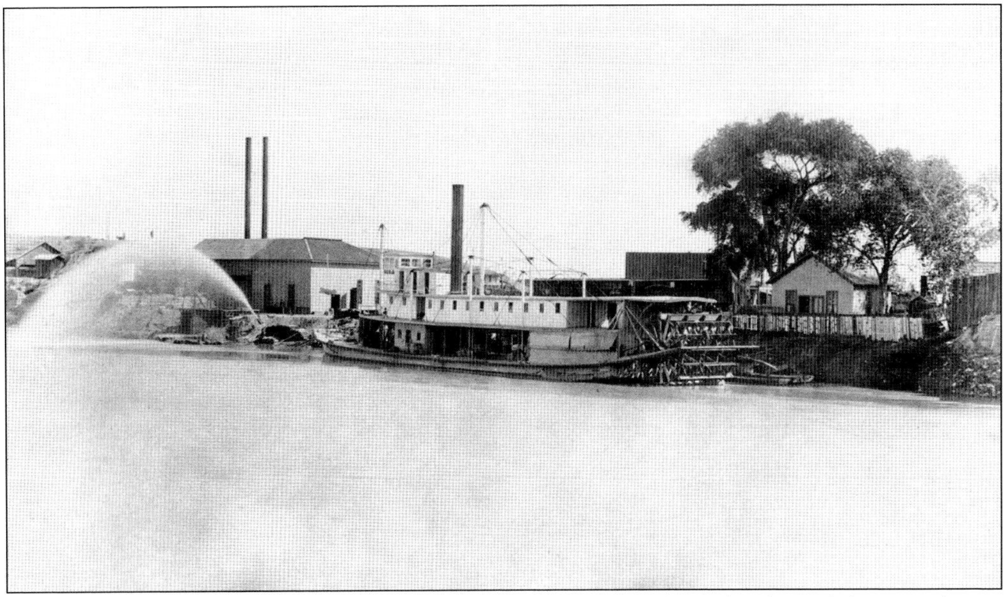

By 1888, when this photograph of the steamboat Gila was taken, the days of the steamboat's supremacy were over. Still, even with the Southern Pacific bringing supplies from San Francisco by 1877, the steamers served a critical role moving supplies up the river to towns without railroad service. For passengers from San Francisco to Mohave County, for example, the trip consisted of 731 miles by train and 255 miles on a river steamer. The total cost, $65, was no paltry sum in that day.

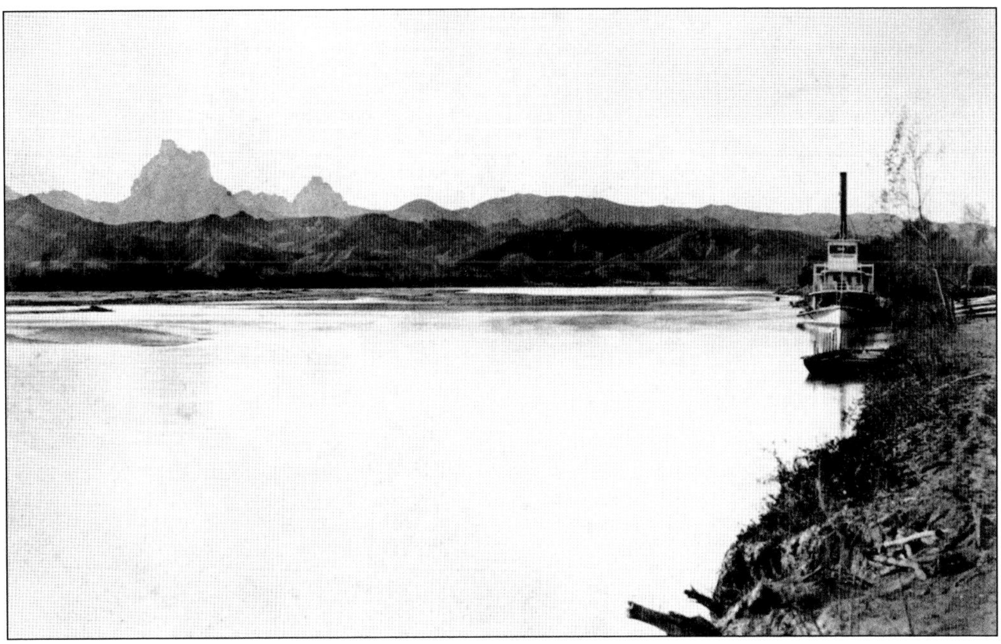

The steamer *Colorado* is docked amid the rugged mining country north of Yuma.

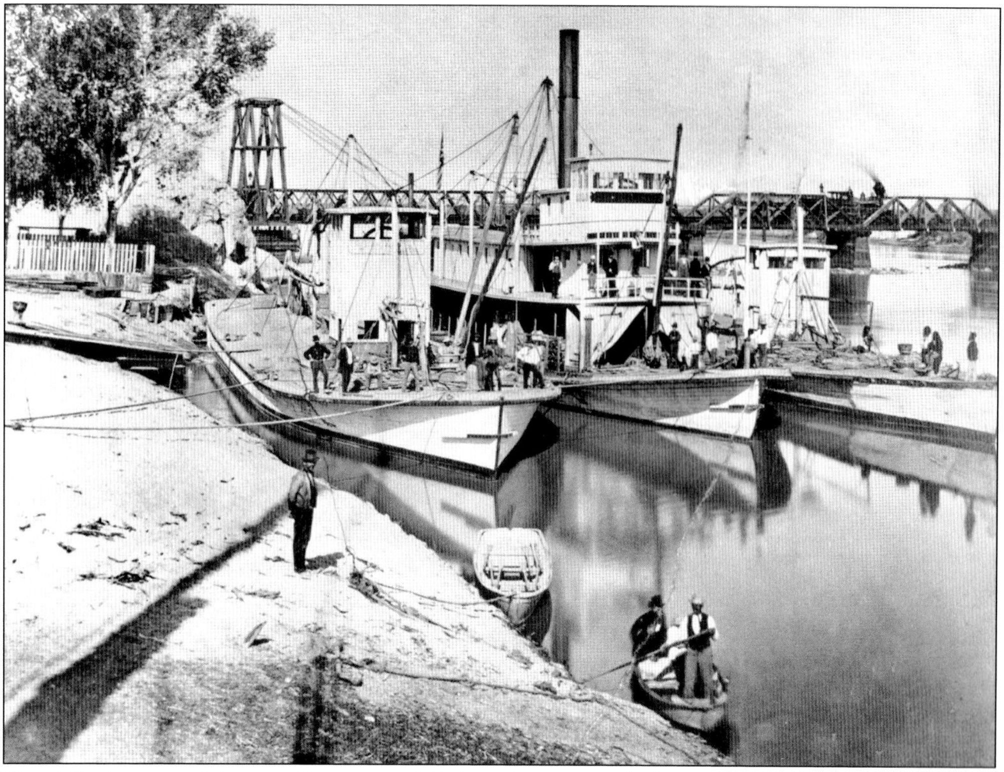

The *Gila* is moored here at Yuma, straddled with two supply barges. In this scenario, supplies would be discharged to the ship heading to the products' final destination. The Colorado Steam Navigation Company, born from the old George Johnson company, had as of 1875 four steamers weighing 400 tons each. The company had four barges, like the two pictured here, that weighed 800 tons each.

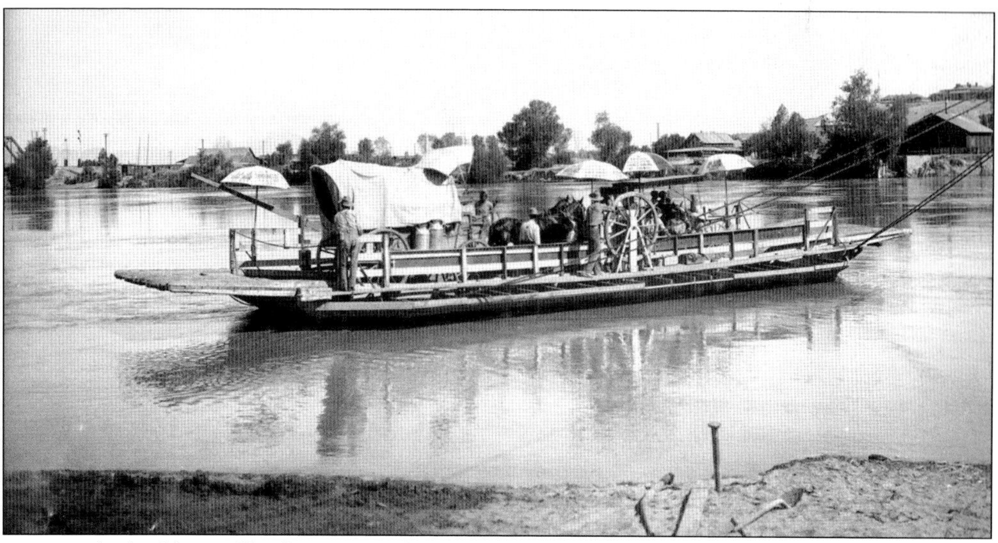

Prior to the building of bridges across the Colorado River, travelers crossed by ferry. One of the earliest ferrymen was John Glanton, a larger-than-life scoundrel who, before taking up the ferry business, led a band of scalp hunters through Chihuahua.

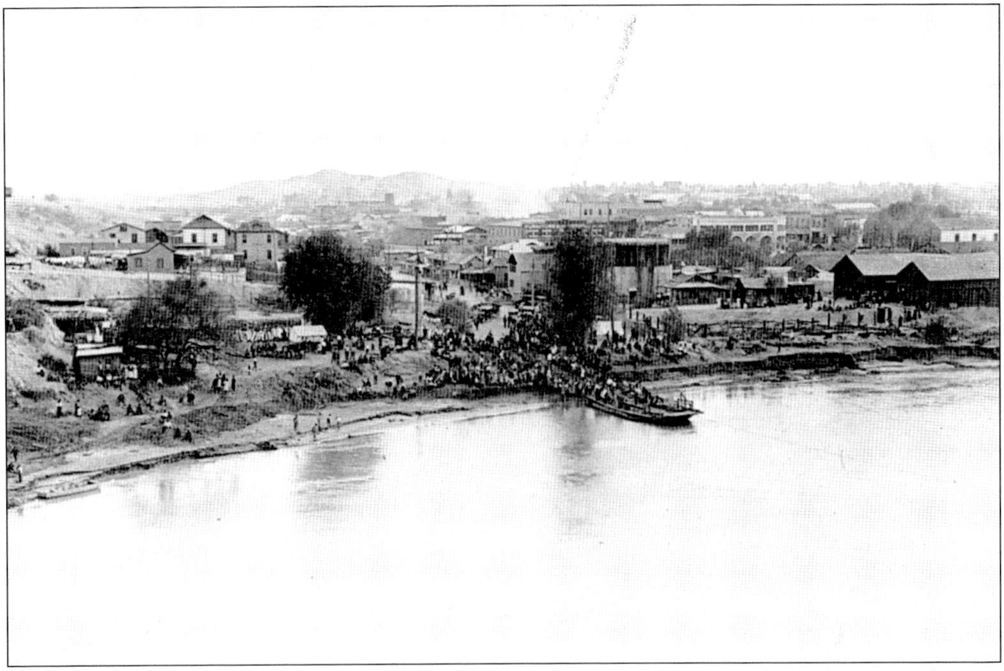

Glanton attempted to bully the Quechan, who, instead of cowering, killed Glanton and many in his gang.

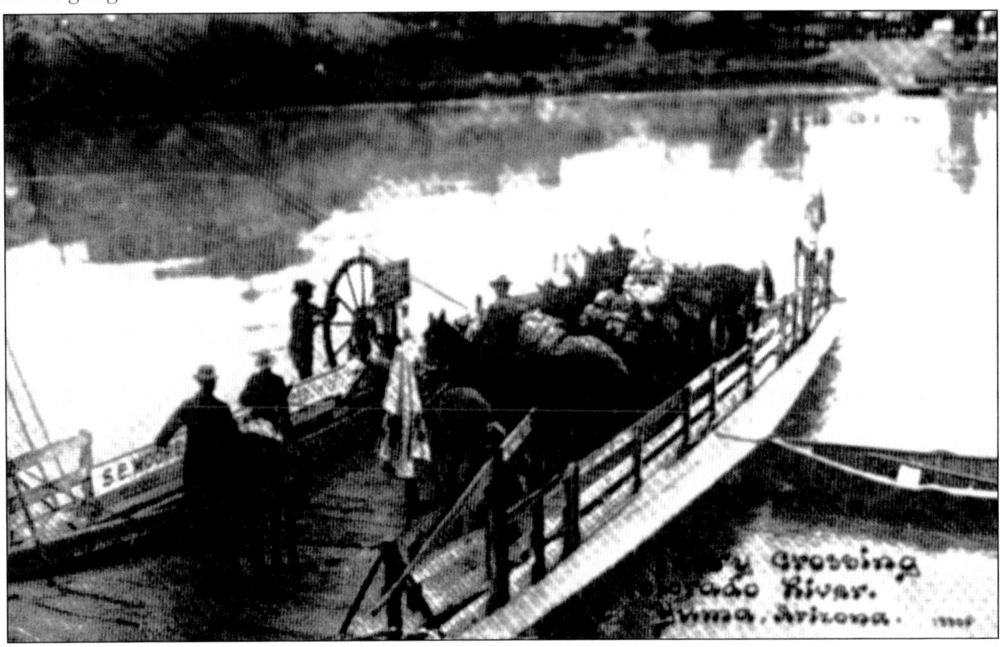

Louis Jaeger first started his ferry near Fort Yuma in 1850. When the army realized it couldn't get supplies from the coast, they closed the fort for a short time and Jaeger headed back with the soldiers to California. After steamboats successfully made the run up the Colorado River, the military returned in 1852 and, with the hope of a military contract, so did Jaeger. The problem: When he returned, he found the Quechan had burned the raft he had left on the banks of the river.

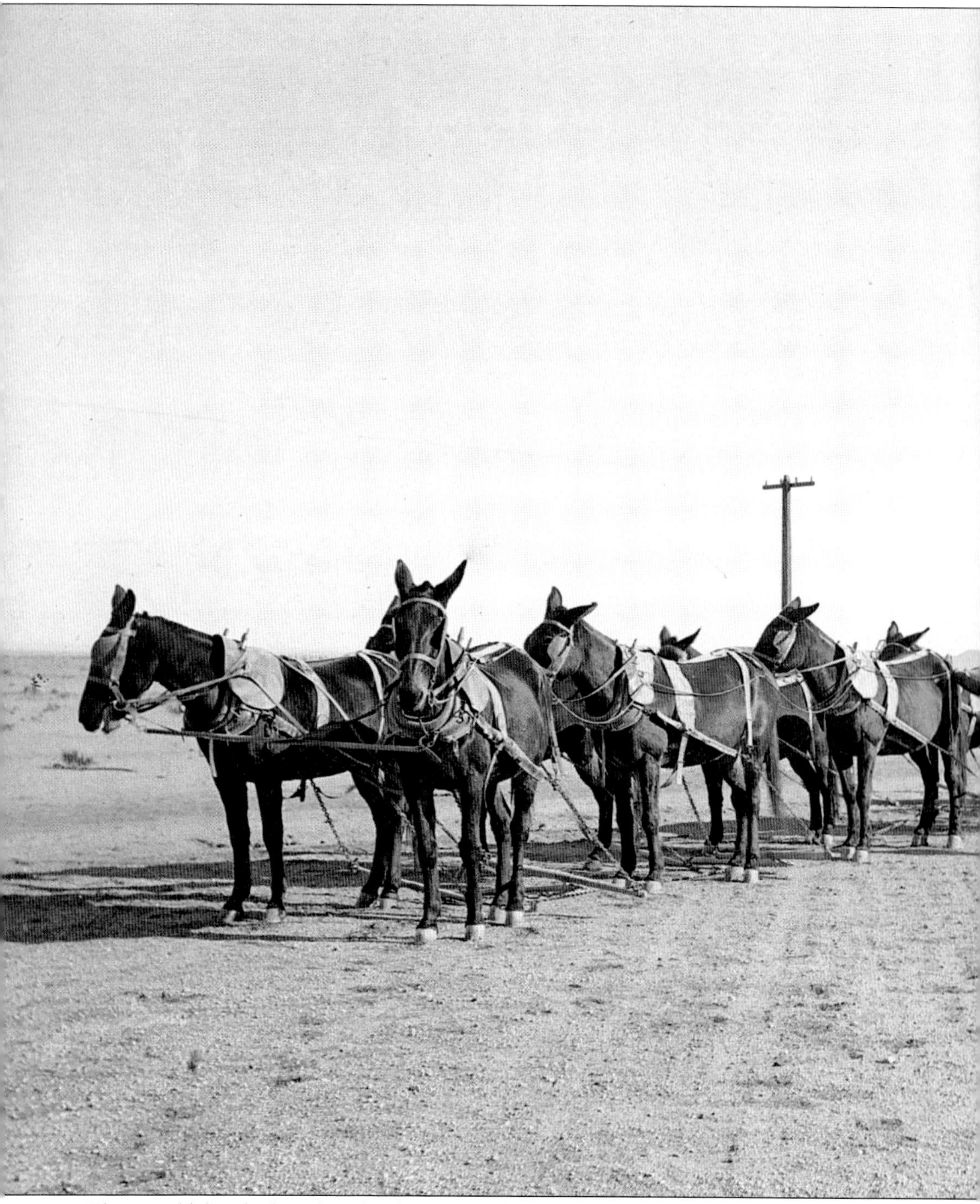

They would first be heard in the distance with the slightest rumble, like thunder in a far-off canyon. But as the sound grew, the early settlers began to rejoice. Supplies were on the way. Very often, the arrival of the freight wagon meant the arrival of new life, as early settlers were often short on food, low on ammunition, out of horseshoes, and out of dynamite. The largest freighter was the Murphy wagon, with a box measuring 16 feet long, 4 feet wide, by 6 feet tall. It

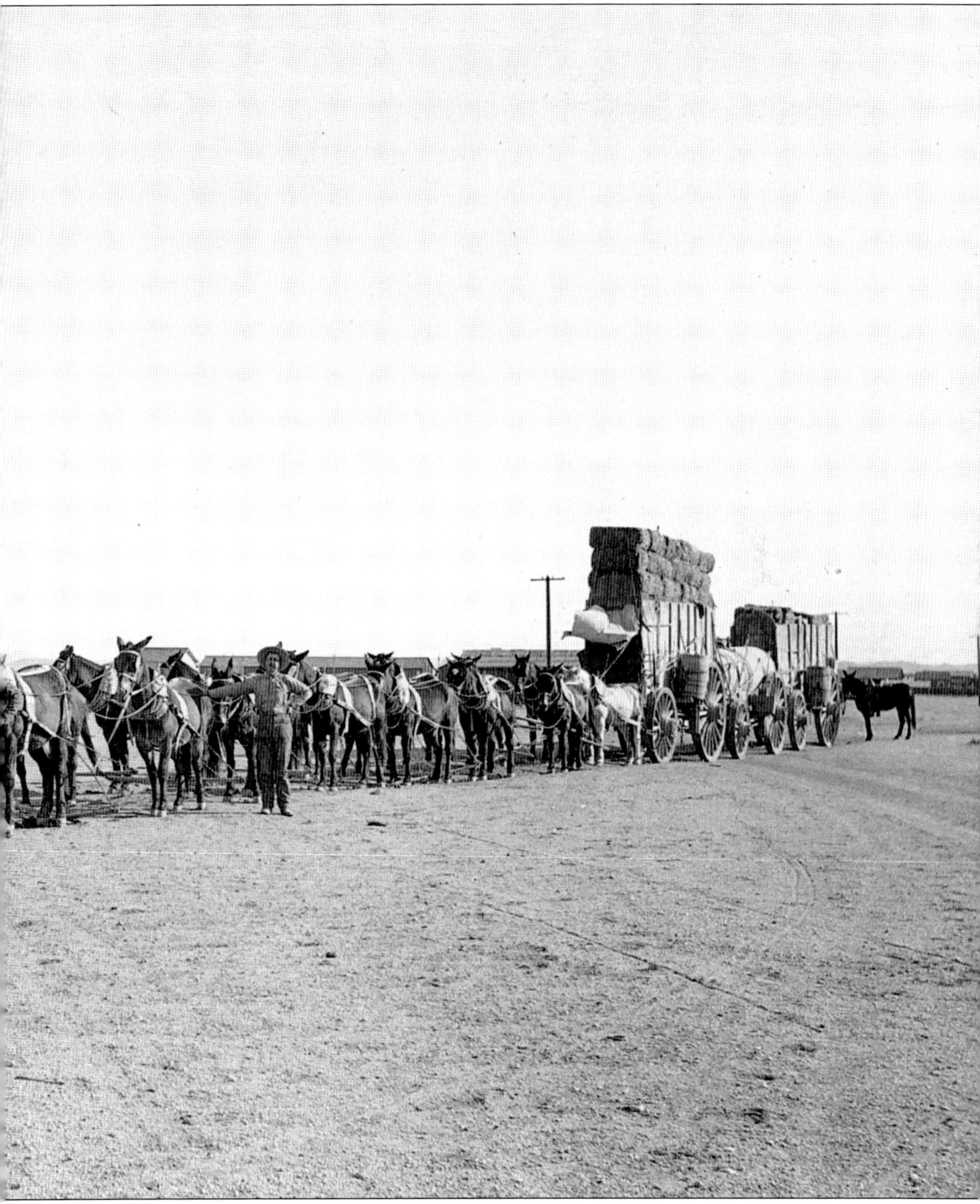

took 12 to 20 mules to pull these wagons, depending on the weight of the load, which could be as much as nine tons, and the incline that had to be climbed. Some of Arizona's mining towns, high in the mountains on roads of rock shard, provided severe challenges for even the most experienced wagoneer.

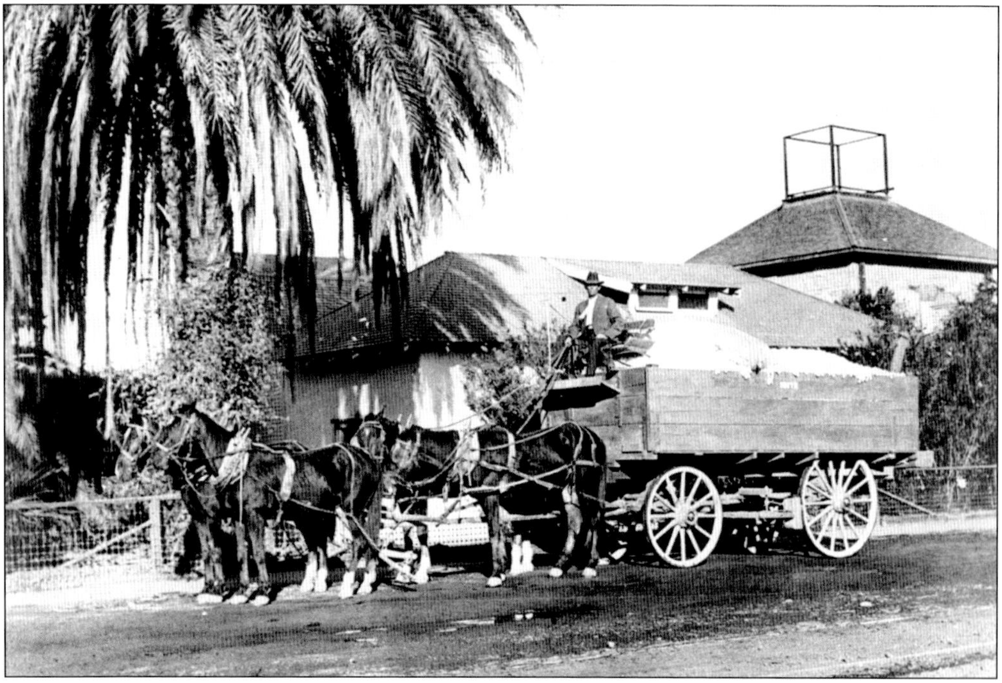

This farm delivery wagon likely just left the store of E. F. Sanguinetti since it stopped for a photograph in front of Sanguinetti's home, now the home of the Yuma branch of the Arizona Historical Society.

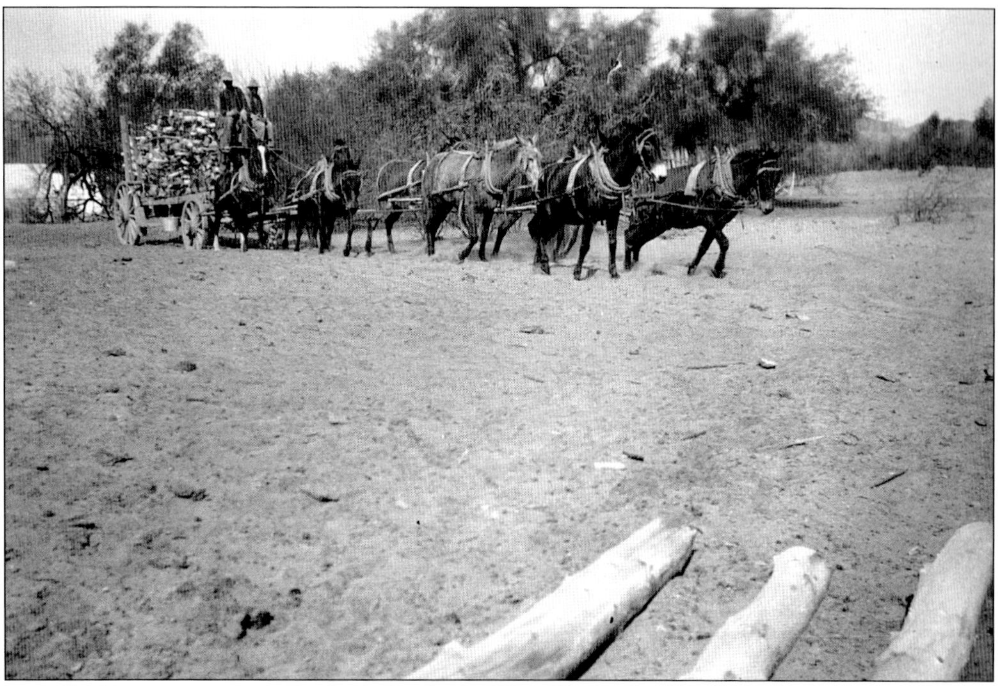

Not all of Arizona's mining camps, and certainly not all of its lowland villages, were well situated for wood. Thus it was not uncommon to see a freight wagon loaded with nothing but wood bound for fireplaces, stoves, and especially the mining steam engines in the territorial interior.

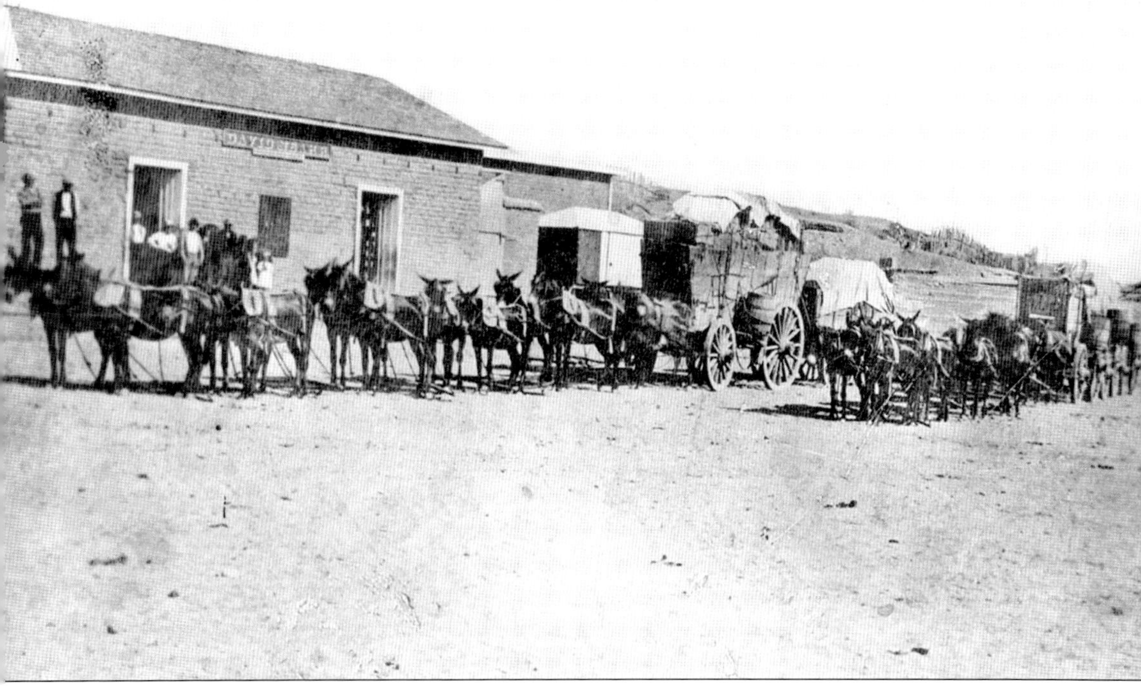

This photograph of a heavily loaded freight wagon was taken before the arrival of the Southern Pacific line, likely in the early 1870s. Behind the wagon is the store of one of Yuma's earliest and most respected businessmen, David Neahr, who also played a critical role in the early political history of the town. Neahr also served as a freighter, often bringing furniture and other goods from San Francisco not only to his store, but for sale to stores in faraway Tucson or Phoenix. This load was bound for the young Phoenix district. Neahr's early store was on the corner of Main and First Street down near the river. Notice the wide streets that gave plenty of room for a freight wagon to make a turn, a common scene in a village where cargo was constantly being loaded and unloaded. Neahr, like many of Yuma's early prominent citizens, was himself a steamboat man prior to becoming a successful businessman supplying the growing territory.

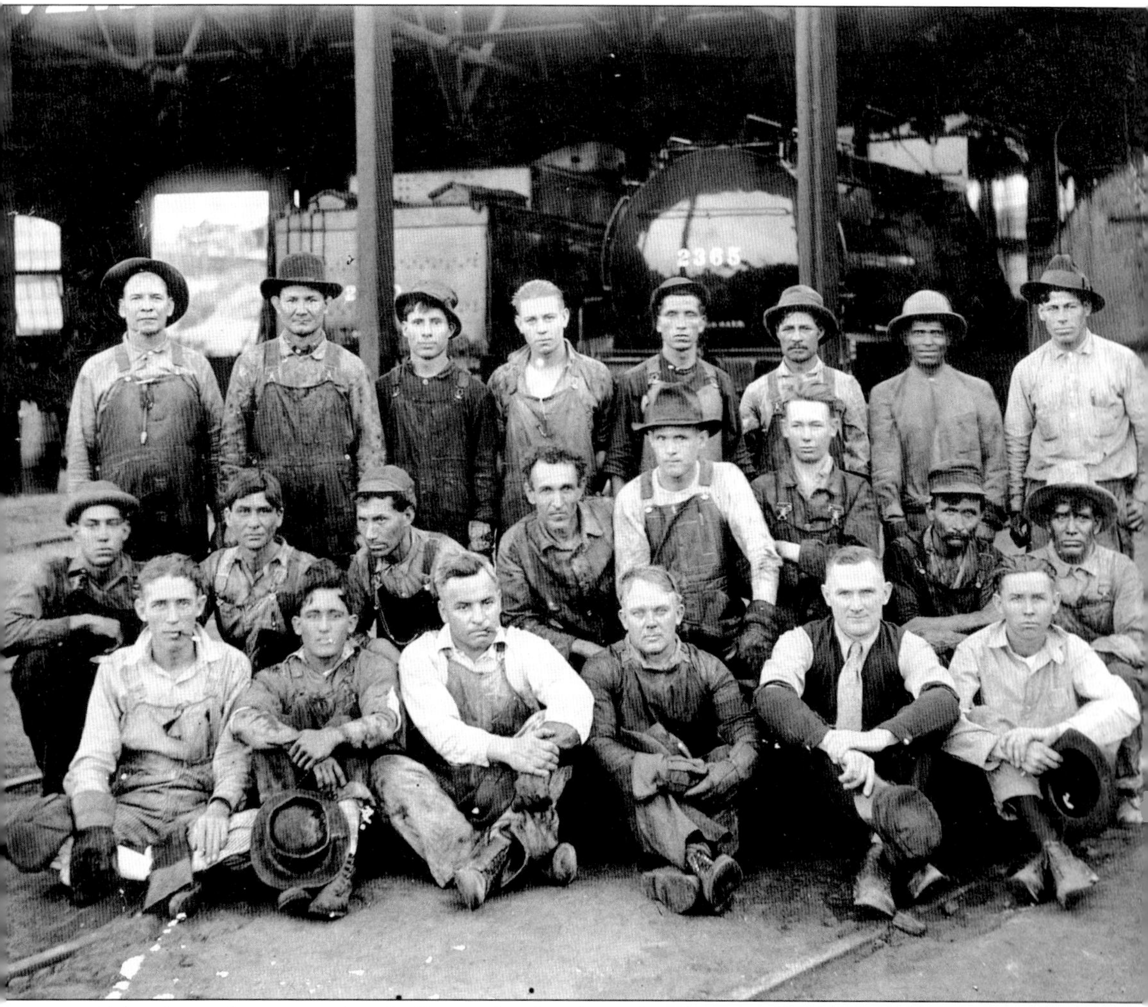

Like the wide streets of early Yuma, the Southern Pacific Roundhouse provided the means to turn around and get freight heading in the opposite direction. Also, these men kept the engines and cars in top shape for the sometimes brutal temperatures through the desert on both sides of Yuma. Unlike the Chinese men brought east to build the rail lines from San Francisco through Indio to Yuma, the yard workers, particularly the electricians at the Yuma roundhouse, made good money. The electricians in this image, for example, made $150 a month, twice what they could make in Los Angeles at the time.

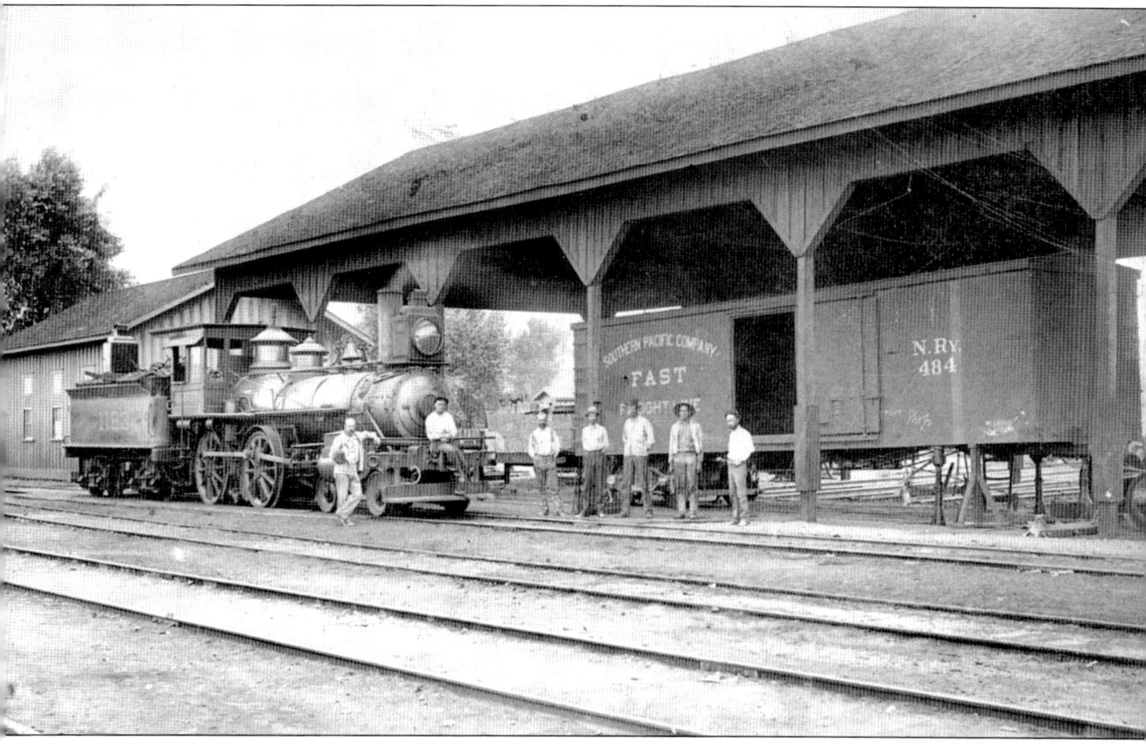

Pictured here is the car shop of the Southern Pacific Company's facilities at Yuma. Here managers of the yard, usually out from California, made $100 a month. Although wagon freighting survived, and in fact thrived, after the arrival of the train, the Yuma Quartermaster Supply Depot did not do as well. After the railroad reached Tucson in 1880, the depot's pumps, steam engines, and other equipment were removed to Fort Lowell near Tucson. The Yuma Quartermaster Depot was terminated in 1883. After the train arrived in Yuma in late 1877, the village remained the eastern terminus of the line for more than a year. Finally, in November of 1878, the process of laying track began east of town toward Tucson. Less than two years later, a train entered Tucson from Yuma to great fanfare.

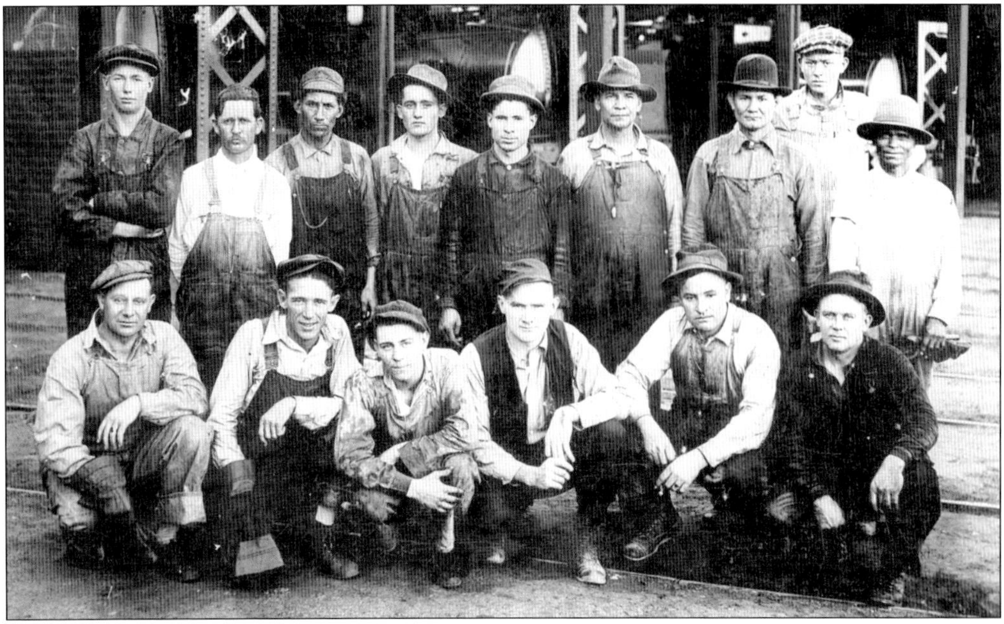

In the year following the arrival of the rail line from San Francisco, the Yuma rail yard saw intense activity as the South Pacific went on a track-building race against the Texas & Pacific Line pushing west from central Texas. The two companies were in competition to be the first to Sierra Blanca, Texas, southeast of El Paso, where the company that got the line laid in its key mountain pass would have undisputed right-of-way from Sierra Blanca to El Paso.

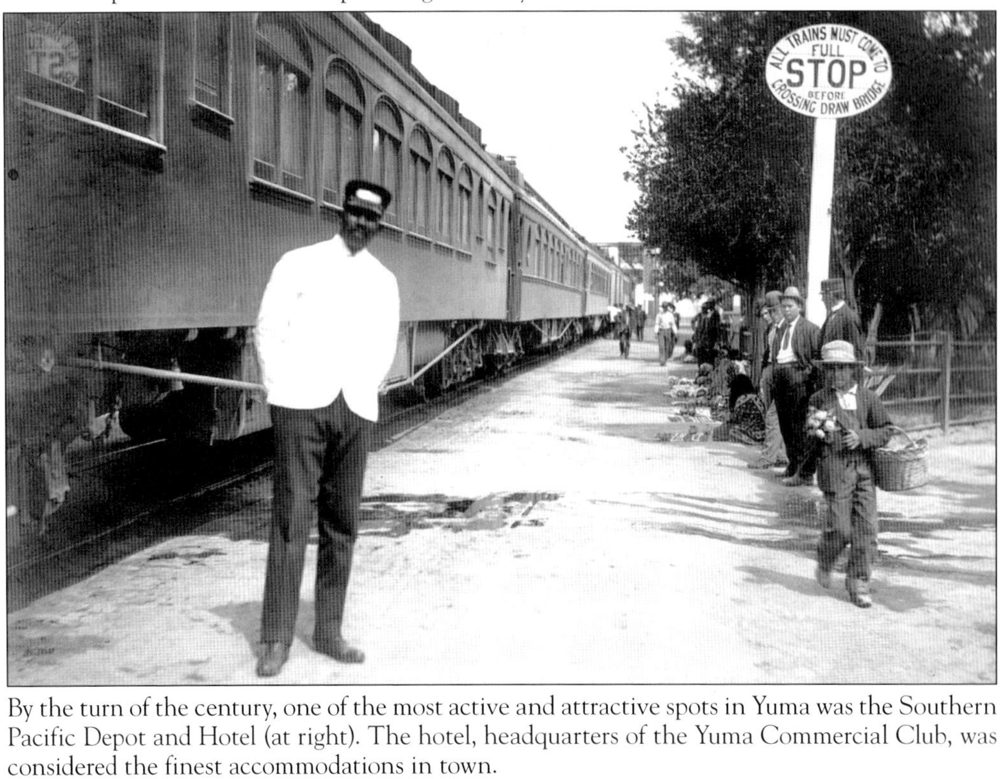

By the turn of the century, one of the most active and attractive spots in Yuma was the Southern Pacific Depot and Hotel (at right). The hotel, headquarters of the Yuma Commercial Club, was considered the finest accommodations in town.

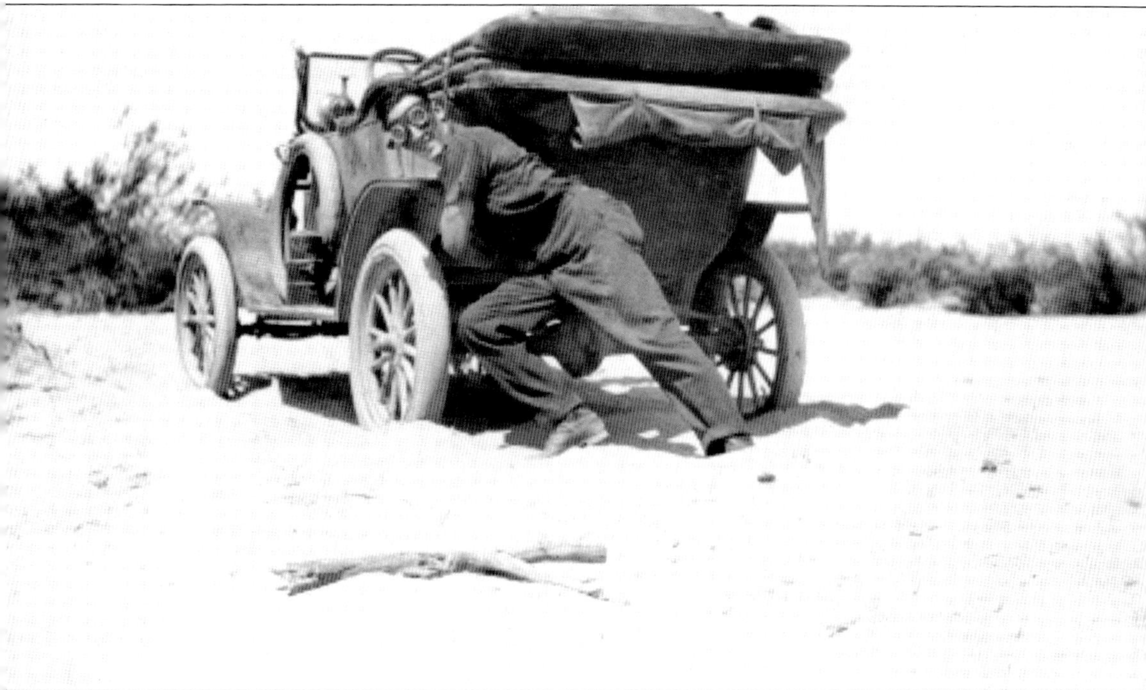

As the completion of Laguna Dam forever ended the days of the steamboat, automobiles began establishing themselves in Yuma as the transportation mode of the future. But much of the terrain in all directions of Yuma didn't readily accommodate the new vehicles. The worst of all roadbeds were the sand dunes west of Yuma that stood between the town and San Diego. In this 1914 photograph, a young Otto Enderton is likely pretending to be stuck in the sand for the benefit of the camera. (In his later years, Enderton would become known not for his driving skills but for his ability and courage flying airplanes.) A few miles of sand dunes could not stand in the way of progress, so engineers went about developing one of the strangest stretches of highway in the history of the United States—the plank road.

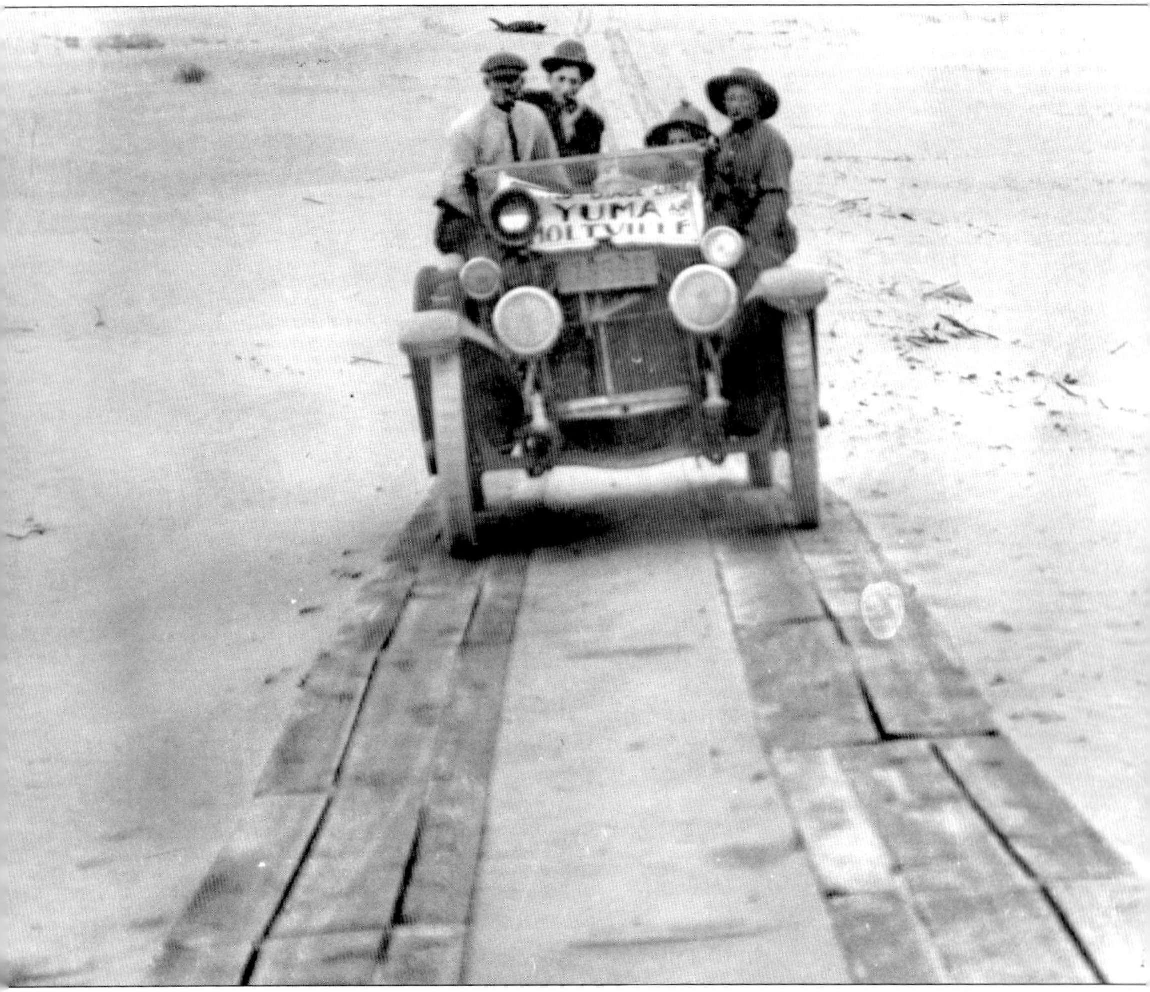

The Algodones Sand Dunes, or Imperial Sand Dunes, cover 1,000 square miles, making it one of the largest sand dunes in North America. For travelers heading west from Yuma, it was also one of the greatest barriers in North America. In early Yuma, travelers heading west were told of whole wagon trains being swallowed up by the sand. In 1912, San Diego businessmen hoping to attract visitors from the east came up with the idea of a wooden road across the dunes. Support grew for an east-west route from San Diego to Yuma, and on February 14, 1915, the first of 13,000 planks were laid in the dunes. Work on the two parallel plank tracks, each 25 inches wide, ended two months later. A week after the road's completion, 100 riders in 25 cars broke out across the sand dunes and successfully reached their destination. This rare photograph from 1915 shows one of the cars as it makes that inaugural trip between Yuma and Holtville.

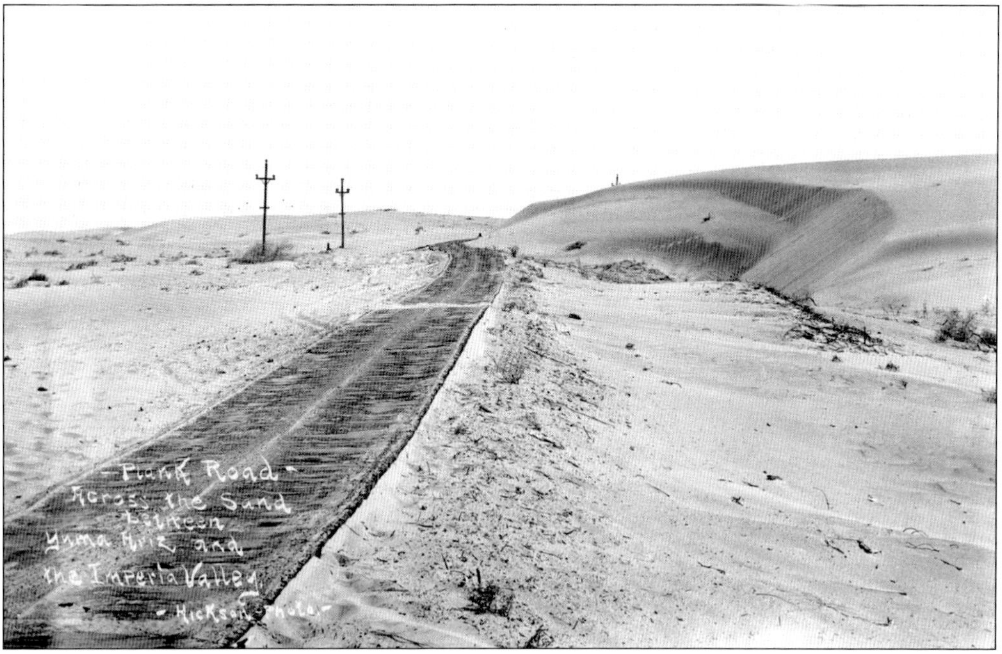

Within a few months, this version of the plank road began to break down under the weight of heavy travel and the scraping of road crews trying to clear sand from the planks. A year later, with the road degrading as support for the route grew, the California State Highway Commission began work on an improved version of the road.

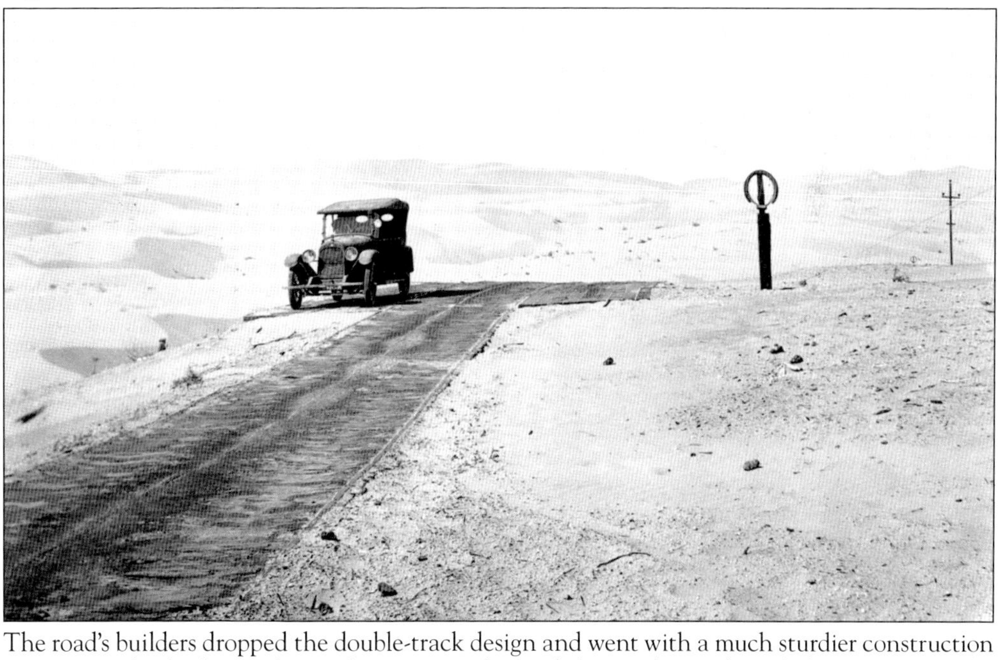

The road's builders dropped the double-track design and went with a much sturdier construction consisting of eight-foot-wide wooden cross ties laid tightly together with underlying support. The road was built in 12-foot sections at a fabricating plant in Ogilby, California. The new road was built with 16-foot-wide turnouts every 1,000 feet. Still, as traffic grew on the road, the plank road became notorious for fist fights between drivers vying for the right-of-way.

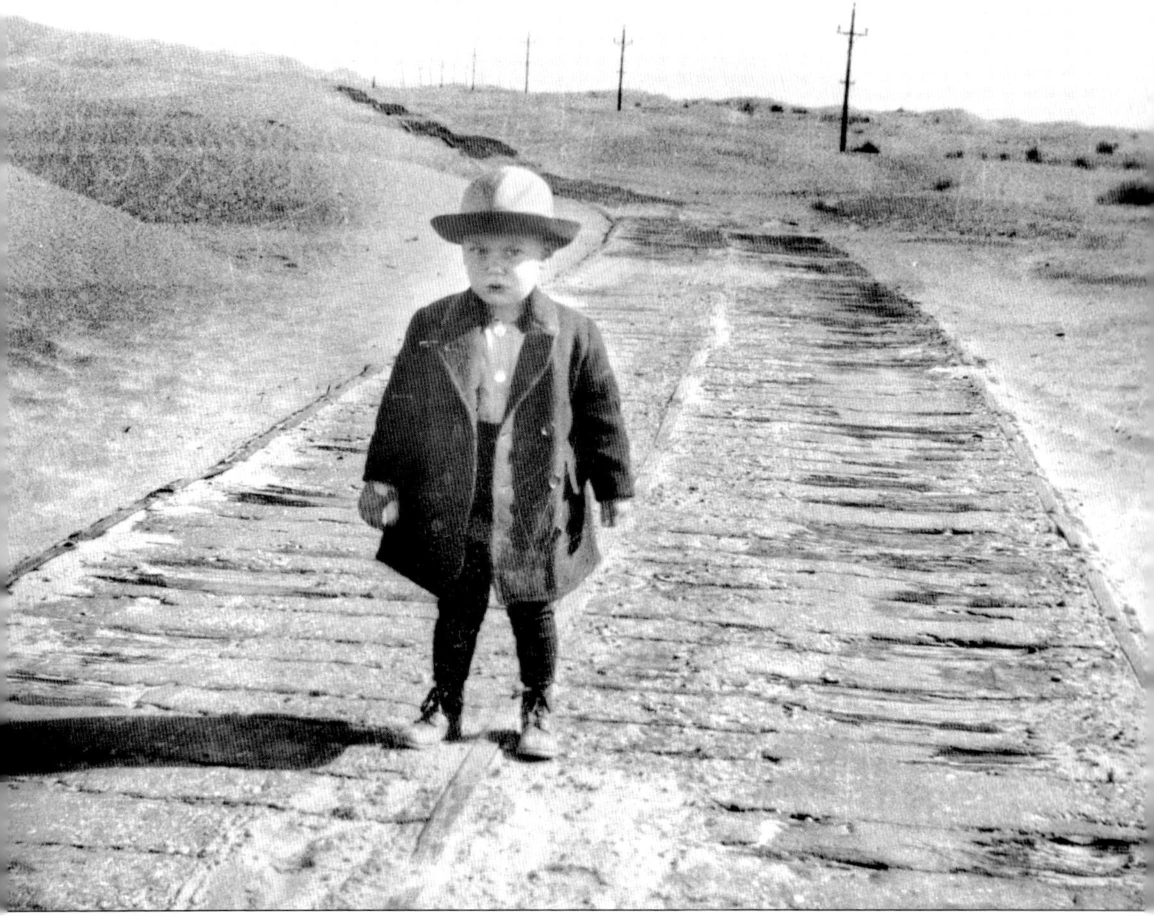

Hopefully, this was a quiet day on the plank road. There were many such days, even in the cool winter months. The plank road was simply a tough, seven-mile racket of a trip in a Model T even when it was cool and the wind was still. By the 1920s, alternatives to the high-maintenance plank road were being pursued by California officials. In the early 1920s, a road official wrote, "The final solution of the problem appears to be to locate the road south of and away from the shifting sand dunes." To do this, however, would require that for a distance of approximately 15 miles the state highway be built in Mexican territory. But engineers once again came to the rescue and devised an ingenious roadbed, which was essentially a massive sand berm compacted and sealed with asphalt.

Three

Building Yuma

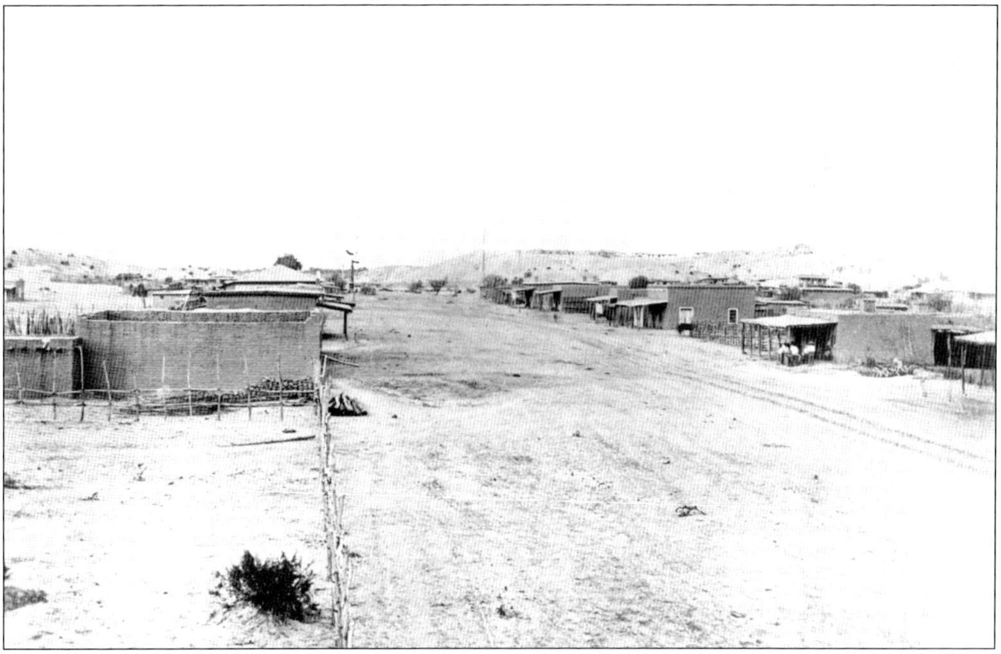

From the slaughter of 1781, through hundreds of deaths from drowning, disease, and violence of every sort, through flood and earthquake, through a landscape seemingly made of knives, it is amazing that something built in Yuma actually survived. This dispatch from the *Alta California* newspaper in March 1862, reprinted in the Yuma County Historical Society's 1976 book on the city, sums up the devastation of those early years:

> Colorado City is entirely washed away. . . . The principal losers are Messrs. Hooper and Hinton's store, entirely washed away. The steamboat company's machine shop and store, with all its contents, washed away. . . . The whole country is submerged between here and Pilot Knob and impassable for anything but boats.

In 1891, the levees broke. In 1916, they did so again (burrowing gophers were blamed the second time). In each instance, the town was inundated with water, drenching and shifting frame structures while melting adobes like butter on a warm skillet. And each time, the people of Yuma rebuilt, promising to build bigger and better and a little smarter.

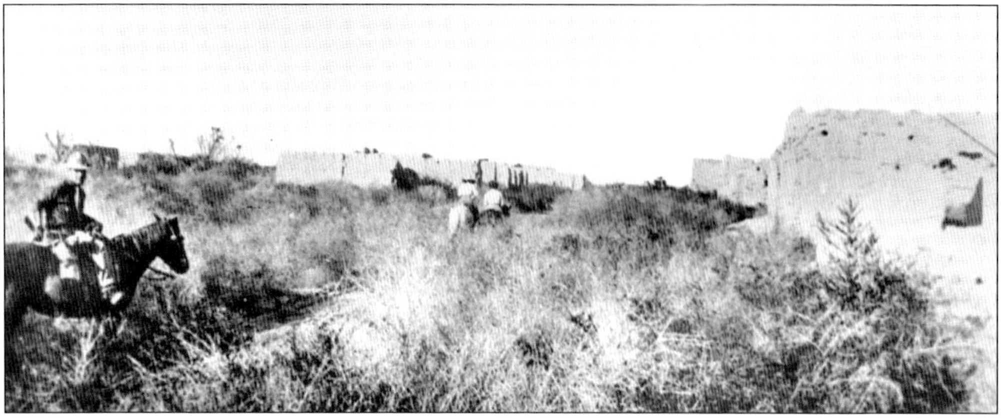

The boom of Yuma in the second part of the 19th century probably would not have been possible without the death of one of the region's first boomtowns, La Paz. La Paz, an early mining town up the Colorado River from Fort Yuma, had 3,000 residents during its heyday in the 1860s. As La Paz died, many of the merchants and workers there began moving downriver to the village by the fort. This photograph of the ghost town was taken in 1903. Remnants of the town have long since disappeared.

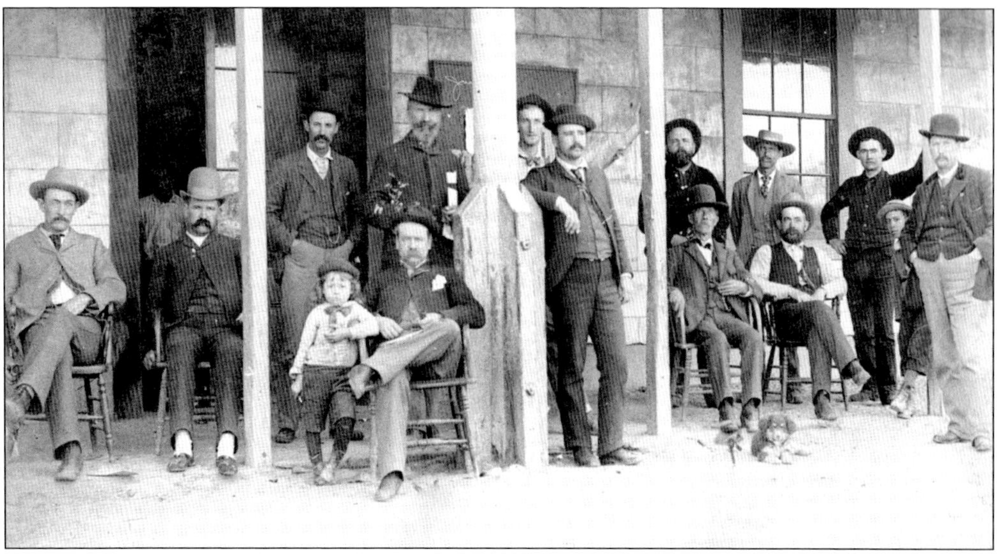

Another boost for the young village was the army's decision to locate its quartermaster depot for the territory in Yuma. The depot ensured that hundreds of tons of supplies would be moving off the steamboats at Yuma bound for the interior.

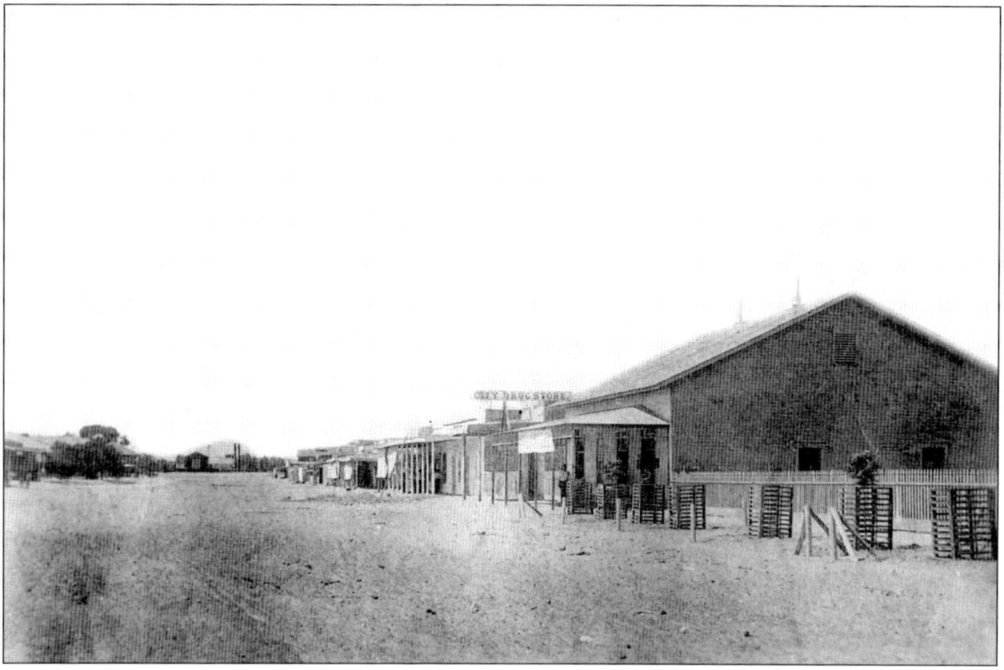

This rare image displays why Main Street was truly the main street of early Yuma. The street, wide so 20-mule freight wagons could make a clean U-turn, leads directly down to the dock where the steamboats stopped with their supplies. In the background, two steamboats are docked side by side.

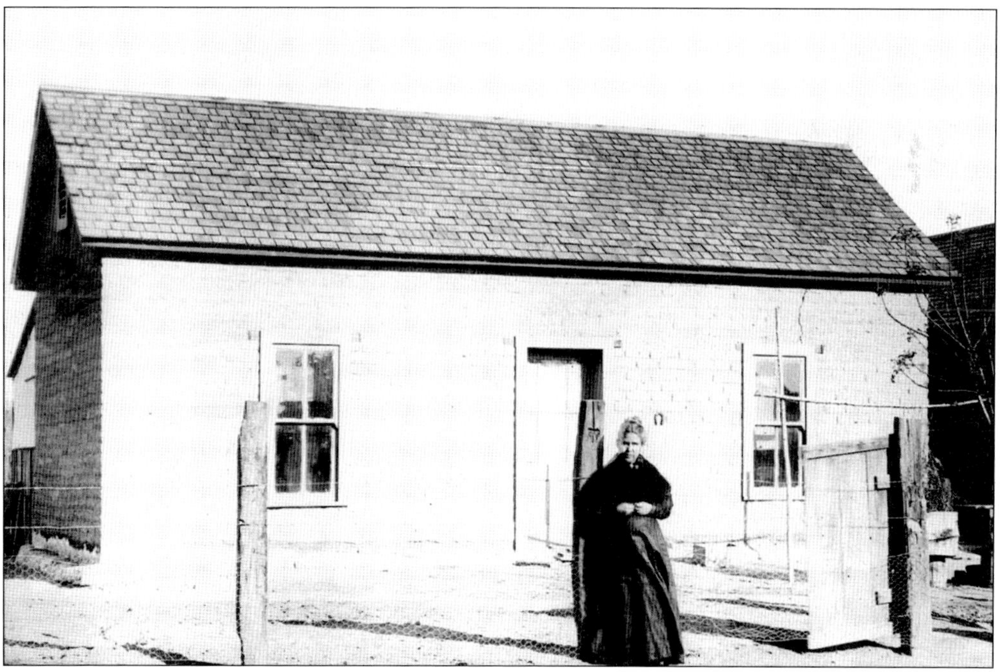

This very early frame structure at 485 Gila Street was the home of pioneers Salvador and Concepcion Contreras. The Contreres family was an important farming family in the area. Piedad Contreras married Jose Maria Redondo.

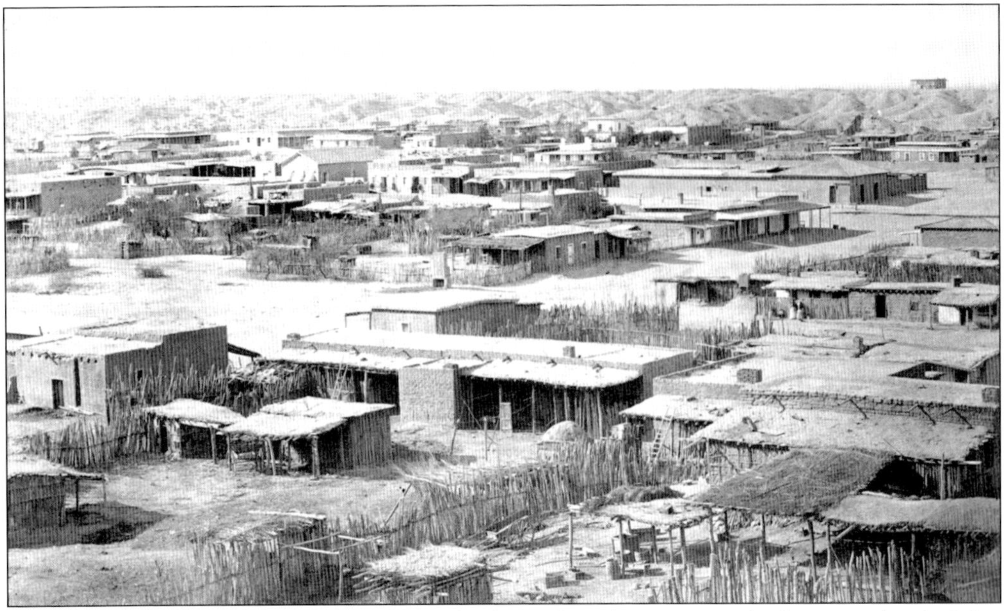

This panorama from 1880 shows Yuma in the days when the town was built primarily of adobe. The 1891 flood washed away much of what is seen here.

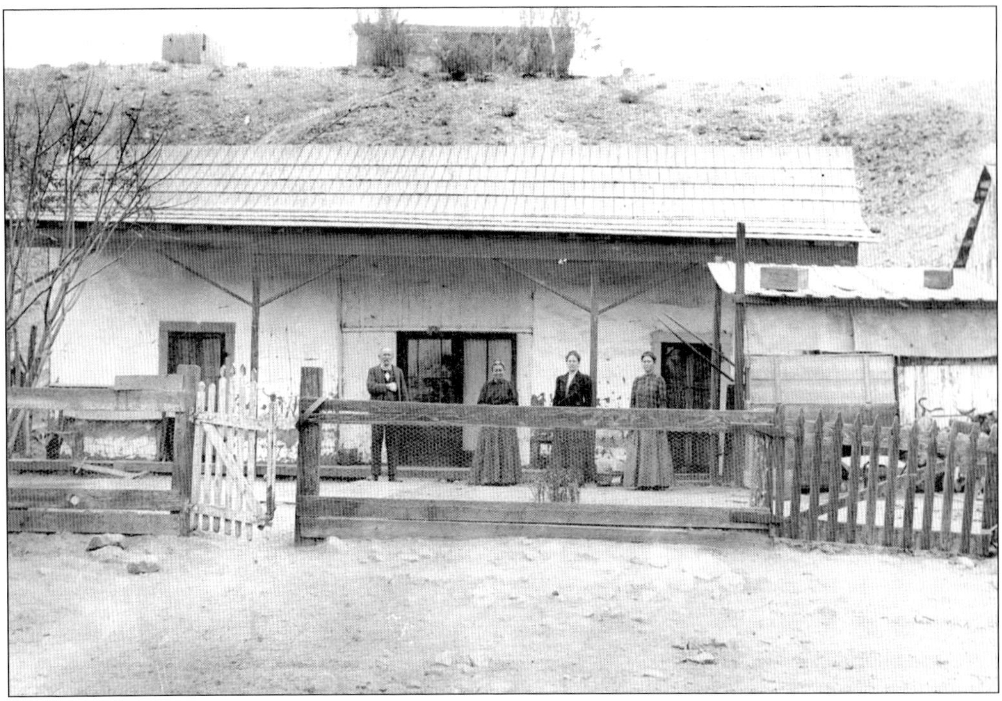

This is the home on Gila Street of David and Luz Redondo Balsz, important pioneers in both the history of Yuma and Phoenix. David Balsz (shortened from the German name Bialasiewiez) came to Arizona territory and built an extensive sheep and cattle business. In the 1880s, seeking educational opportunities for her 11 children, Luz Redondo Balsz started one of the first schools in the Phoenix area. Today the Balsz School District in Phoenix has four schools, 400 staff members, and 3,000 students.

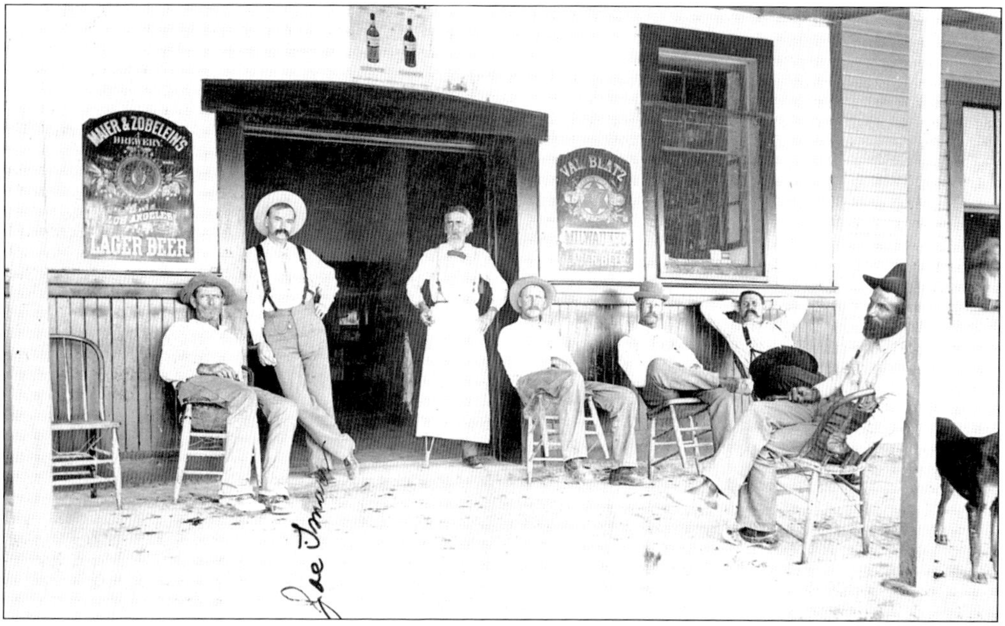

Early on, before the railroad, the bars of Yuma would draw patrons from miles away, especially from the mining camps to the north. Yuma, before any other spot in the territory, had top-shelf liquors, beers, and wines brought by boat from San Francisco.

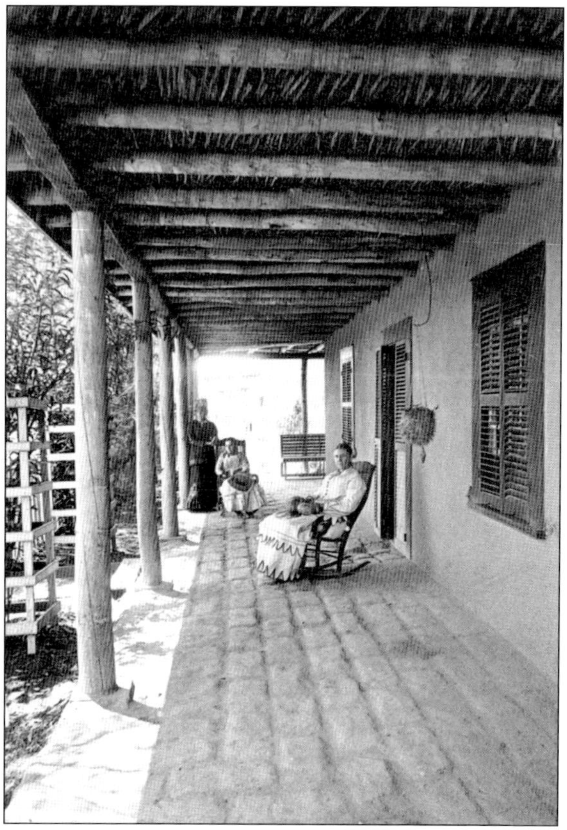

This is the home of leading businessman E. F. Sanguinetti as it looked in the 1880s. Known as the Century House, it is now the Sanguinetti House Museum, which houses the Yuma Branch of the Arizona Historical Society. The historical society is currently busy refurbishing other early Yuma structures in the vicinity of the Sanguinetti House to expand the society's displays and archival space.

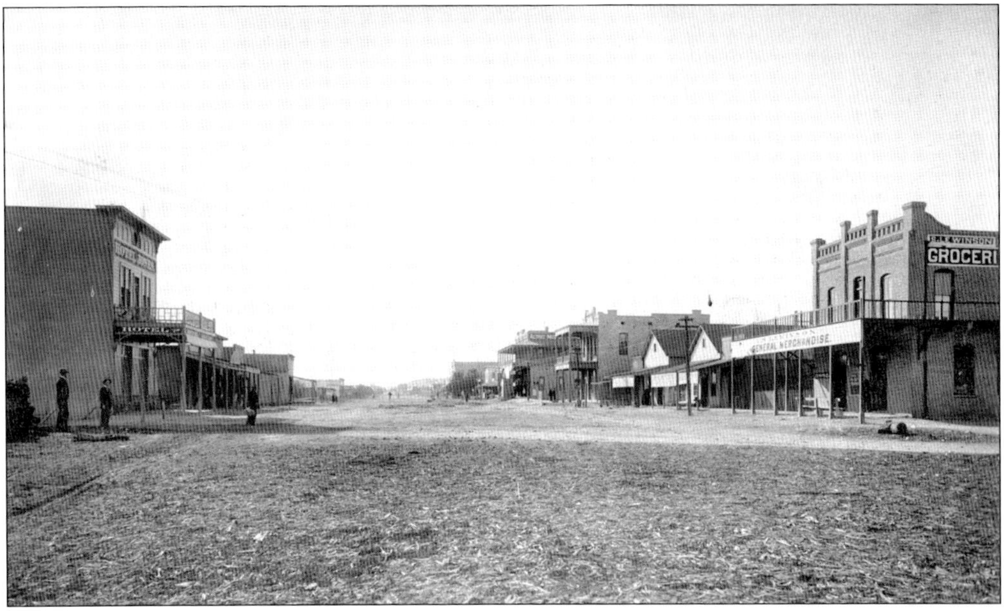

By the time this photograph was taken of Main Street in 1896, flood and fire, as well as strong profits, led many of Yuma's business owners to build with brick. Another indicator that Yuma was prospering, and prepared for the new century can be seen on the right-hand side of the street. It's Yuma's first power line.

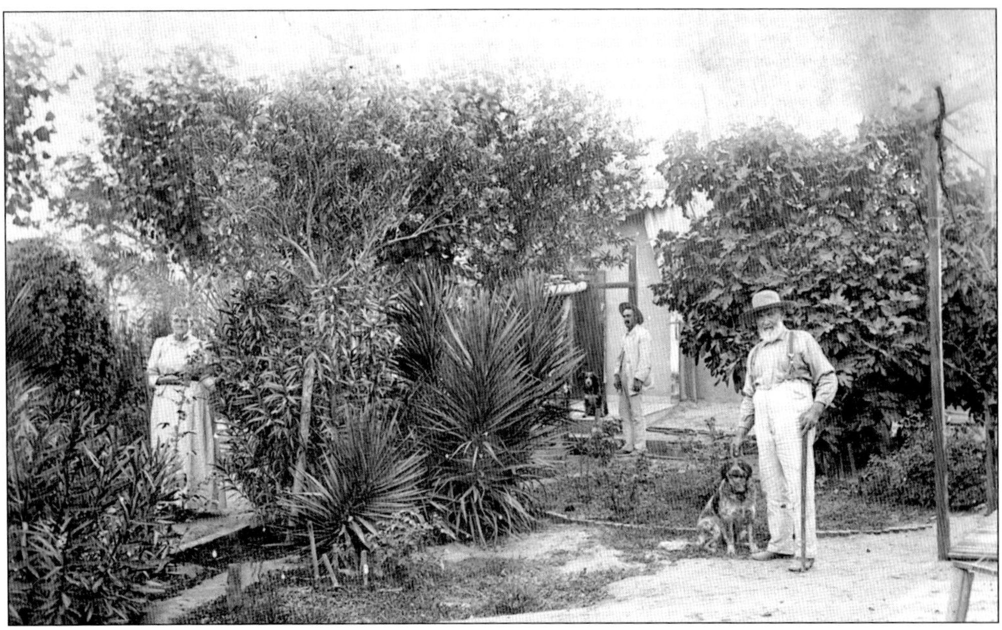

As Yuma prospered and matured, residents began taking pride in their backyard or side yard gardens. Fruit trees were particularly prized, providing both food and shade. Notice also the yucca in the garden of Mr. and Mrs. Harry Carpenter, pictured here with their gardener, Gabriel Martinez.

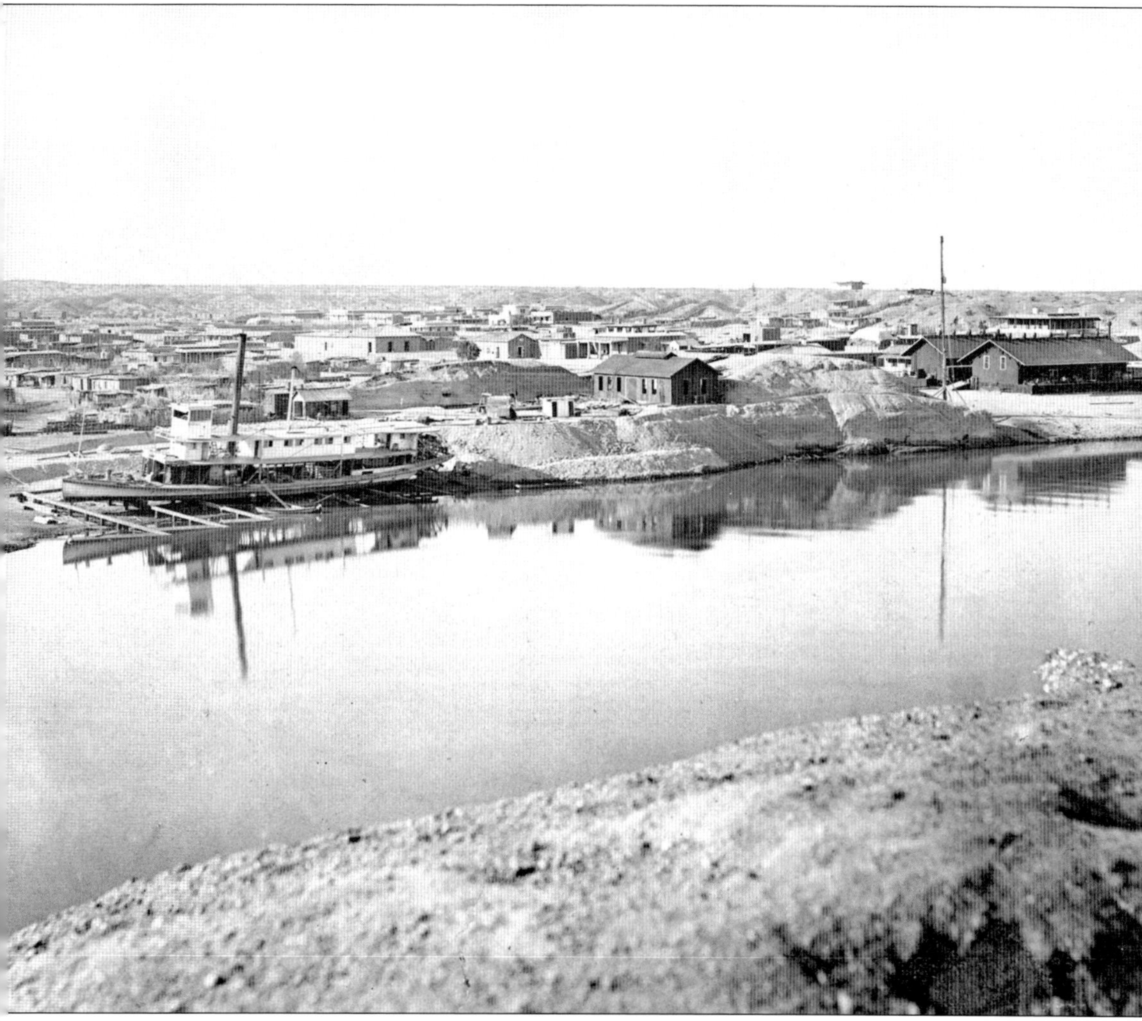

The river was in one of its better moods in this photograph of the village and the *Mohave I* from what is likely the late 1870s. It was a quarter-century earlier that George Johnson argued that the military compound here could better be supplied by schooners and steamboats. "I felt sure it must be navigable at least to its mouth," Johnson wrote in his memoirs. He also stated:

> I laid my plans before Major Robert Allen, who was at the time quartermaster general of the Pacific Coast. Shortly after Major Allen was called upon to ascertain the expense of transporting across the desert to Yuma. I figured on this and finally proposed that if they would furnish the vessel with a master I would man and provision her. My proposition was accepted and early in October 1851 they furnished the *Sierra Nevada*.

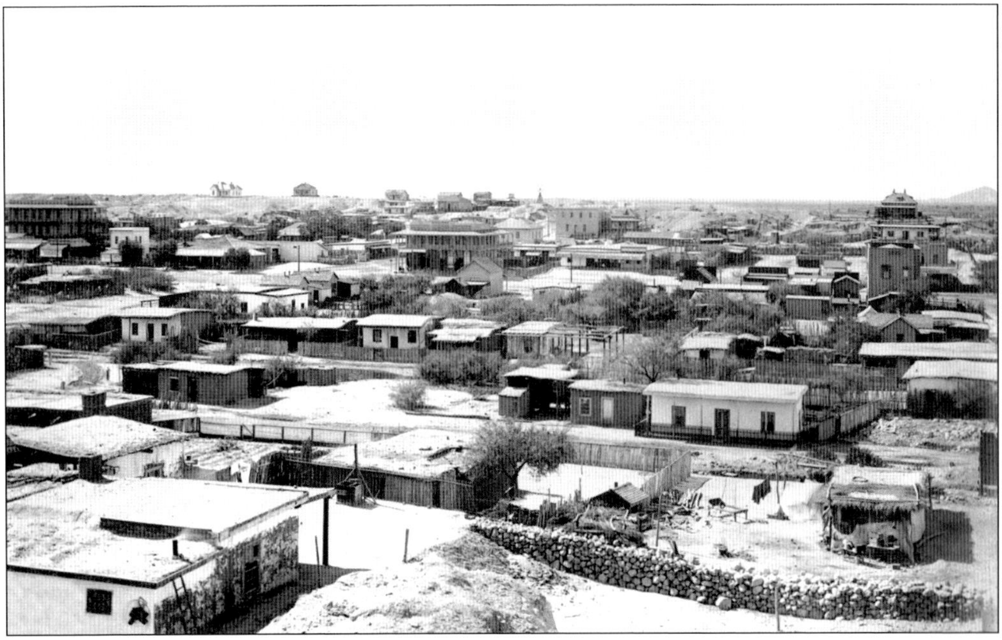

The influence of Mexico on early residential Yuma is obvious in this image as dozens of spare, flat-topped, mud-and-willow adobes with properties fenced off with whatever building supplies were available are scattered throughout the area. Notice the rock wall at the bottom right, while most yards, many with gardens, were surrounded either with sticks from native trees or upgraded with boards or wire fences. Most of the structures in this image vanished in the flood of 1891, which reached the rooftops of the adobes in the forefront.

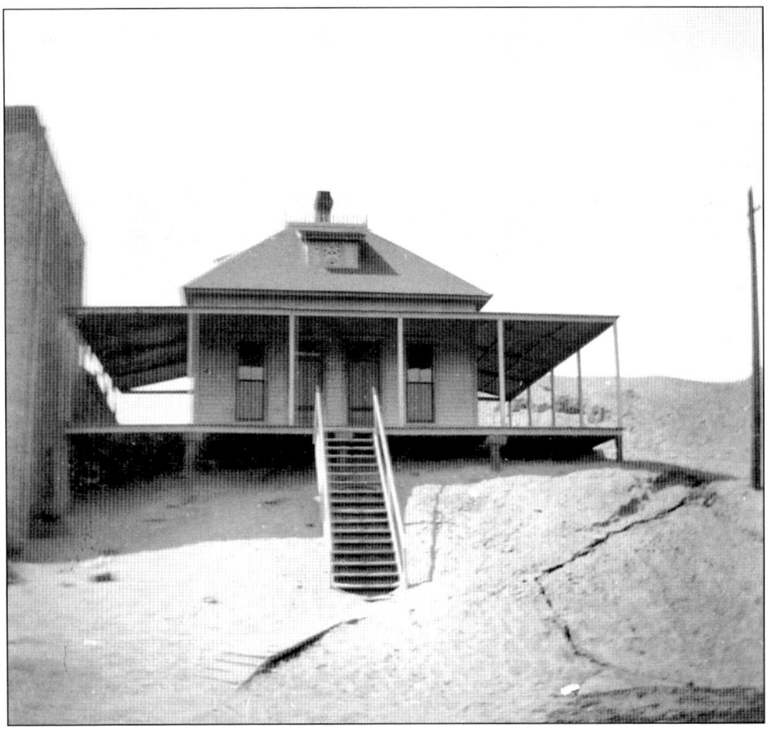

After losing enough homes to flood, Yumans began moving up the hill and building with wood. This home was also notable for the wide porch surrounding the entire house. In some cases in Yuma, the square footage of the porch was greater than the square footage of the house itself.

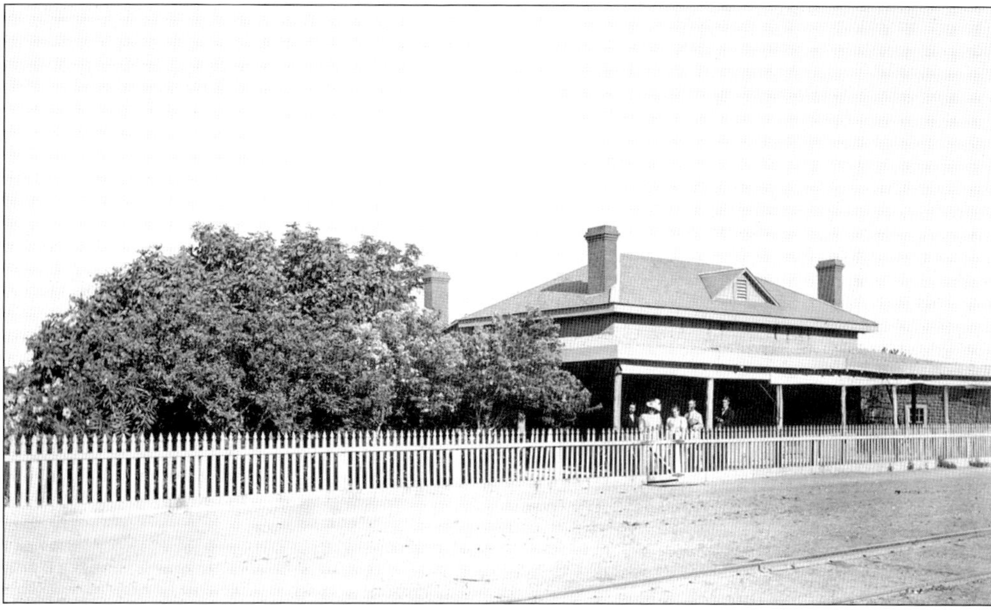

As the century came to a close, homes in Yuma began to look more like homes back east and, in many cases, like the homes these transplants lived in as children. As soon as it was financially feasible, many Yuma residents began building houses that mimicked styles from their homeland. Notice the Blaisdells added a front porch that spans the complete length of the house.

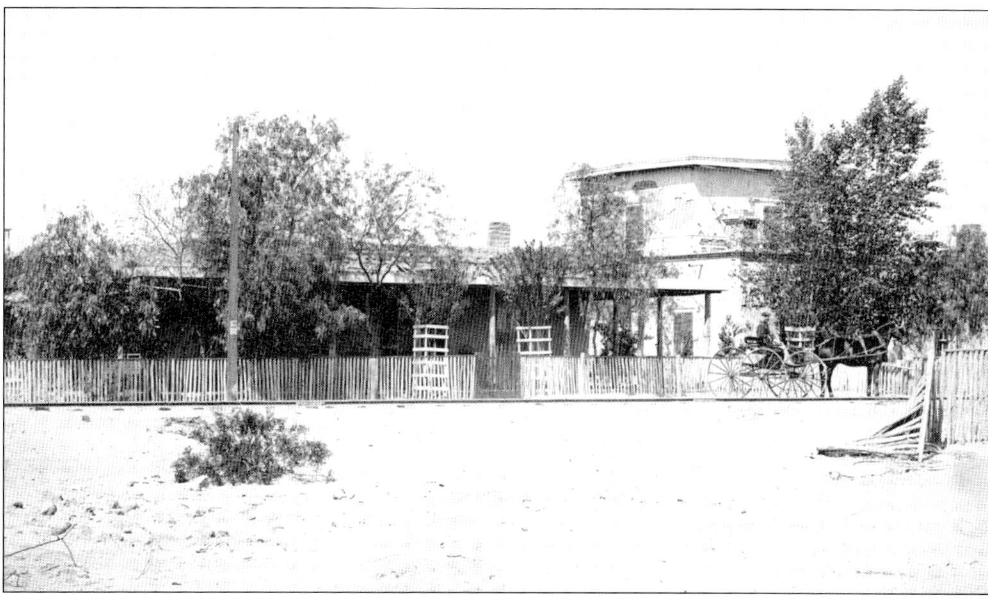

Dr. J. K. Corson, the surgeon at Fort Yuma from 1878 to 1882 who owned this house, provided medical help at the battles of Gettysburg, Falling Water, Manassas Gap, and several others, earning him the Congressional Medal of Honor. The doctor can be seen here with his horse and buggy, the preferred mode of transportation for doctors of the time.

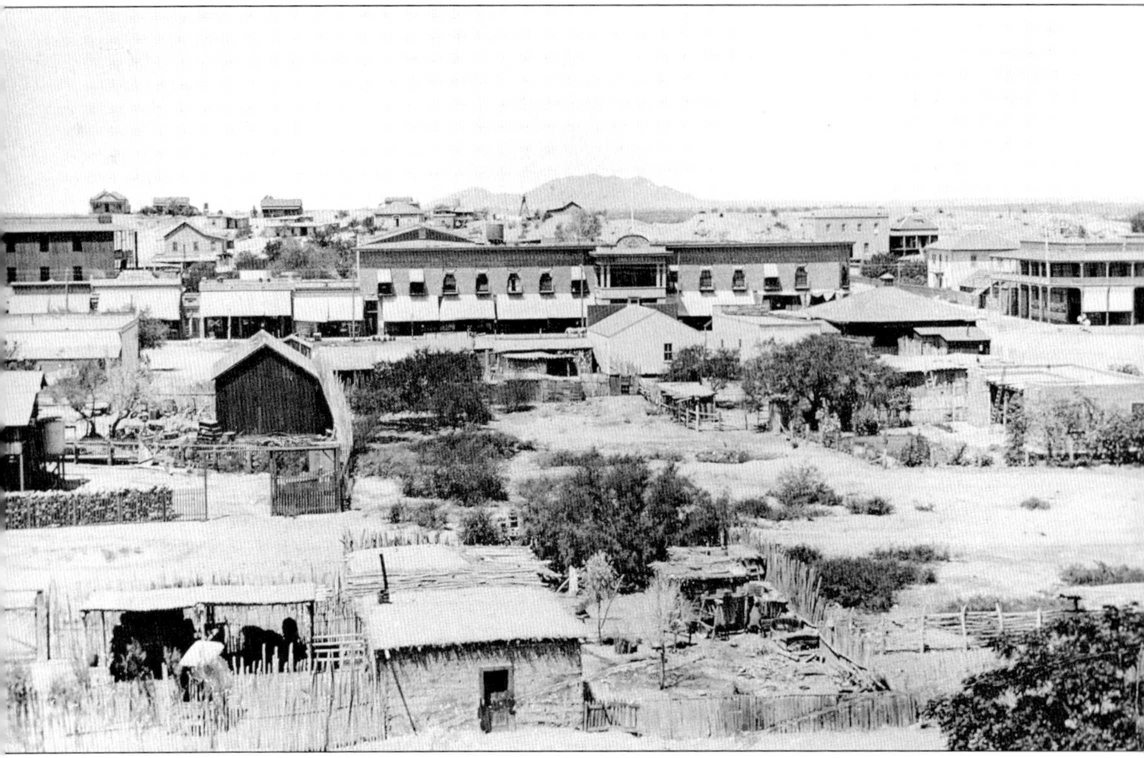

In this panorama of turn-of-the-century Yuma, the sprawling two-story hotel of John Gandolfo stands out in the center of the photograph. Gandolfo was one of several Italian immigrants who became prominent in Yuma. At the turn of the century, Gandolfo built this hotel, which prompted this playful review in the Phoenix publication, *Arizona Graphic*:

> Mr. Gandolfo and his architect evidently went to sleep at one point in the planning of the building, as there is no interior communications between the hotel office or guest rooms and the dining room. The guest goes out on the street in order to enter the dining room. As the weather is always ideal in Yuma the guest suffers no inconvenience by the arrangement.

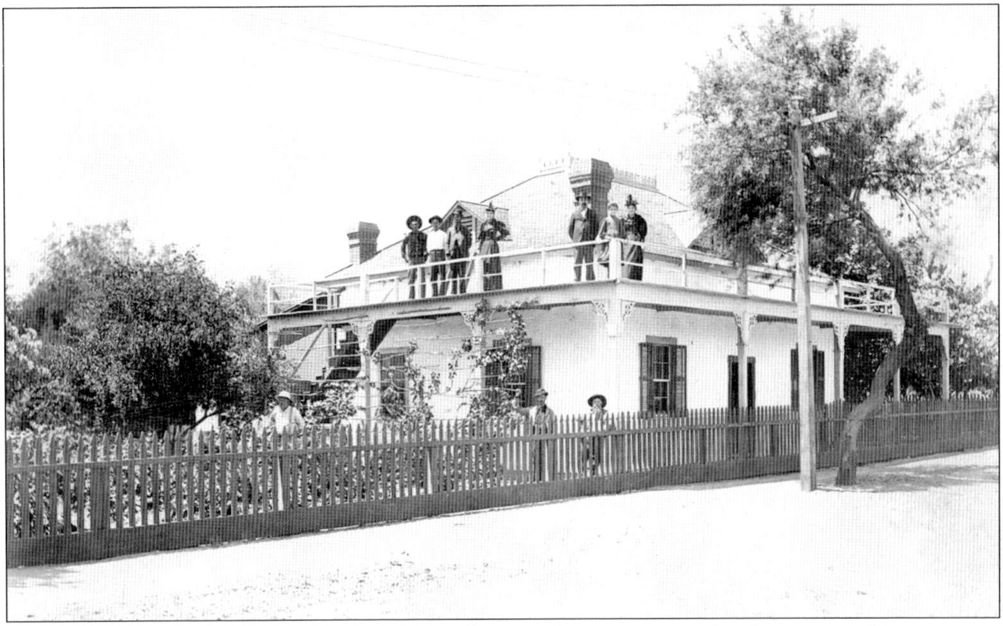

Sentinel owner John Dorrington was a strong booster for progressive development in Yuma except when it came to cutting down the mesquite tree at right in this photograph. Dorrington fought to save the tree by writing numerous editorials, and he went so far as to post a guard at the tree at night. Dorrington finally won the battle, and the road was simply built around the tree.

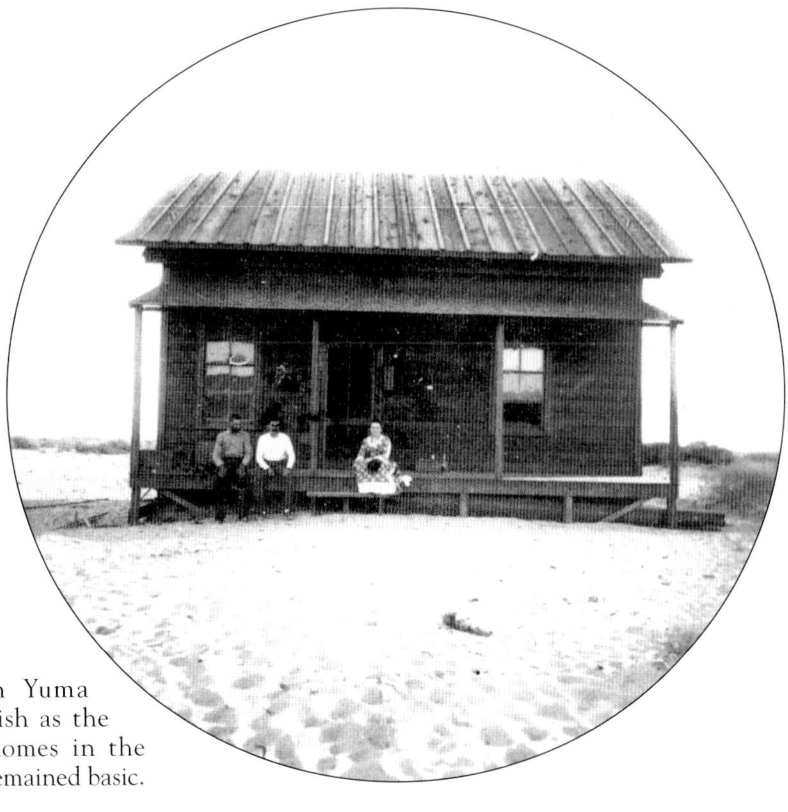

While homes in Yuma became more stylish as the century closed, homes in the country generally remained basic.

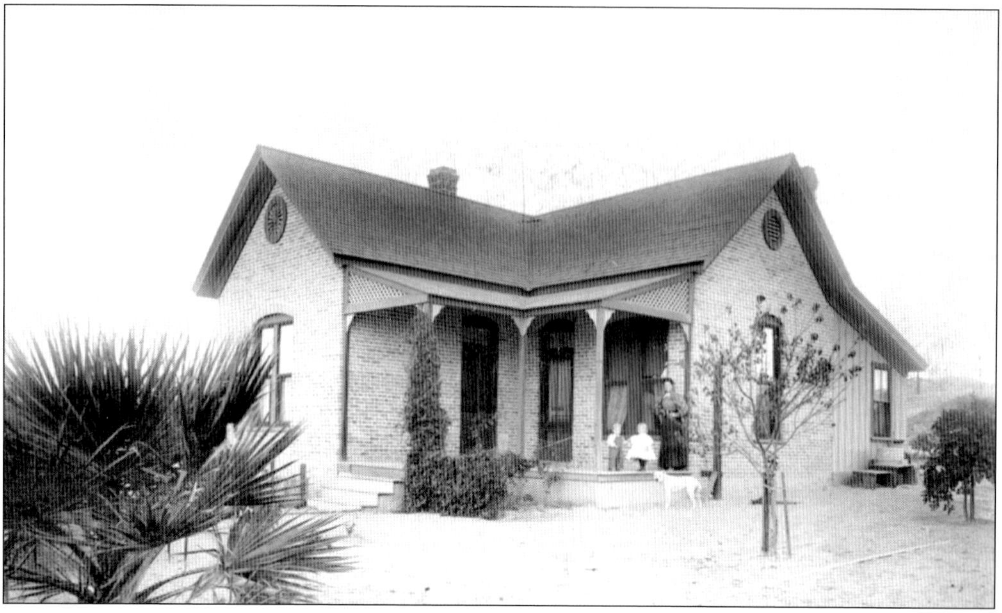

Once Yumans copied Eastern style, they began to realize there was good reason for many of the architectural features designed by the Spanish and Yuma Indians. Now, of course, Southwestern is again the style of the Southwest.

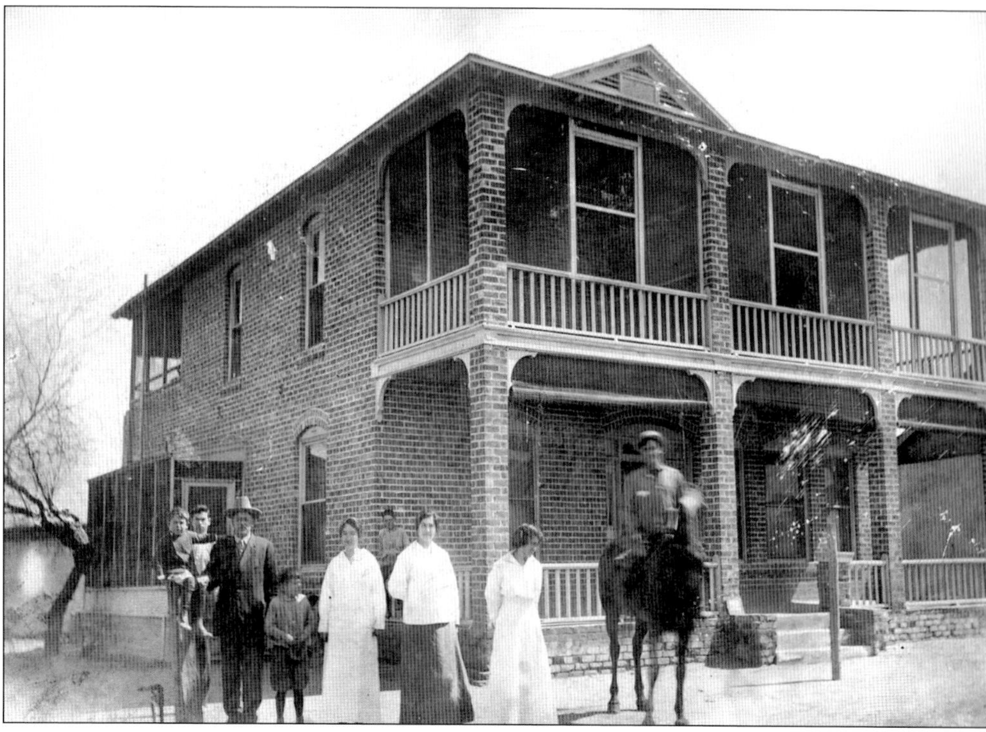

This is the Avila house on Maiden Lane as it looked in 1916. Before air conditioning, upstairs rooms in a two-story brick house would not be tolerable in a Yuma summer. The answer to that problem was the sleeping porch, which was also critical in providing the fresh air needed to ward off the dreaded tuberculosis.

Four

COMMERCE

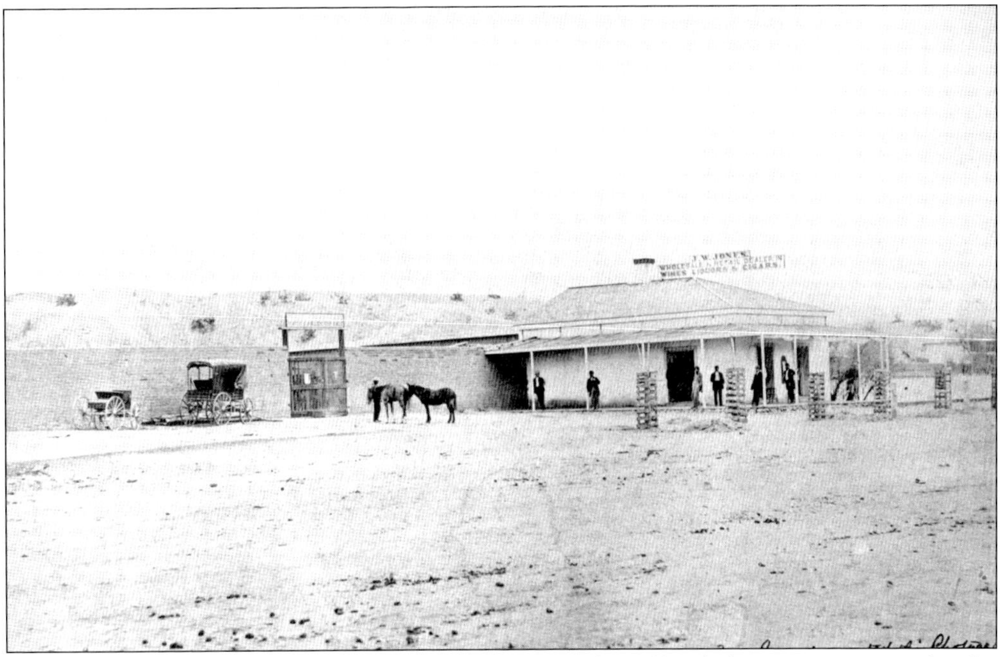

While the wild territory offered many challenges, it also offered the opportunity to be the founding father of any number of businesses, such as the general store, the livery, and the hotel, which generated occupations such as butcher, barber, blacksmith, carpenter, doctor, dentist and, seemingly the most important, bartender. If they prosper, a village becomes a town, and a town becomes a city. One of the earliest businesses in Yuma, then Arizona City, was J. W. Jones's hotel, which also specialized in wholesale wines, liquors, and cigars. Behind his store, travelers could camp in the safety of his adobe enclosure and purchase hay and barley for their animals. This photograph of Jones's one-stop shopping emporium, which sat on the north side of what is now North Main Street, was taken in 1869.

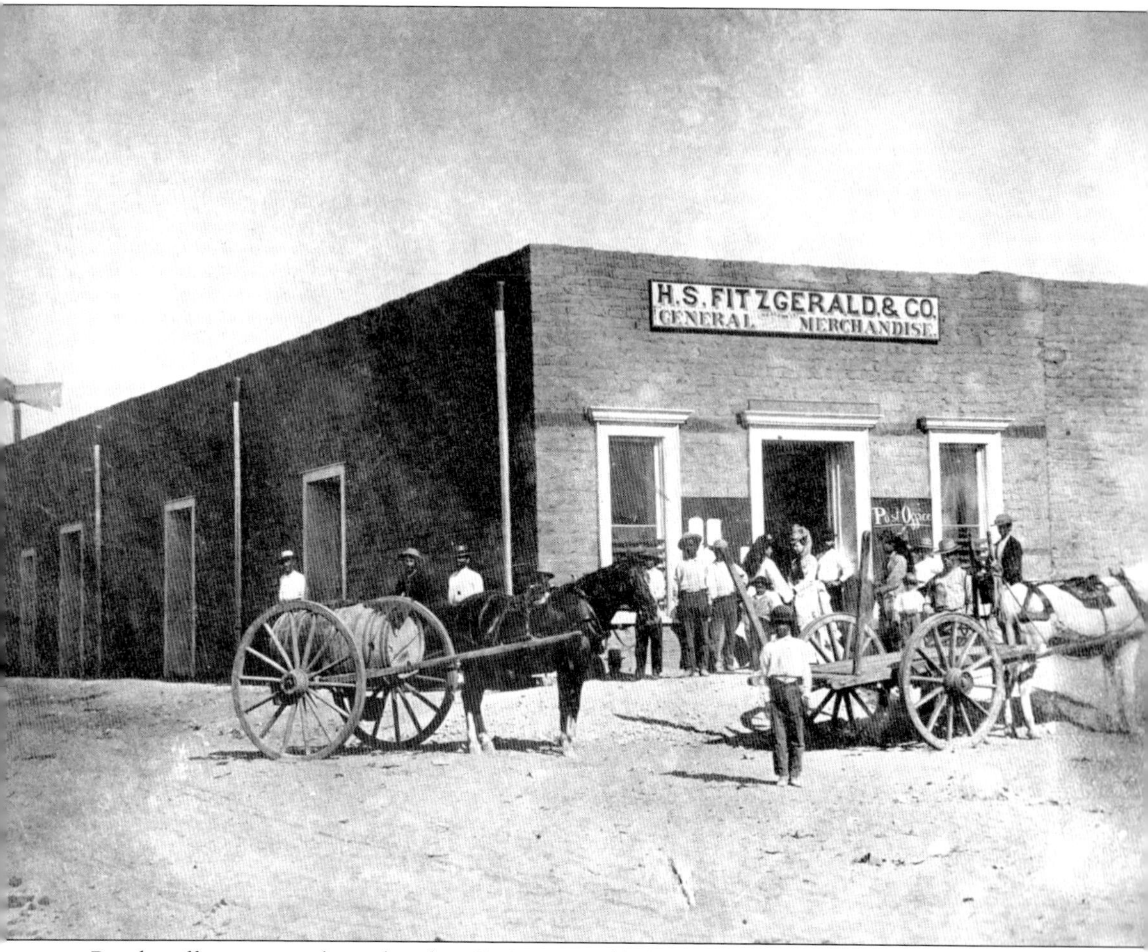

Besides offering general merchandise, H. S. Fitzgerald also held the mail contract for Arizona City, meaning his store served as the village post office. Some of Fitzgerald's most popular items were the jugs of whiskey he had sent to his store from San Francisco. This item from the *Arizona Sentinel* in 1874 gives a small taste of the role whiskey played for men in the early Western town:

> Our excellent and liberal merchant friend Henry S. Fitzgerald, Esq., presented us the other day with a demijohn filled with the finest "Ladies Crusade" that we have tasted lately. It is good to have on hand in case of snake or other reptile bites. It is also good to have when a weary friend calls to pay his subscription and other little things.

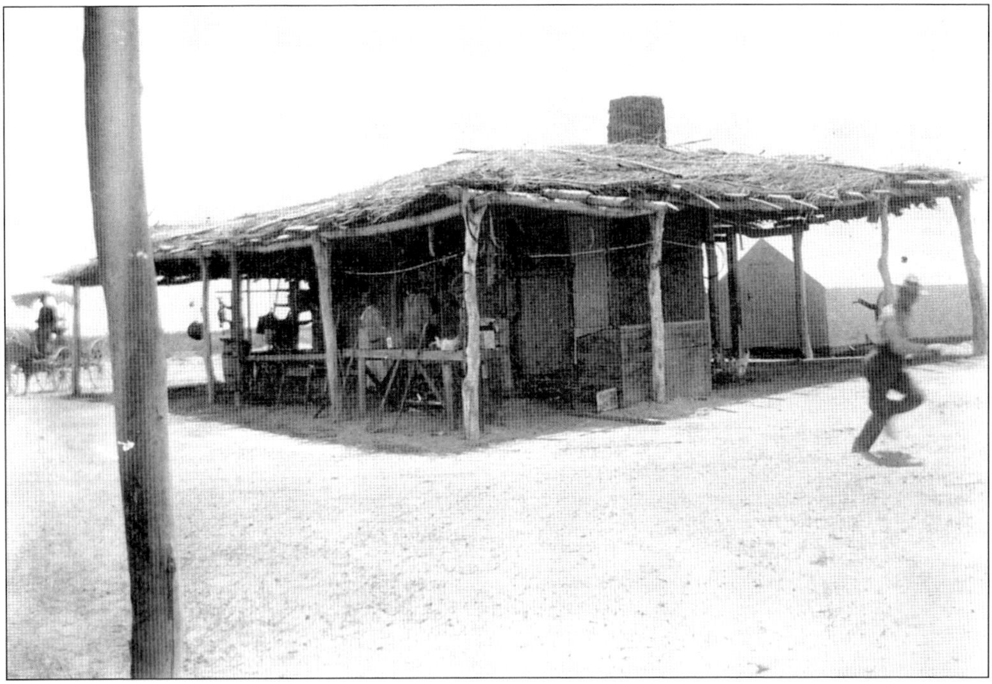

Early taverns were little more than ramshackle hovels of adobe and arrowweed with a man behind a table wielding a demijohn of whiskey. This early bar sat on the outskirts of Yuma into the 1880s, long after the downtown's finer taverns had been built. It likely survived because it provided other entertainment. Written on the back of the original photograph is the following: "Liz Rooming House—not too respectable." This may explain the man seemingly running from the camera's eye.

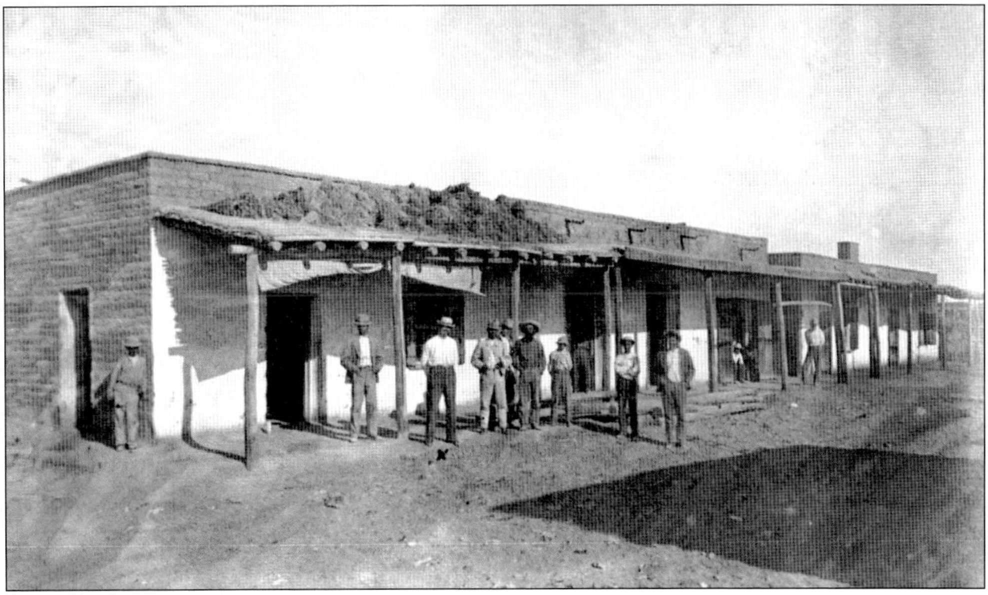

Most of the earliest businesses in town were made of adobe, with little concern for style. Note that only the front of the buildings beneath the awning were plastered. These buildings disintegrated in the flood of 1891.

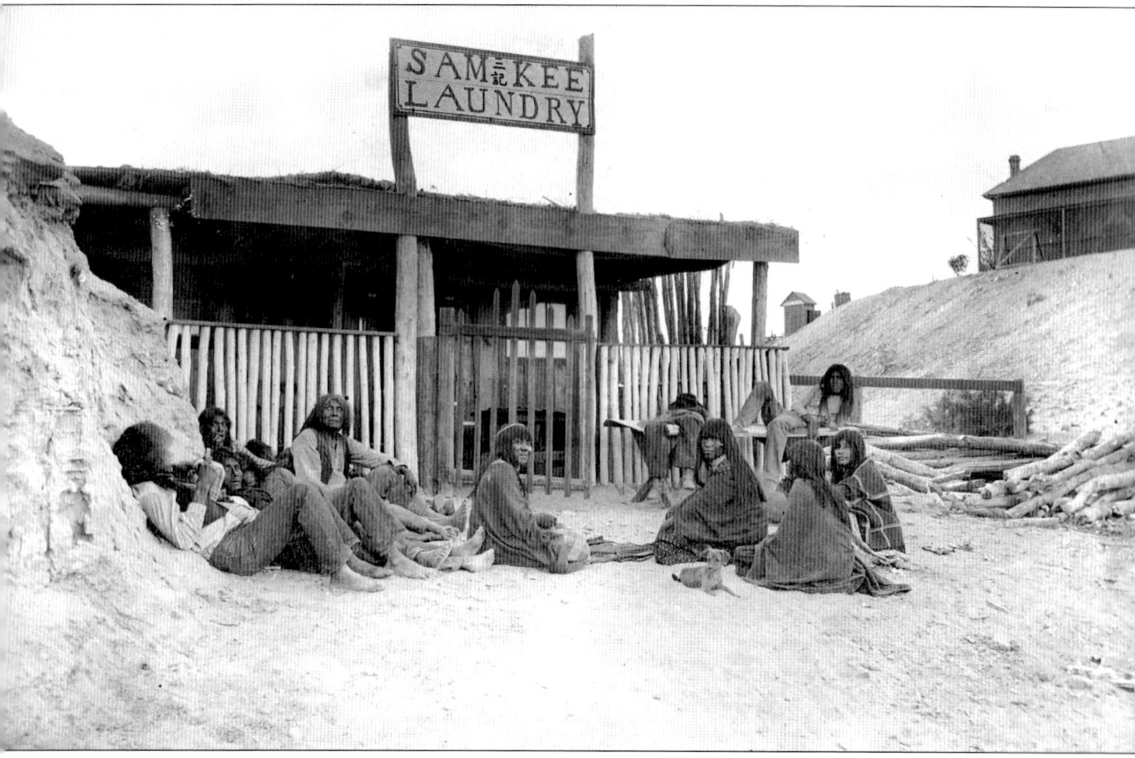

Chinese immigrants, such as the owners of the Sam Kee Laundry in Yuma, which is pictured here behind a group of resting Quechan, found a more welcoming Anglo community in Yuma and the Arizona Territory than in many areas in the West. Some historians attribute this to the fact that Anglos in Arizona Territory saw Chinese immigrants as less threatening politically than Mexican immigrants, who made up much of the population of Arizona and a still larger segment of New Mexico, with which Arizona was often being pitched nationally for combined statehood. The first Chinese immigrant in Arizona was William Tching, listed in the 1860 census as a "steamboat cook," likely with the Colorado Steam Navigation Company. Other Chinese men came as servants to the officers at Fort Yuma. As was true across the Southwest, though, the largest wave of Asian immigrants to Yuma came with the Southern Pacific Railroad in 1877.

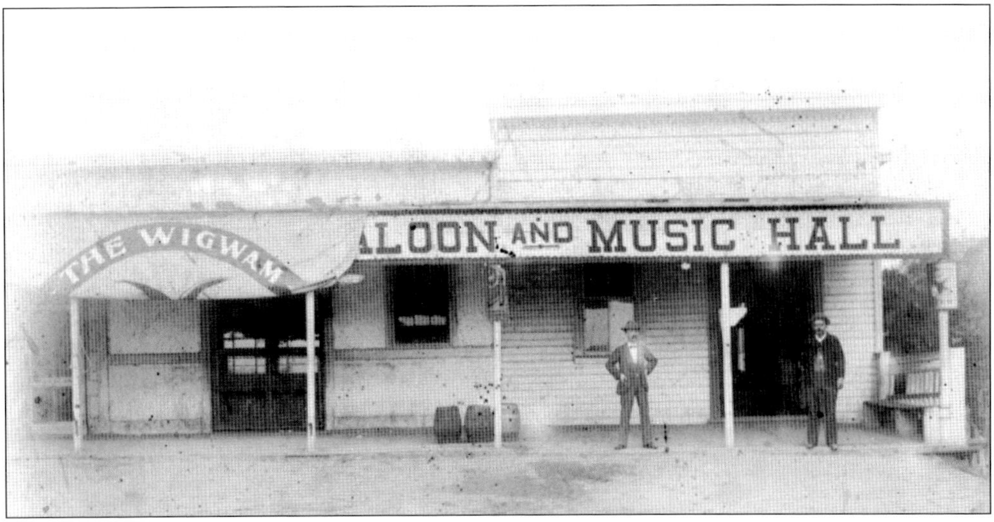

This early saloon was likely the first to include a music and dance hall in Yuma. Musicians would set up in the large hall (left). Note the three wooden kegs, likely for beer, and the bench (far right) for dancers to take a breather with their date.

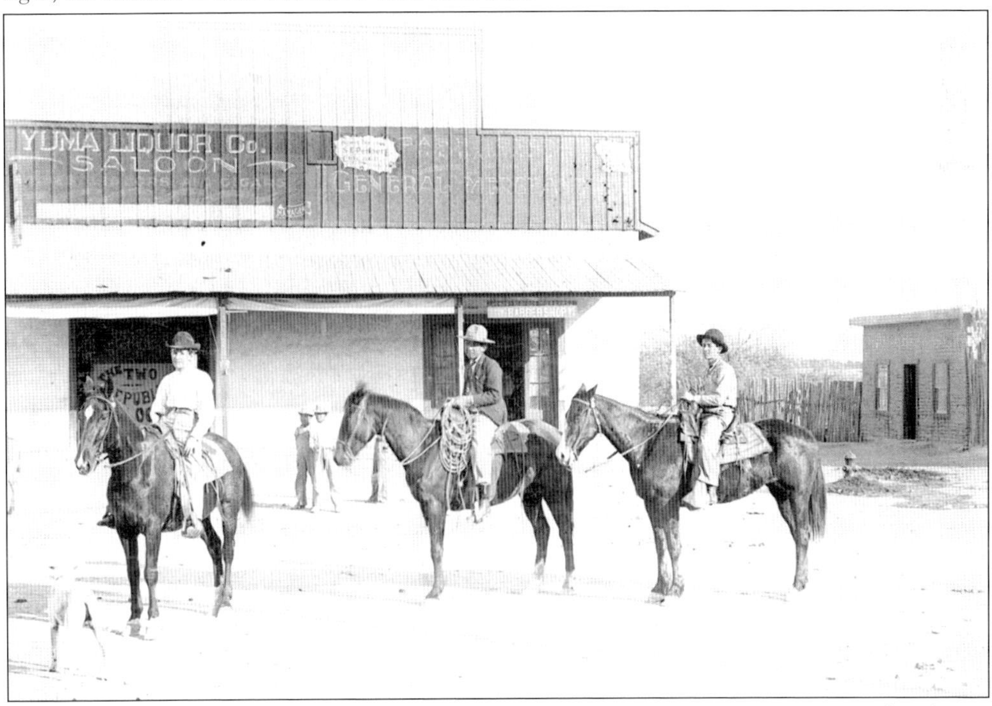

Competition was fierce among bars in Yuma, as this 1881 promotional note in the *Sentinel* explains:

> Yuma has two hotels, one restaurant, four general stores, four grocery and variety stores, two drug stores, one stationery, three butcher shops, one barber shop, two blacksmith shops, two wheelwright shops, two paint shops, one saddle and harness shop, four bakeries, one jewelry, one stable and feed yard, one printing and job office, one gunsmith, one boot and shoe shop, four china wash houses, three physicians, five attorneys, two telegraph offices and 11 saloons.

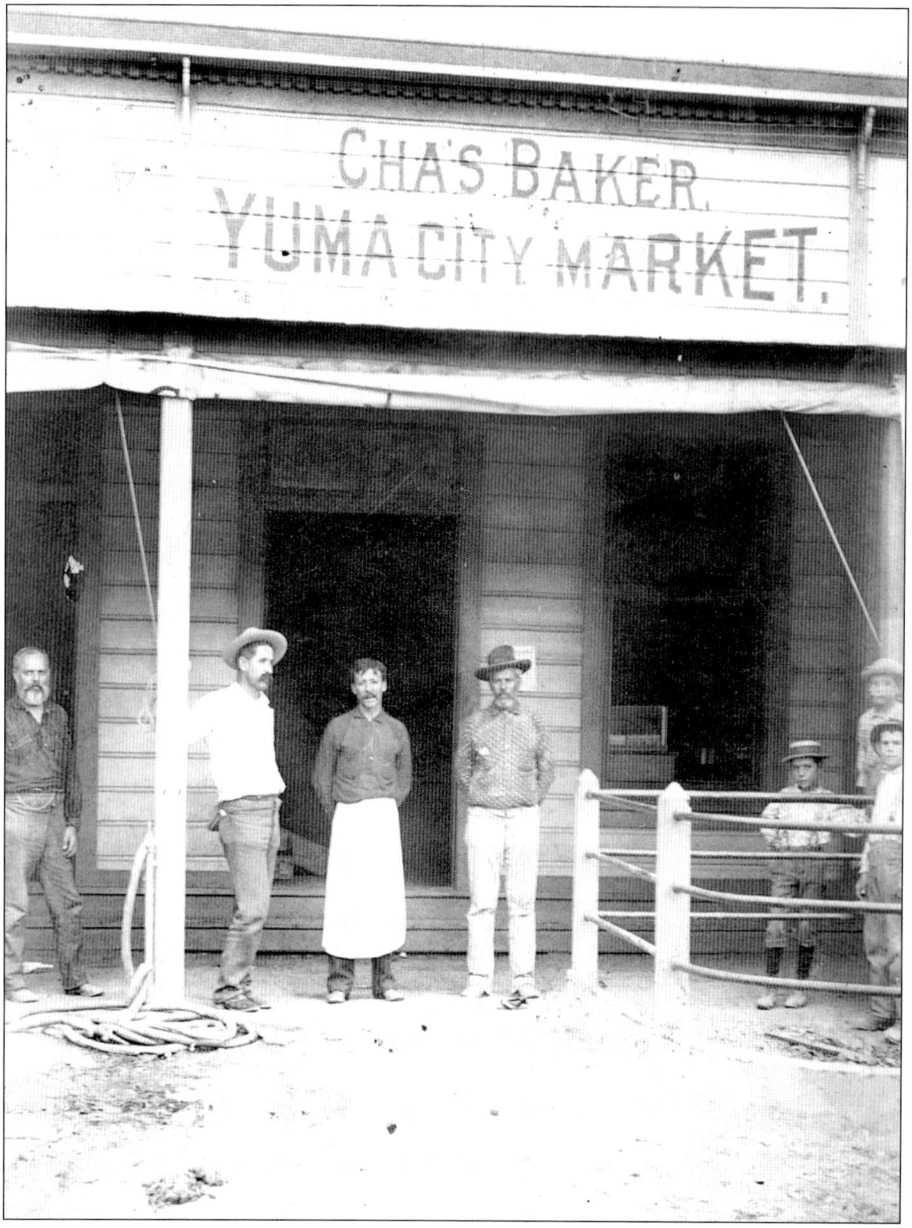

Charles Baker's Yuma City Market, which sold the meat of cattle that Baker raised on his ranchlands around Yuma, was one of those three butcher shops and more than 50 businesses in the thriving town by 1880. More so than in many communities, the businesses of early Yuma were serving people other than those living in the town itself. The following note in the *Sentinel* in 1874 shows how private money was often used in the early days to spruce up the emerging town:

> Hon. J. M. Redondo, our worthy landlord, has laid a fine sidewalk in front of our office. These improvements are not only ornamental but useful. Gradually our enterprising citizens are extending these blue gravel sidewalks on both sides of Main Street, and soon we will be able to walk the whole length of the street without having our nice polished boots soiled by dust.

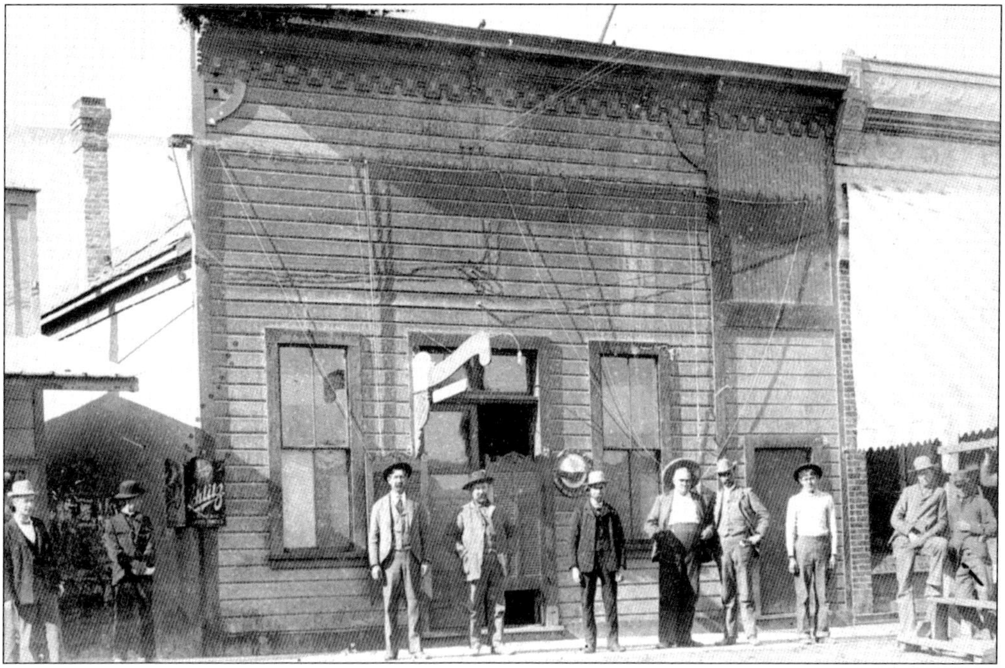

In downtown Yuma, with 11 saloons, a bar owner had to make his establishment stand out from the crowd. One way to do that was to make the bar cooler than the competition. In the 1880s, bars and stores downtown began using what essentially was clipper-ship sail technology to make portable awnings for their businesses. In this photograph, the rigging of one awning can be seen while the neighboring awning is fully extended.

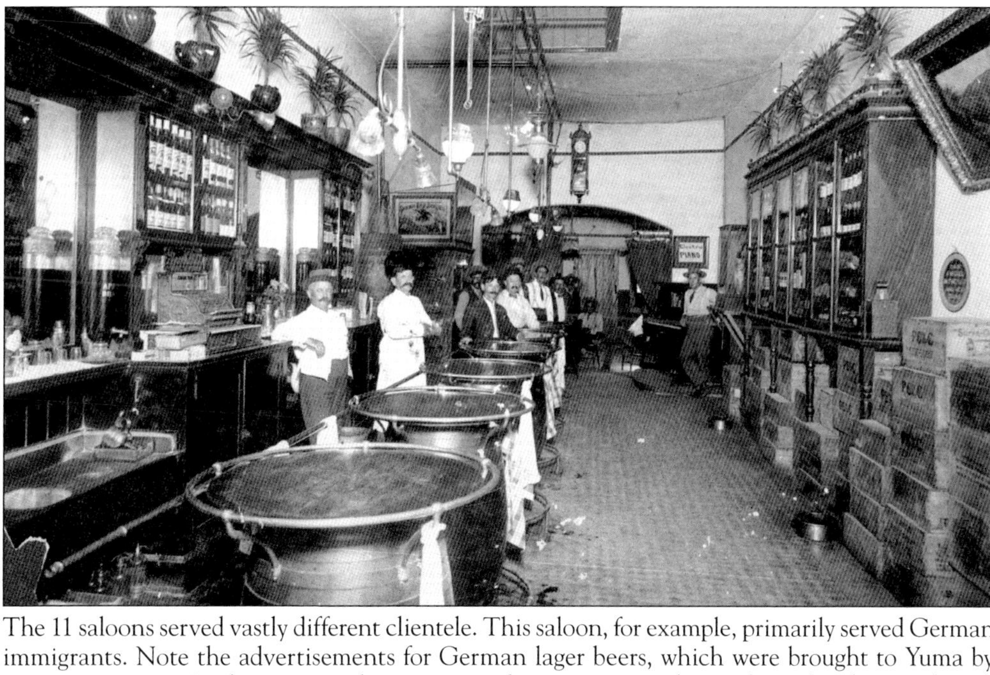

The 11 saloons served vastly different clientele. This saloon, for example, primarily served German immigrants. Note the advertisements for German lager beers, which were brought to Yuma by steamer or train. In the summer, bar patrons often congregated outside under the porch roof or awning.

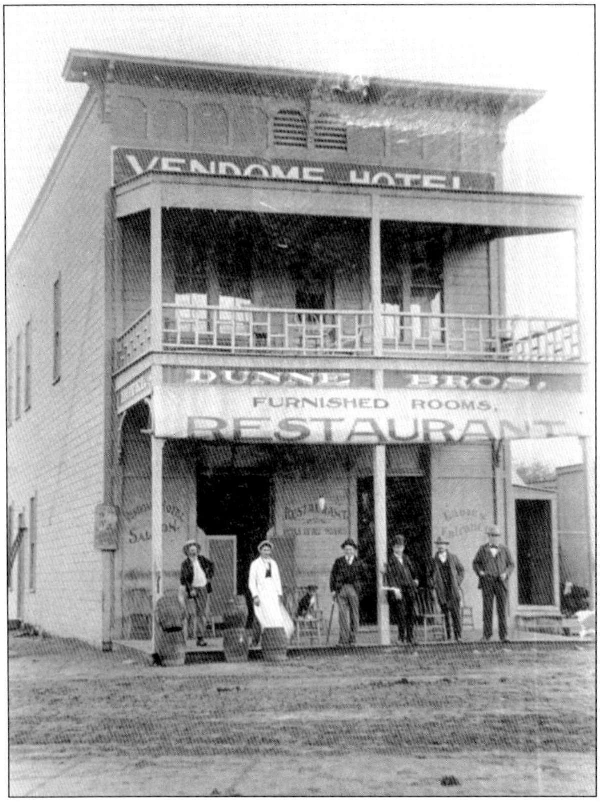

Not quite the Hotel Vendome in France, the Vendome Hotel of Yuma was still considered quite pleasant by frontier hotel standards. Martha Summerhayes, who came to the region with her husband, an army officer, quickly learned the tricks of making life pleasant in the desert. She wrote this in 1874:

> Of course it was hot; it was August, and we expected it. . . . But the heat of those places can be much alleviated by the surroundings. There were shower baths, and latticed piazzas, and large ollas hanging in the shade of them, containing cool water. Yuma was only 20 days from San Francisco, and they were able to get many things direct by steamer. Of course there was no ice, and butter was kept only by ingenious devices of the Chinese servants.

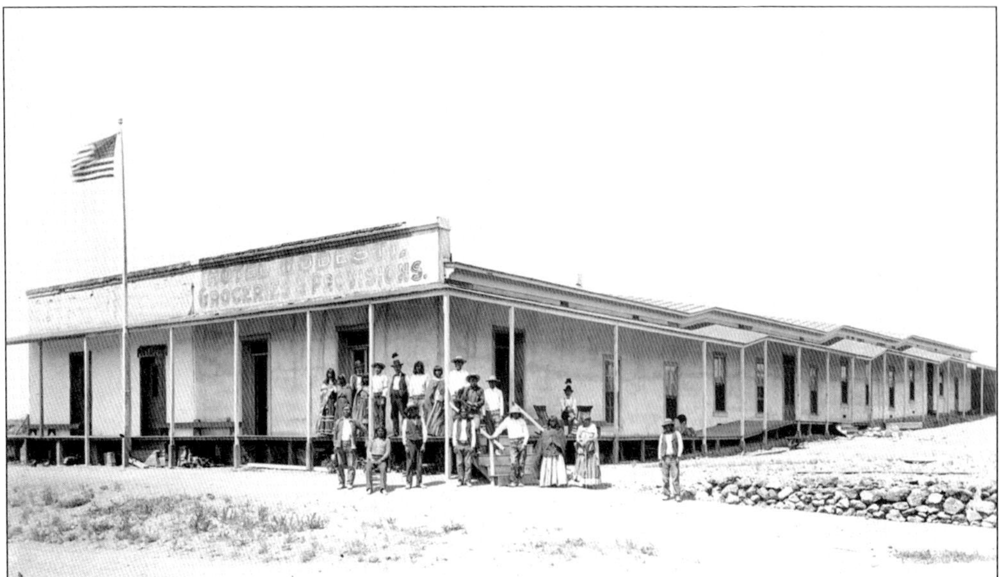

East of Yuma, out on the Gila Trail, was another hotel at Agua Caliente famous for its hot mineral baths. Although the hot springs have since dried up, this building is still standing. The Modesti and Pancrazi families of Yuma ran the hotel and baths for most of the spring's existence.

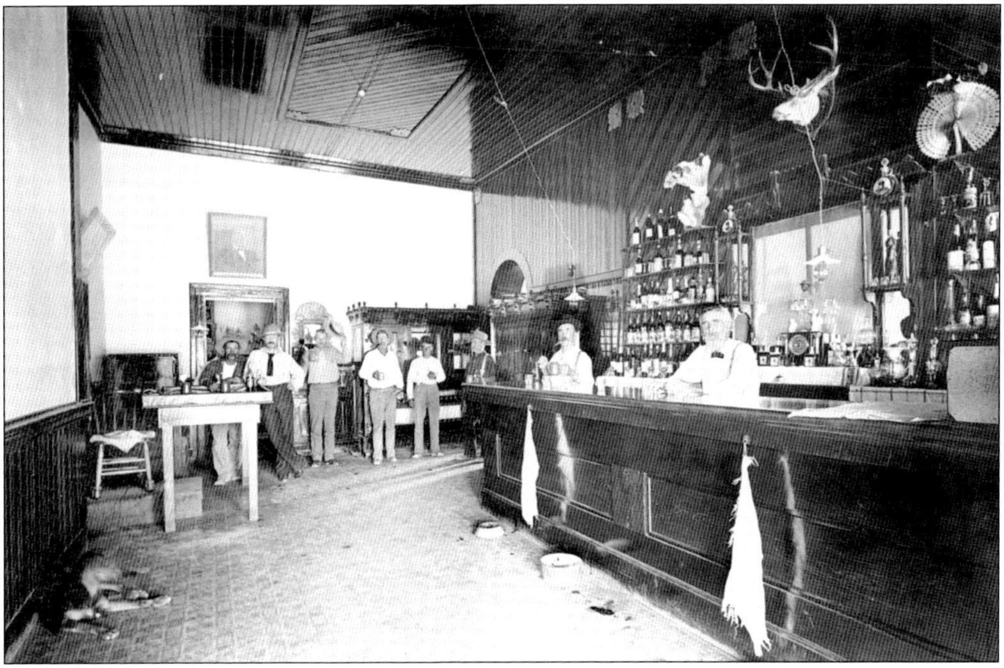

In 1901, one of the most notorious crimes in Yuma's history, the shooting death of Undersheriff Devane, began with a theft of some of a bar's stored liquor. After the theft, Devane spotted three men acting suspiciously. When he told the men he wanted to search them, one of the men pulled a gun and shot and killed Devane. The sheriff took the culprit to the jail for safe keeping, but after he was tried and sentenced, the shooter broke out of the jail, stole a train, and was ultimately killed by posse members and buried where he laid. The culprit ultimately ended up in the territorial prison.

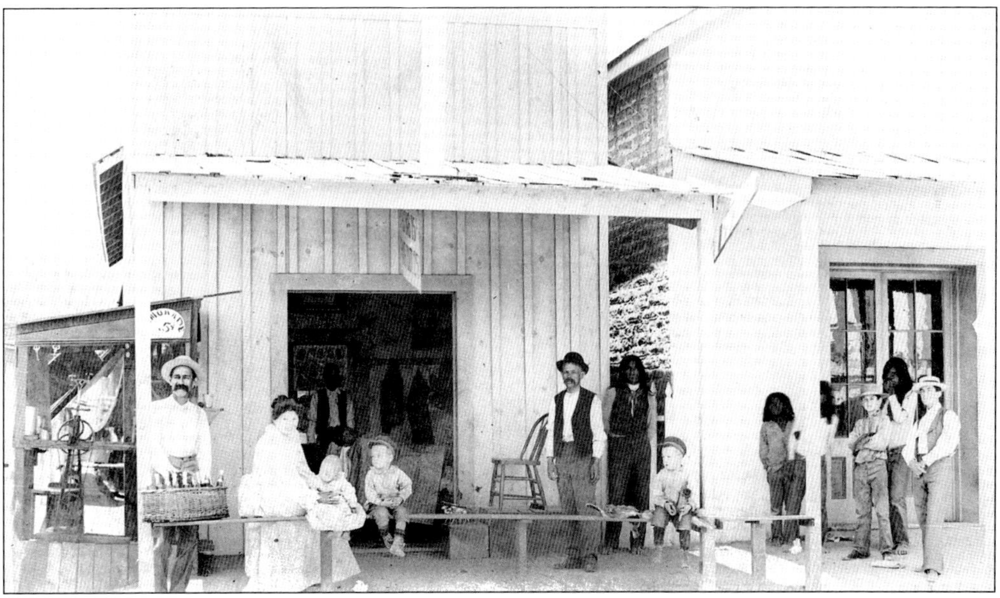

While waiting for a 15¢ haircut, Yumans could catch up on gossip as they waited outside sipping on 5¢ lemonade.

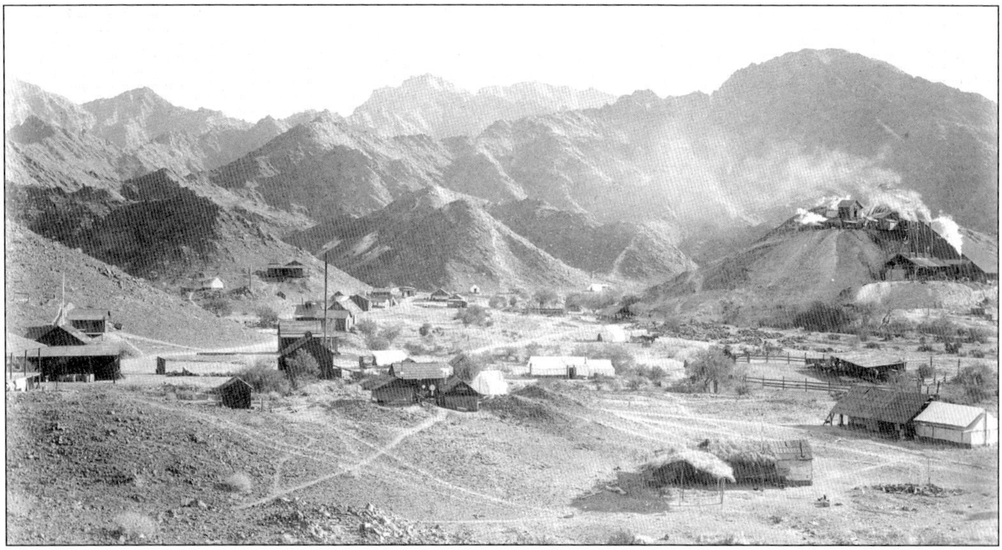

Yuma would have remained a village if not for the immense amount of trade flowing to and from the area's mines. At first, the river crossing was a trading post for prospectors searching for gold, which was first found in Arizona by Jacob Snively about 20 miles up the Gila River from its junction with the Colorado River. Within a year, 1,000 people were looking for gold around Arizona's first boomtown, Gila City, which sprang up around Snively's find. As with most of Arizona's golden boomtowns, a few people became rich while most were fleeced by traders selling goods at grossly inflated prices. In Gila City in the 1850s, beans cost 50¢ a pound, while a loaf of bread cost $1—prices that are still seen in Yuma. By 1864, Gila City, "The promising Metropolis of Arizona," as journalist J. Ross Browne put it, "consisted of three chimneys and a coyote." One of the most enduring of the gold mines was the Fortuna, which employed between 80 and 100 people during its heyday from 1896 to 1904. The mine produced more than $2.5 million in gold bullion.

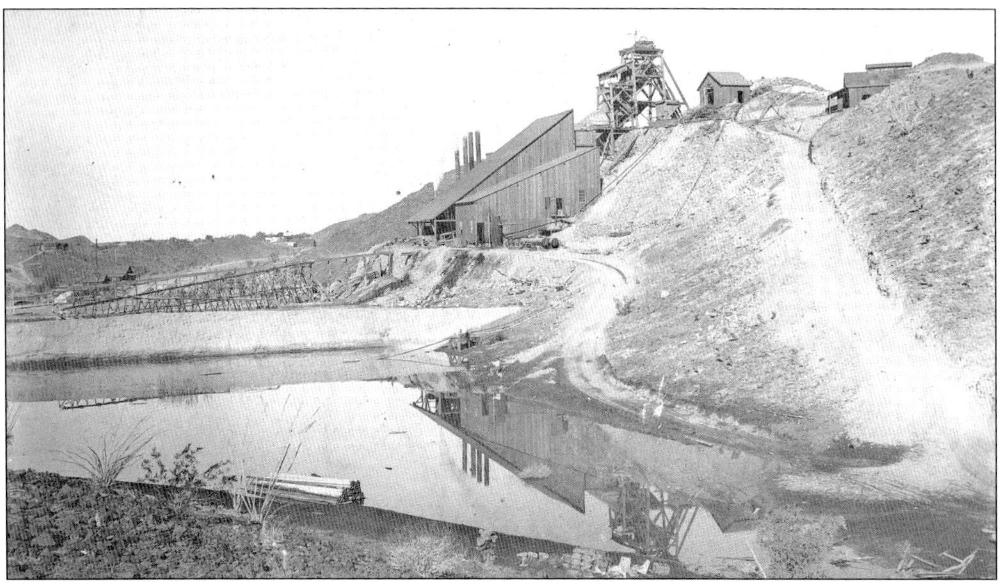

This shack was one of the finer residences for gold miners at the Fortuna Mine. But in time, miners realized that a small, single-story wood shack with little ventilation was just about the hottest structure a person could build in the Sonoran desert. Many miners built a secondary structure of poles and thatch, or whatever was available, to provide shade for their home.

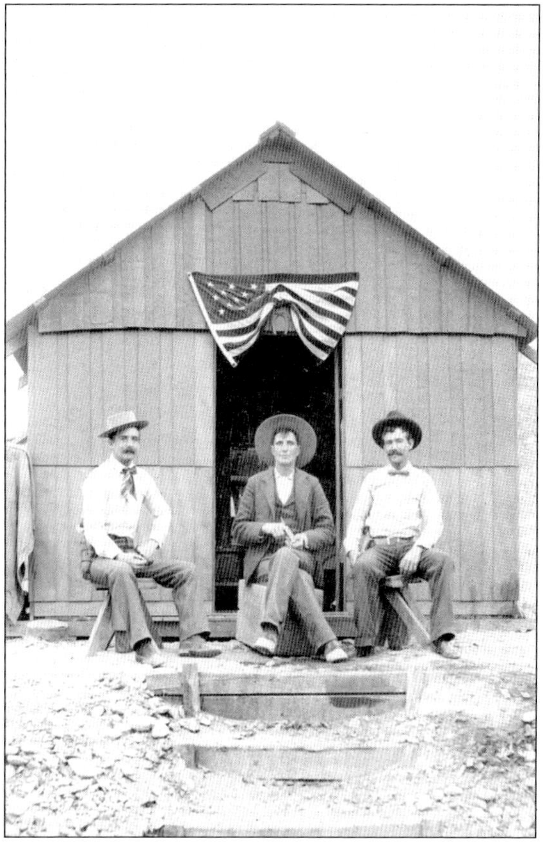

Unlike many mines, the Fortuna and its sister city, La Fortuna, had a strong community life. Besides a school, hotel, and saloon, the people of La Fortuna also held numerous events such as this dance, the "Hard-Time Ball," which brought in the New Year at the mine.

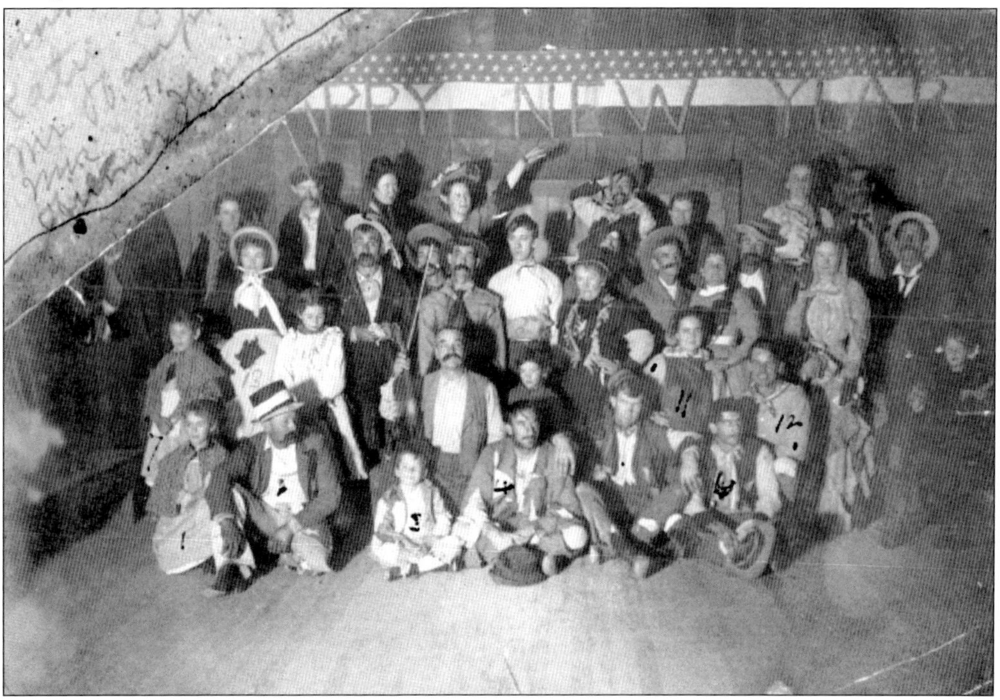

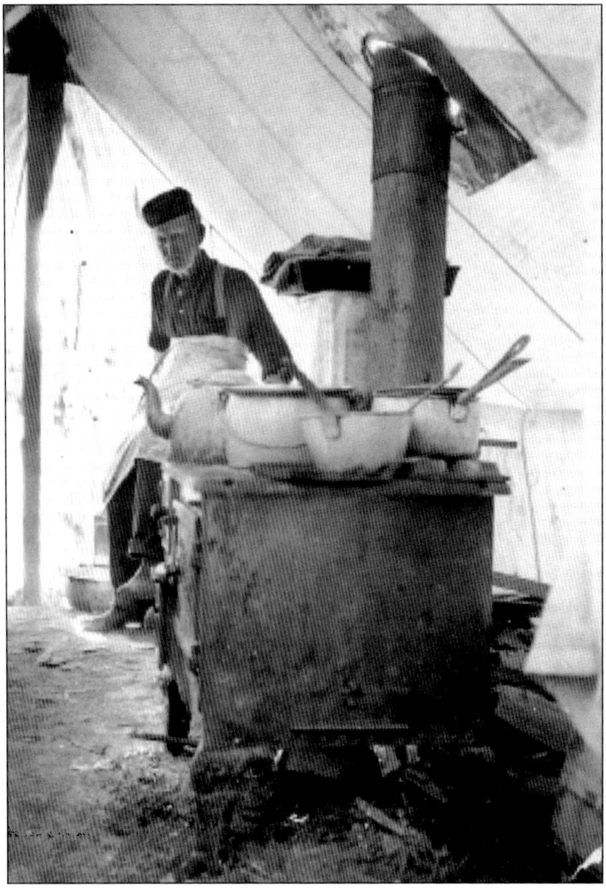

Chinese immigrants moved from California into many of the toughest jobs in the West, particularly in railroad and mining. The older Chinese men likely took the path of many miners and other hard laborers in the West—when they grew too old to work the most demanding jobs, they put their years of experience to work in the kitchen.

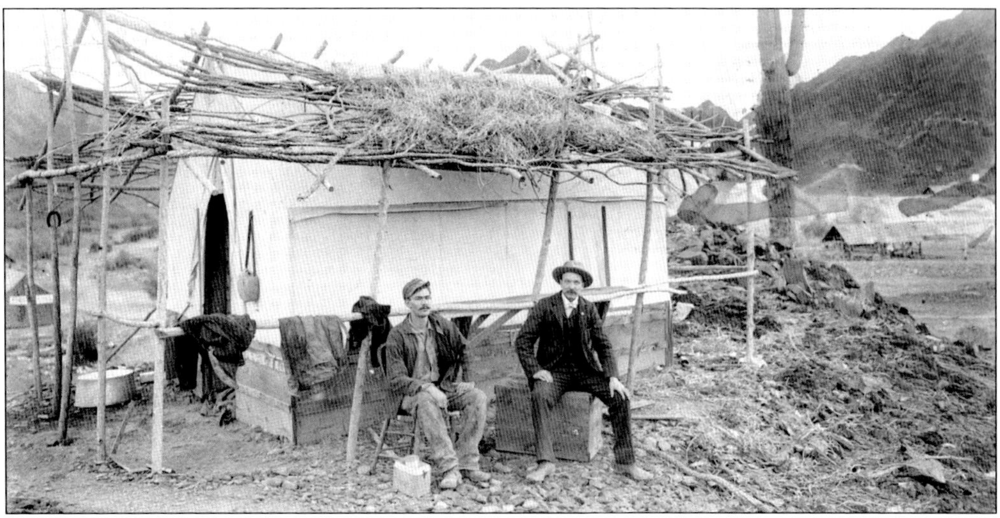

This was the home of miner Charlie Ingalls at the Fortuna Mine. By the time this image was taken in 1897, a year after a large influx of miners to the site, the residents had figured out that canvas and wood shacks needed their own shade structure to make them livable in the intense heat.

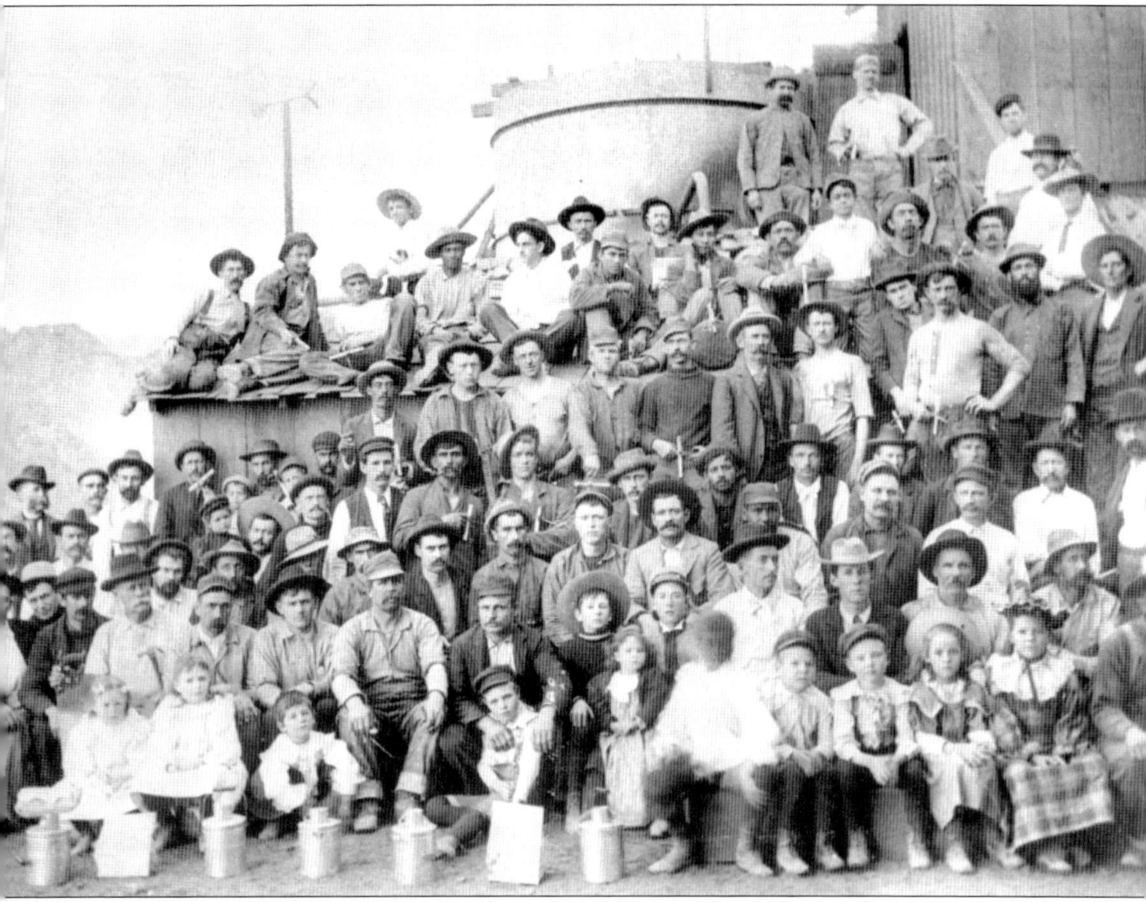

This image from the Fortuna Mine, part of the Enderton-Lancaster Collection at the State Historical Society, was taken between shifts on a Sunday afternoon in 1897. Most of the schoolchildren of La Fortuna are pictured here. Members of the Doan family are identified, including Fletcher Morris Doan (standing at left with Stetson and tie), his son John Doan (left center, wearing white shirt, vest, tie, and small cap), Fletcher Morris Doan Jr. (boy in the front center with the big hat and hand on knee), and Leslie Doan (boy at right of Morris in uniform and cap), who was accidentally shot and killed at La Fortuna shortly after this photograph was taken. The Fortuna Mine shut down in 1904 but was prospected on and off for another 20 years.

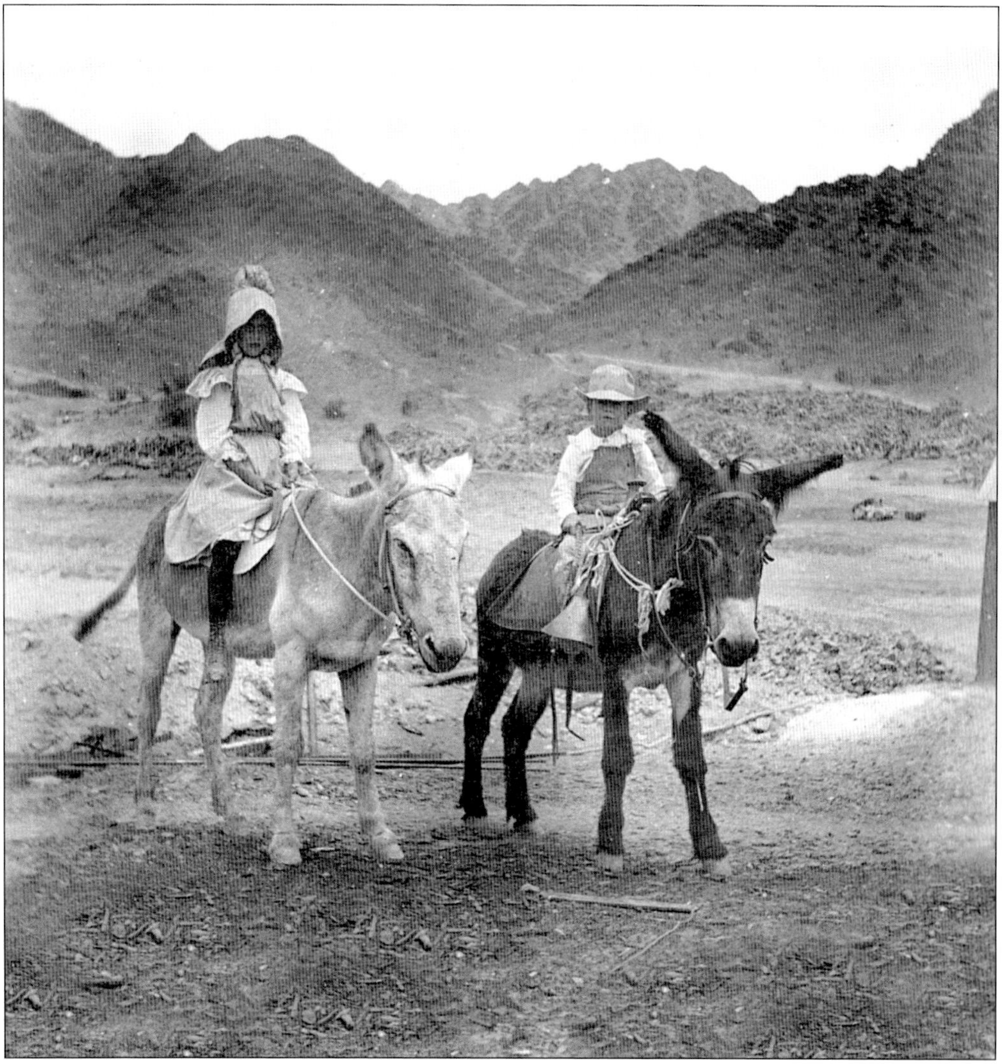

The gold mines of Arizona were not places for children. Leslie Doan, as noted on the previous page, died here, a victim of an accidental gunshot in a place where every shack had a gun. The landscapes surrounding the mines of the Yuma region are some of the most rugged and hostile lands on earth, with every plant designed to stab and every rock jagged to the foot of horse or man. This unique photograph from the Enderton-Lancaster collection gives a taste of life for a child at an Arizona mining town, which in this case is La Fortuna.

To maintain some semblance of civilization and some order in the classroom, the schoolchildren at La Fortuna wore uniforms to school. As is clear from this image, there were precious few other bits of niceties in the mountain camps.

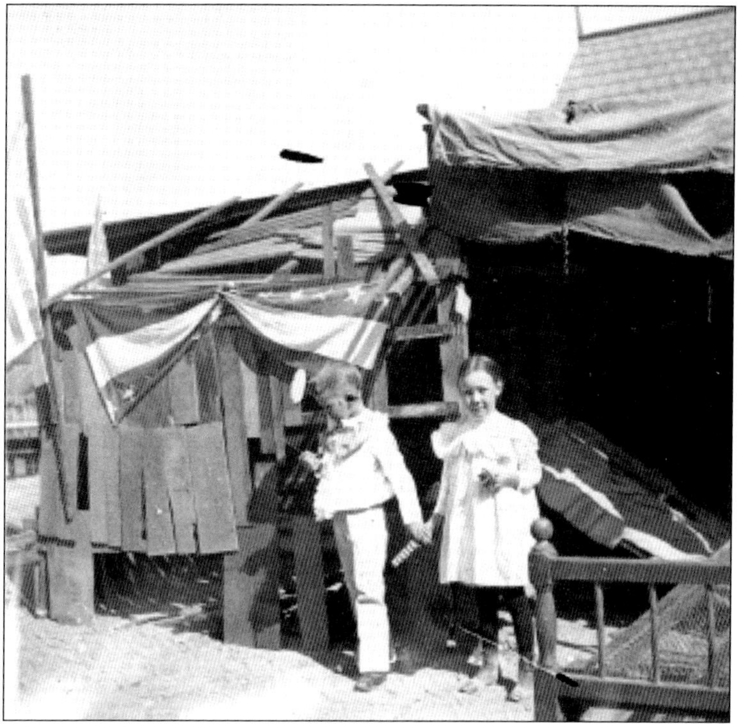

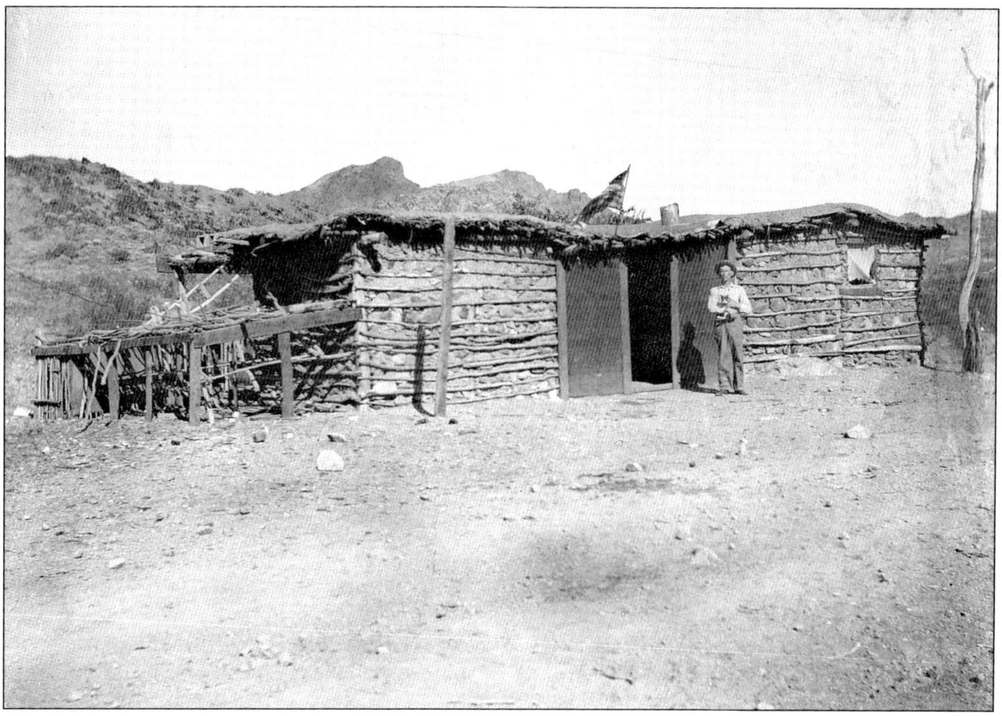

The miners of the brutal mountain terrain near Yuma used whatever materials they could find to build structures. This comparatively large home at the King of Arizona Mine was built with layers of large stones supported by thin poles.

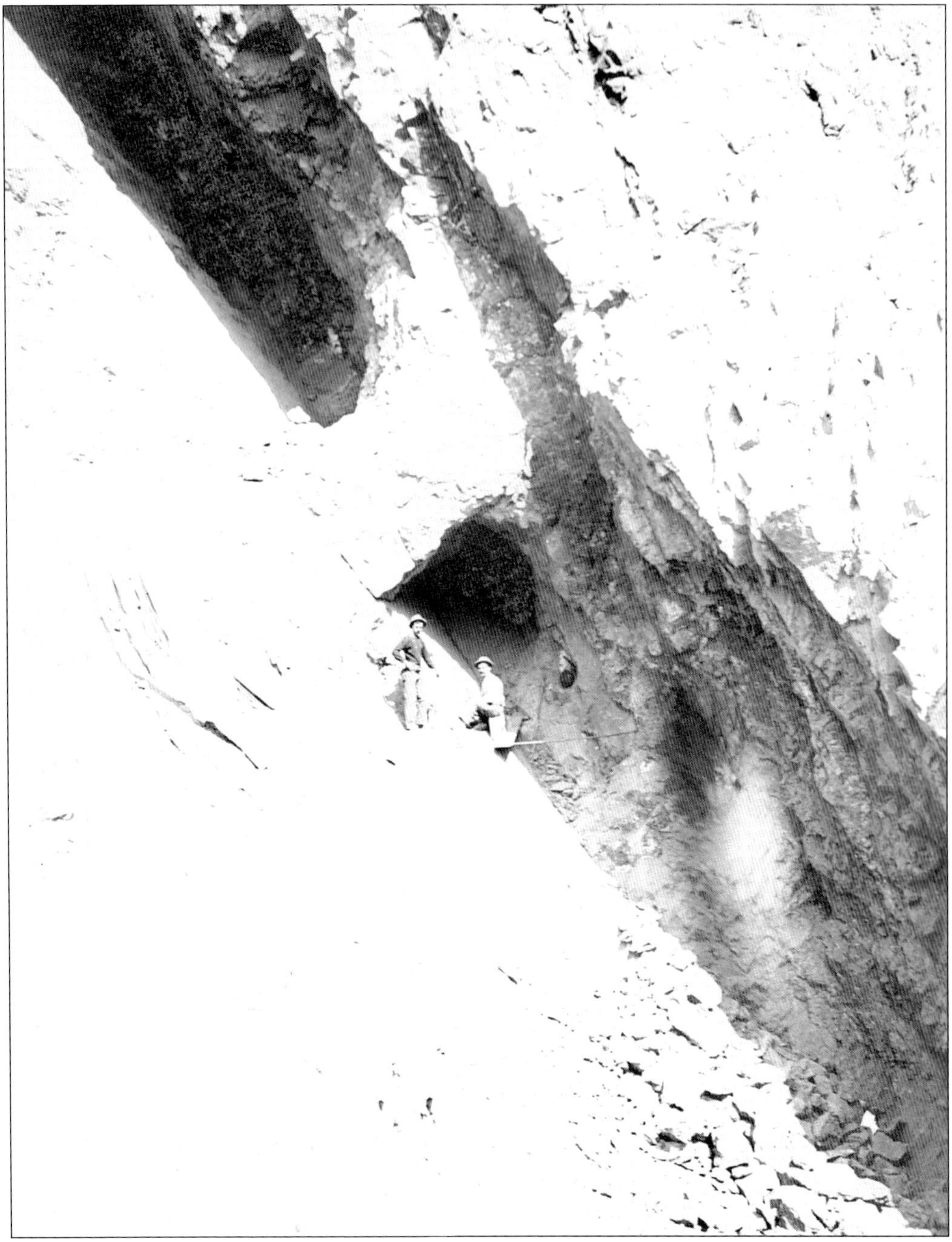

Two men stand in the "glory hole" of the King of Arizona Mine. The name for the mine is said to have come from the editor of the *Arizona Sentinel*, who, after the owner of the King Mine won a hotly contested vote one year by making all his miners register and vote for him, wrote, "Who does he think he is? The King of Arizona?" Locals have long since abbreviated the name to Kofa, which adorns numerous businesses, schools, and streets in the region. The small town that eventually sprang up near the King was itself simply named Kofa. This village, like La Fortuna, also eventually became large enough to have its own elementary school. The school opened in 1900 with an enrollment of 16 students.

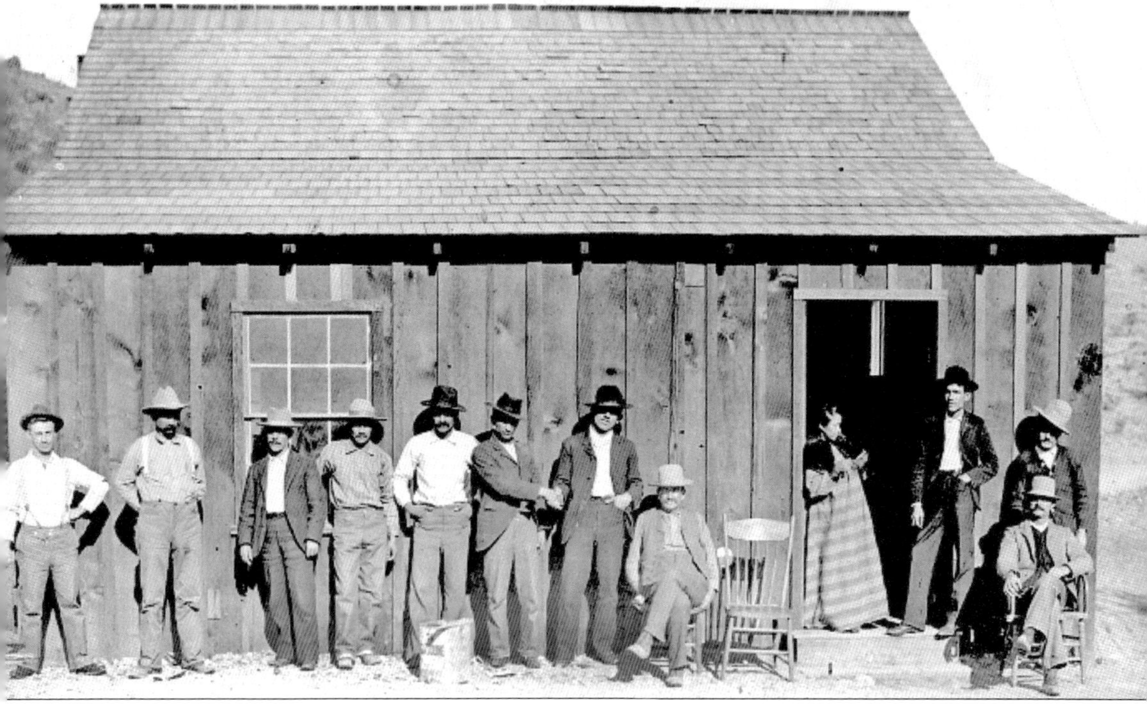

These miners stand outside the saloon at the King of Arizona Mine. The gold mining excitement in the Yuma area was not limited to the boom following the Snively discovery near Gila City. Near Yuma, the turn of the century found the area in the midst of yet another gold rush. The following story is taken from the pages of the *Arizona Republican* (now the *Arizona Republic*) in March 1897, when Yuma's newspaper editor visited Phoenix and told the story of the emerging gold excitement in his home, "Editor John W. Dorrington of the *Arizona Sentinel*, who came up from Yuma yesterday, said that the mining excitement is consequence of the late gold strike in the country between Castle Dome and Eagle Tall Mountains." The article continued with Dorrington describing a discussion he had with an elderly Apache man who told of the location of the famed Lost Frenchman Mine: "The Apache said he was a member of the band of Indians who had attacked the Frenchmen and seven of their number were killed before they succeeded in ending the lives of the wiry Frenchmen."

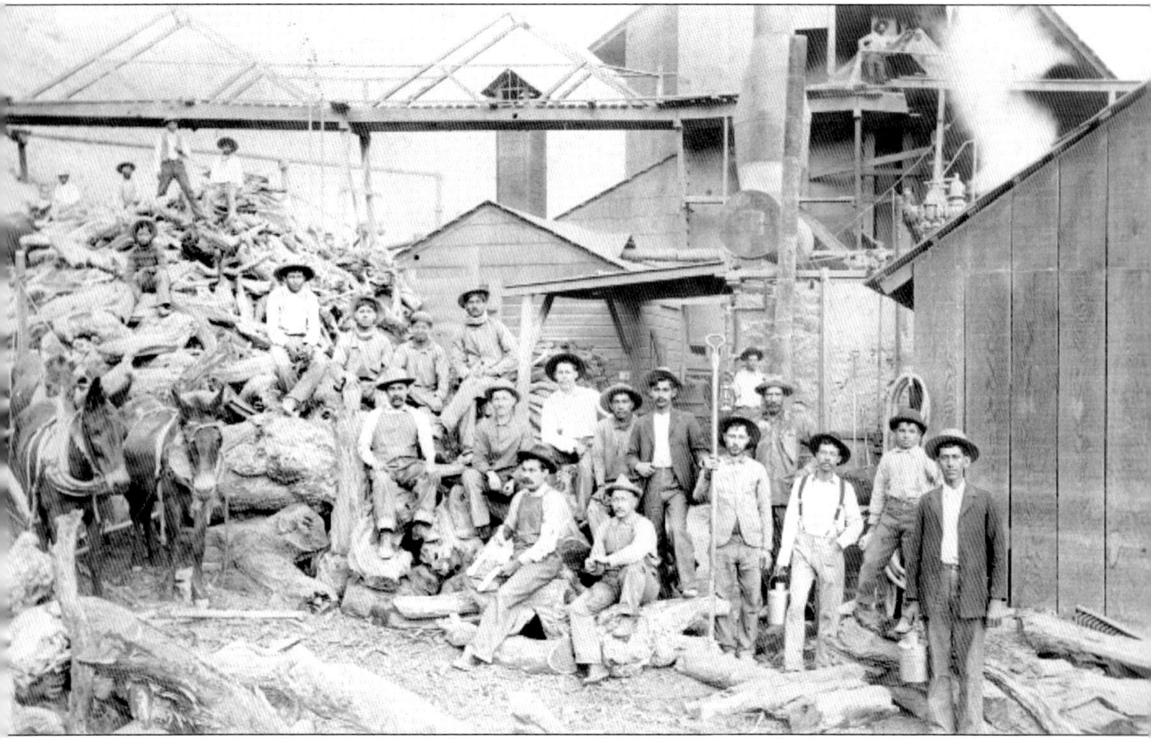

The *Arizona Republican* article continued with Dorrington explaining how most of the gold near Yuma was discovered:

> It is in such localities that all the great strikes in Arizona have been made and almost without exception they have been accidents.
>
> The latest discovery, the Pearce Mine, has been tramped over by prospectors since white men first came into the country, and La Fortuna lay on the old Sonora Road traveled for years by thousands of men. The discoverer of La Fortuna was in the frenzy of delirium tremens and he afterward admitted that if he had been in his right mind he wouldn't have been in that neighborhood looking for gold.

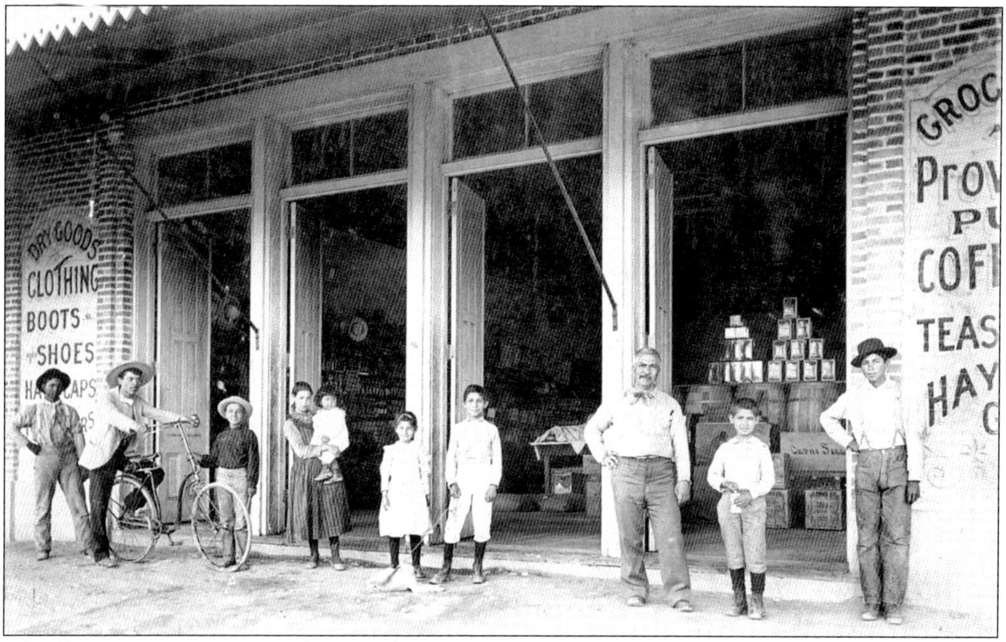

Like George Norton, most of Yuma's businessmen were at one time involved with mines in the region. Isaac Levy, owner of this general merchandise store, provided supplies for the mines, a lucrative business that allowed him to build this fine store, pictured here in 1896.

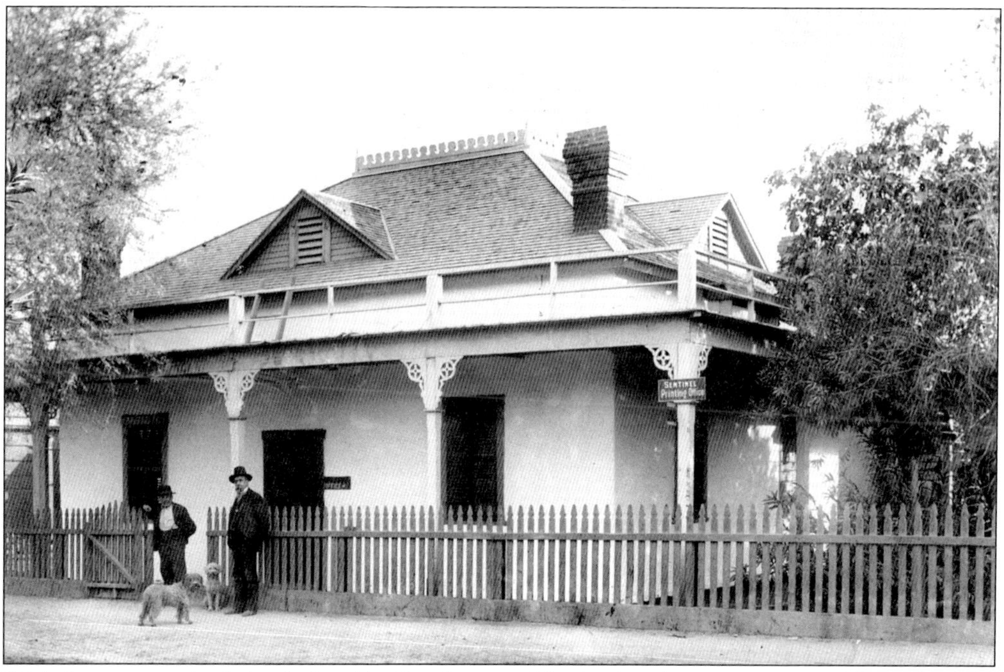

With Dorrington (right) is Judge Abe Frank, one of the leading businessmen in western Arizona in the 19th century. In 1869, Frank followed Jack Stewart, W. W. Jones, and Morris Goldwater to their new town of Ehrenberg, where Frank ultimately ran the largest mercantile business in the county. After coming to Yuma in 1883, Frank, along with Dorrington, represented the region in the territorial legislature while also serving as territorial prison commissioner.

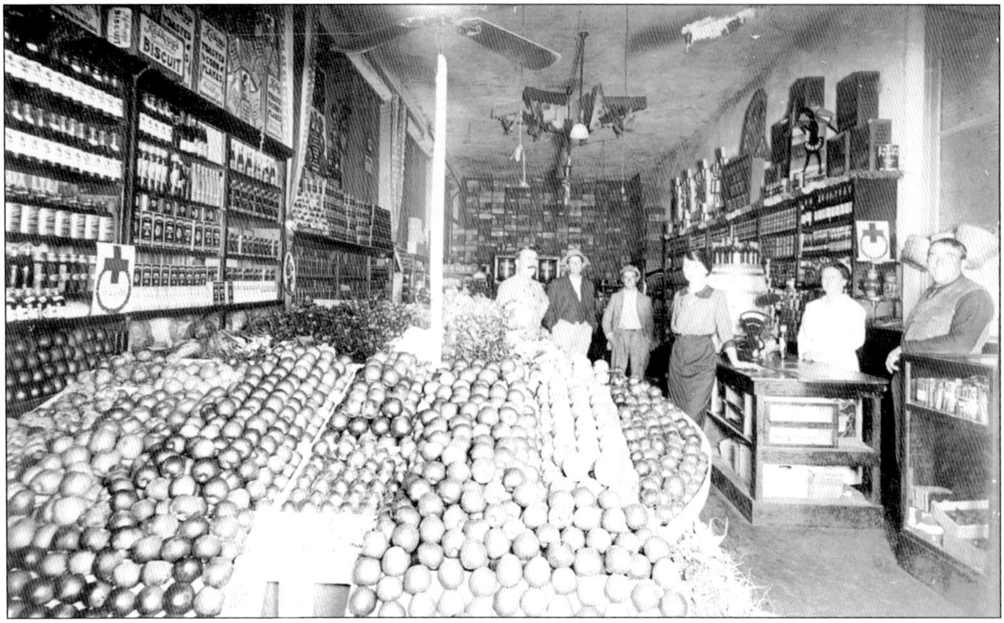

The retail stores of the Gateway City like the Ghiotto Store, pictured here, were known as the best of their kind in the territory. Not only did they have the obvious advantage of receiving goods directly off the steamboats (without freighter markup), as well as supplies from Southern Pacific trains, the verdant valley, once irrigated, produced wonderful fruits and vegetables.

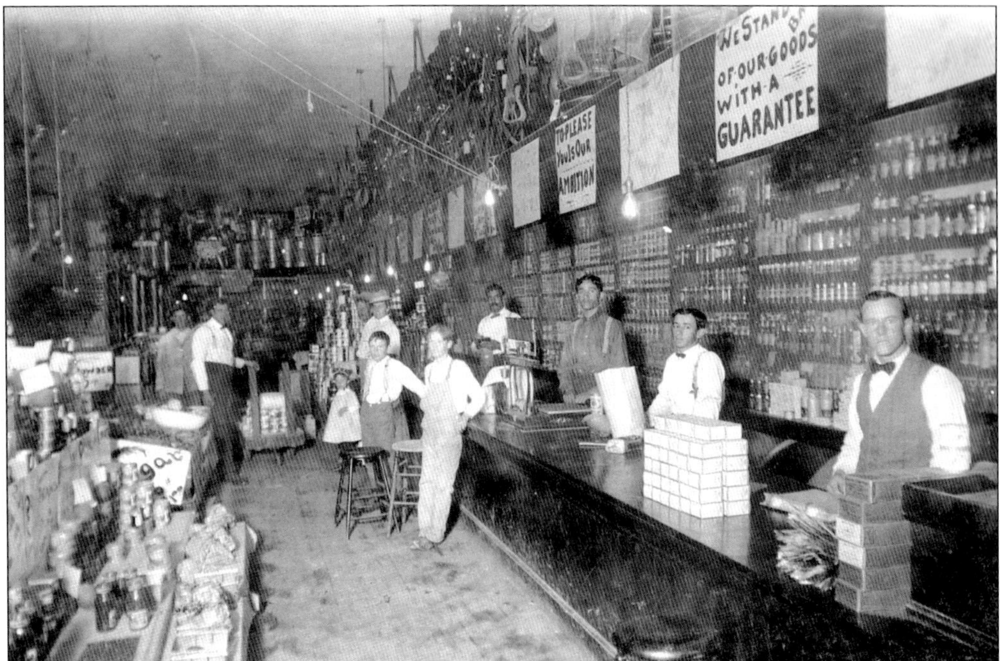

Unlike many retailers throughout the territory, Yuma's businessmen rarely had a monopoly over business in their community. They had to fight for customers. Note the signs on the wall behind the clerks at E. F. Sanguinetti's store at Second Street and Main: "We stand back of our goods with a guarantee," and, "To Please You Is Our Ambition."

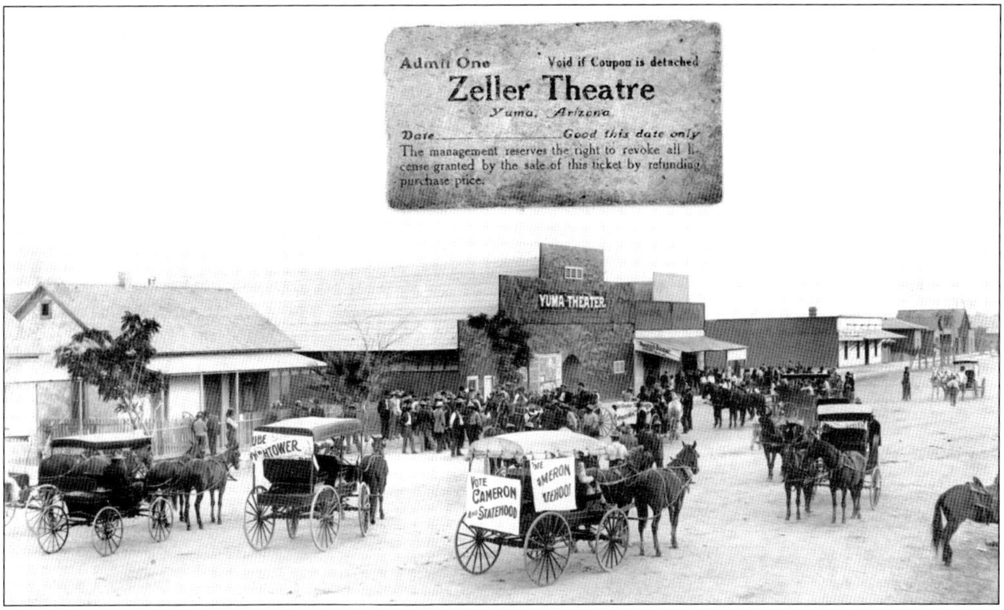

The Yuma Theater hosted many entertaining events, but nothing compared in raucous energy to the evenings when the theater would be packed to hear visiting politicians battling for the seats of power in the territory. In this case, it was the race for a delegate to the U.S. House of Representatives for the territory. In the forefront, a buggy can be seen with a poster arguing to "Vote Cameron and Statehood." On this day, Ralph Cameron, a top politician, orator and, many would argue, blowhard of the day, came to town to convince Yumans that he would bring back statehood from Washington.

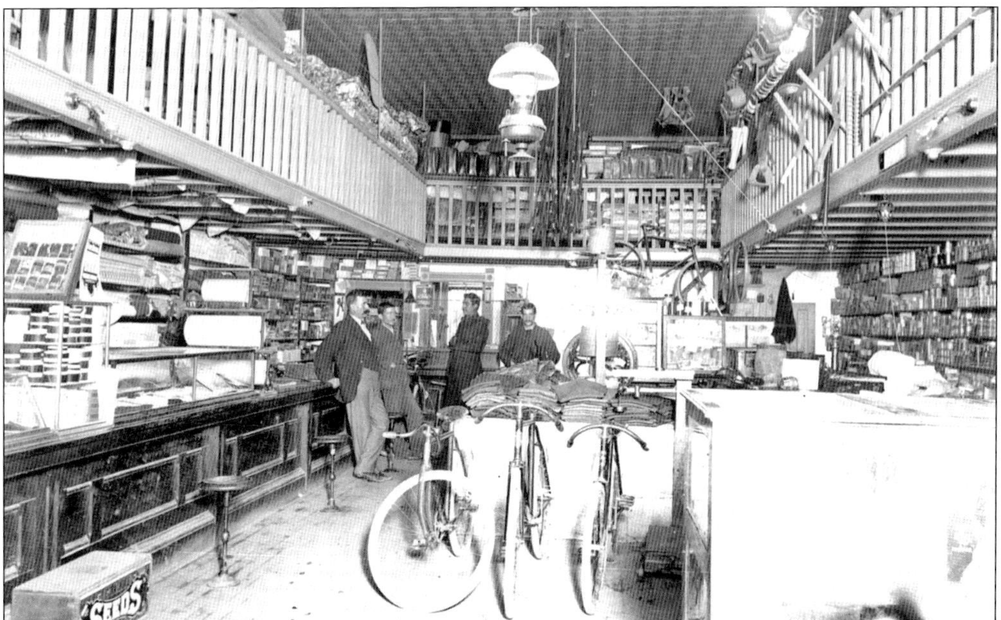

As Yumans began to prosper near the turn of the century, they demanded more goods from their general stores. Besides the bikes and jeans, the store is literally stuffed to the rafters with merchandise.

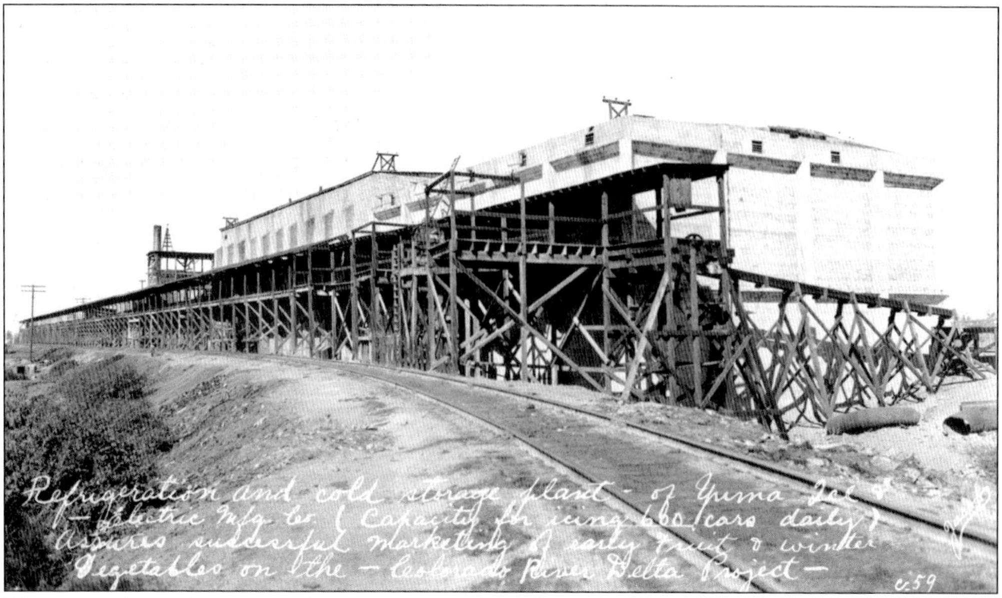

There may be no invention that greater impacted the prosperity of Yuma than refrigerated air. First it was ice making of the Yuma Ice Company, which, by shooting ice onto train cars full of melons and other fresh produce, assured that Yuma's crops and meats could reach far-off destinations without spoiling. This cold storage unit vastly expanded the markets that could be reached by the agricultural producers of the area. In its heyday, this plant could load 600 railroad cars a day. These early refrigerator units used toxic gases such as ammonia, methyl chloride and sulfur dioxide as refrigerants. Because of this, the employees of the cold-storage units in Yuma held some of the town's most dangerous jobs.

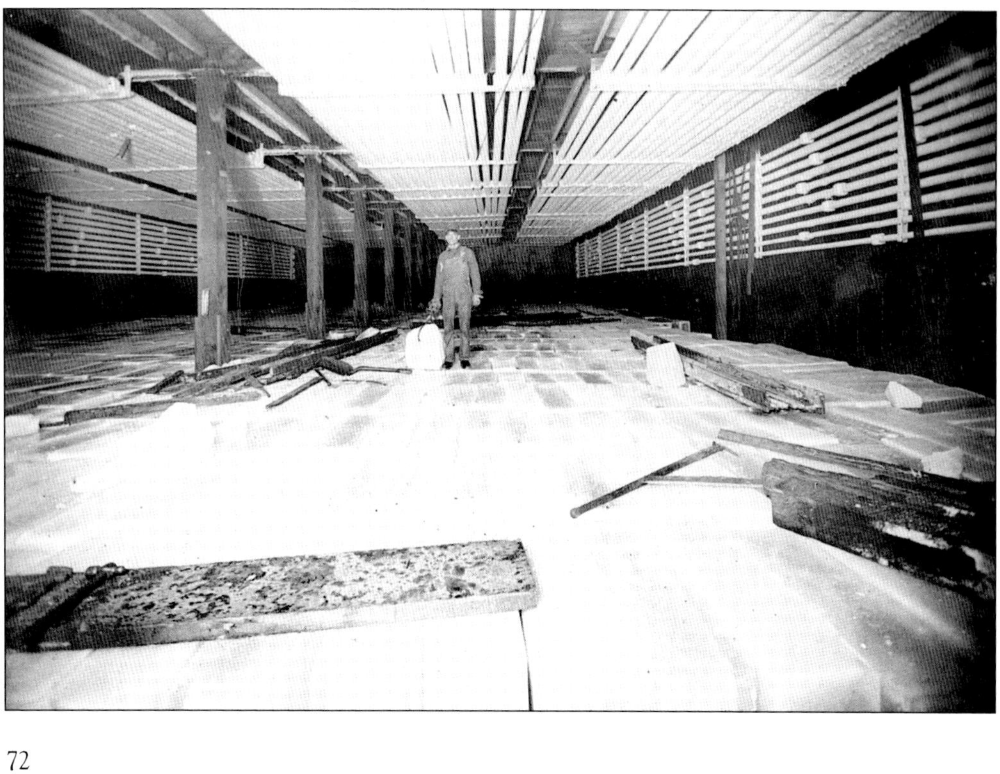

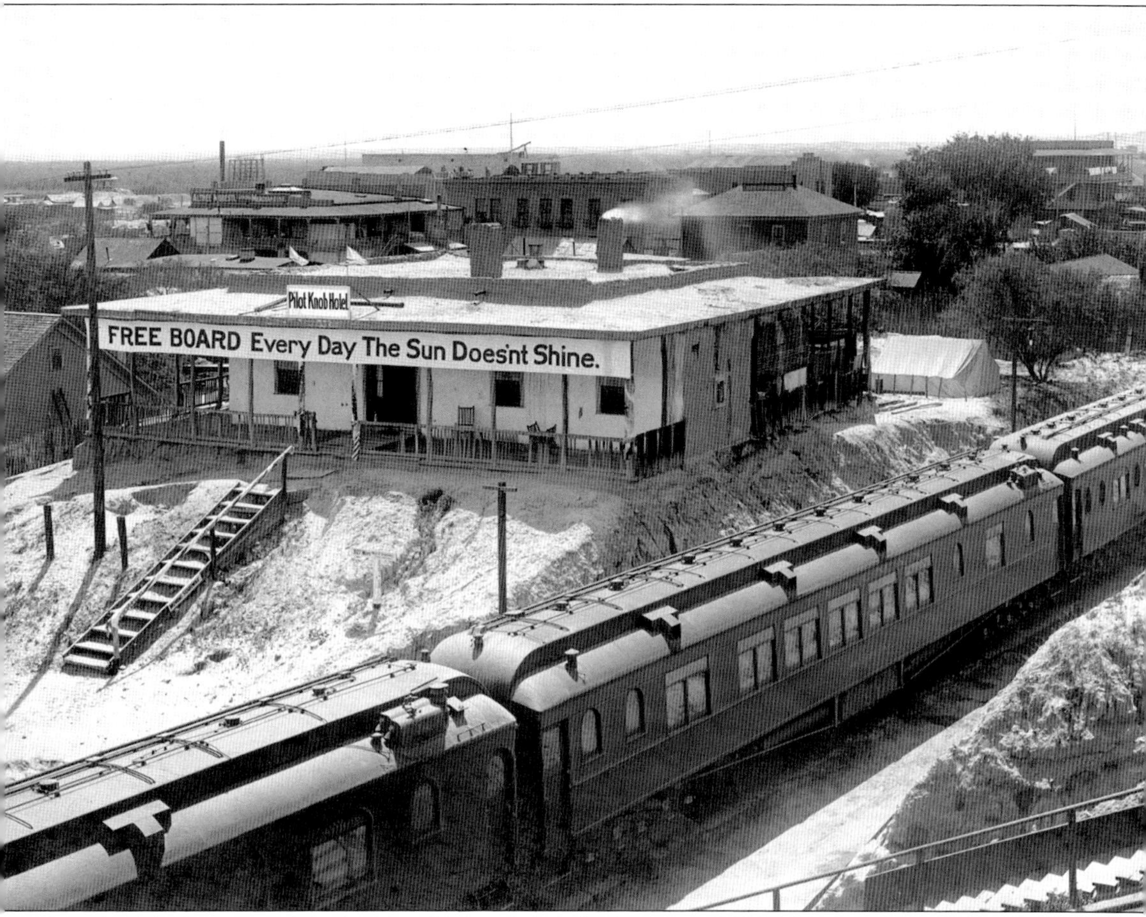

It is said the owner of the Pilot's Knob Hotel never had to pay up on his offer of "Free Board Every Day The Sun Doesn't Shine." Of all of Yuma's hotels, the Pilot's Knob worked the hardest to entice travelers on the Southern Pacific line, which provided most of the overnight guests until the highway to San Diego became more feasible to drive. A later sign on the hotel explained to visitors that Yuma was "3127 miles West of Broadway," which was a bit sobering if train passengers were heading east to New York. This photograph looks south along Madison Avenue.

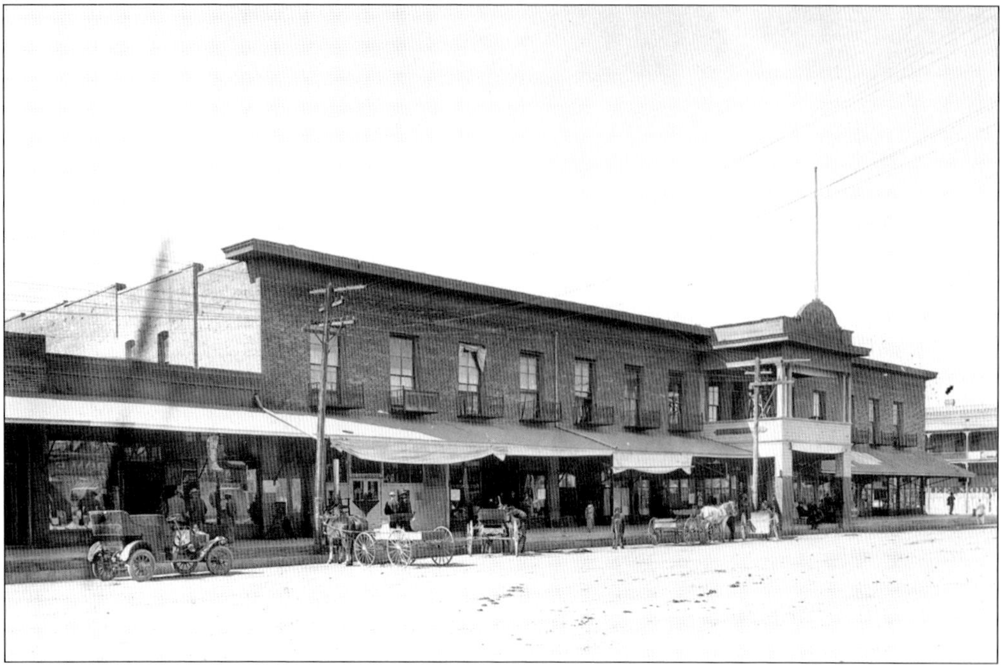

John Gandolfo owned numerous businesses in and around town. One of his earliest in Yuma after he arrived in 1876 was a general merchandise store. The most impressive structure was the Gandolfo Hotel, pictured here in 1910.

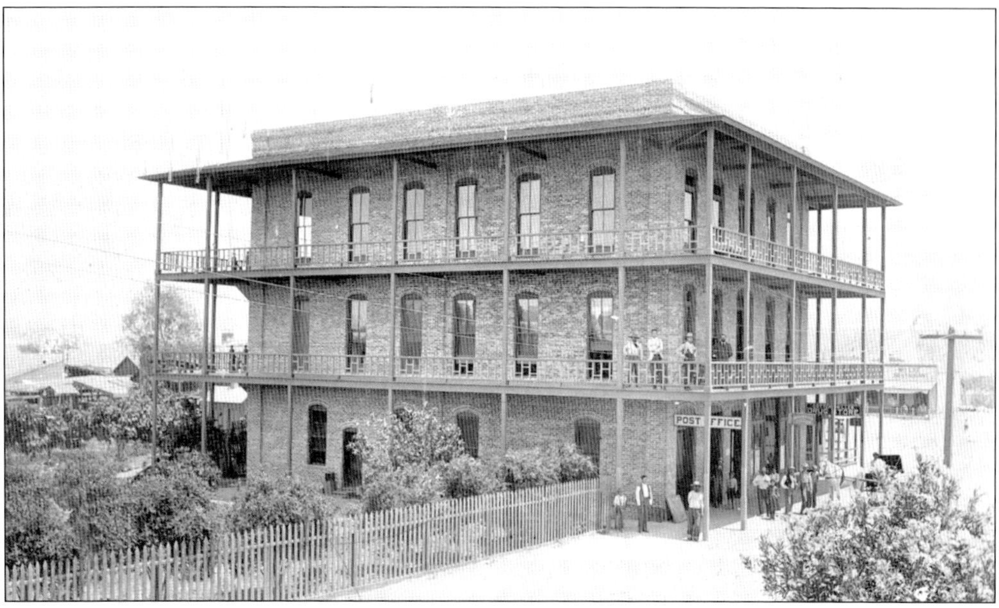

The three-story Cotter Building, Yuma's first skyscraper, housed the post office, the Wells Fargo, and a drug store that was not unlike many modern grocery stores. The remarkable structure, pictured here just after it opened in 1897, burned down a quarter-century later in 1923 and was one of the great losses of the many notable buildings in the city's downtown.

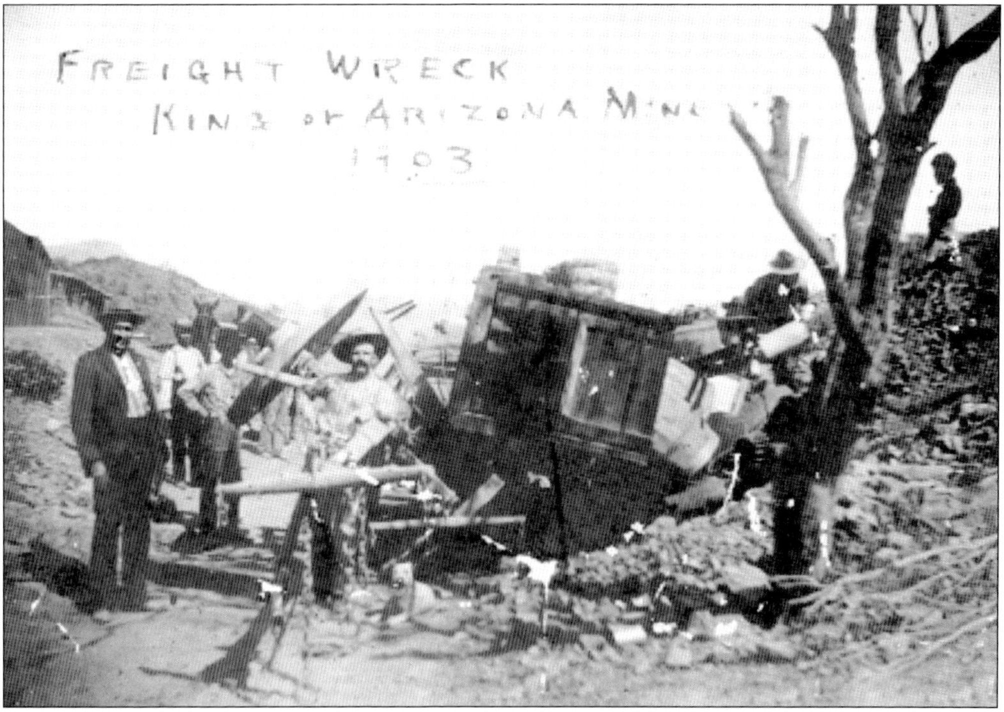

With an economy based heavily on transportation of people and goods, wrecks were common and, without insurance, sometimes devastating to a young business. In this photograph, George H. Rockwood and several miners from the King of Arizona look over the wreckage of a freight wagon headed to the mine in 1903.

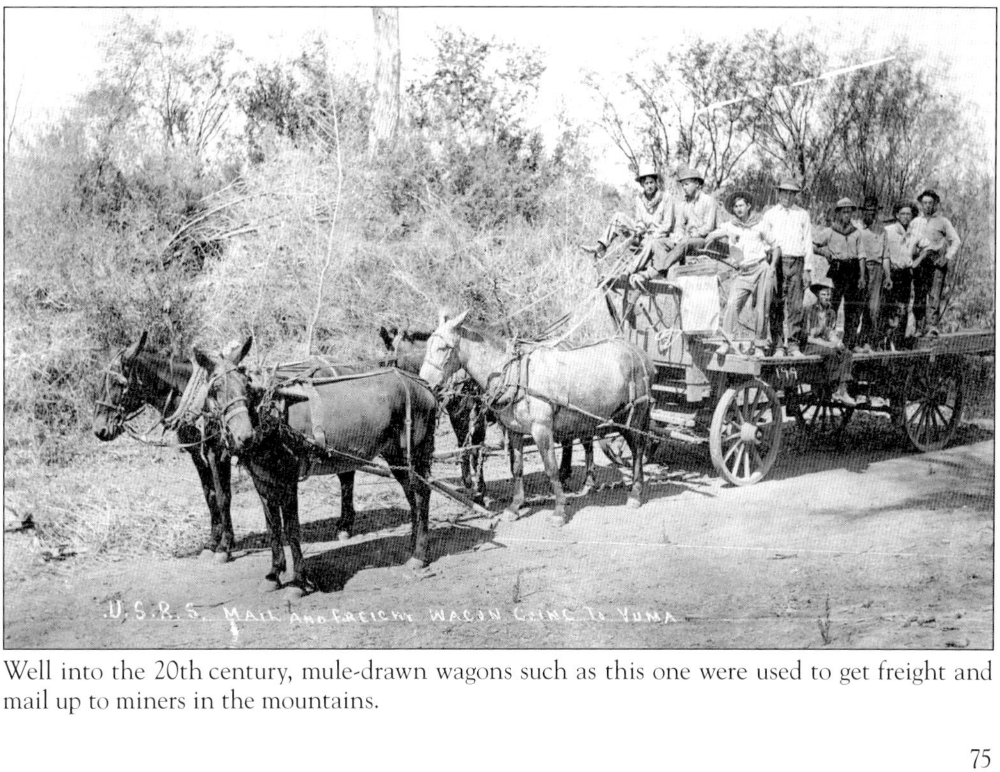

Well into the 20th century, mule-drawn wagons such as this one were used to get freight and mail up to miners in the mountains.

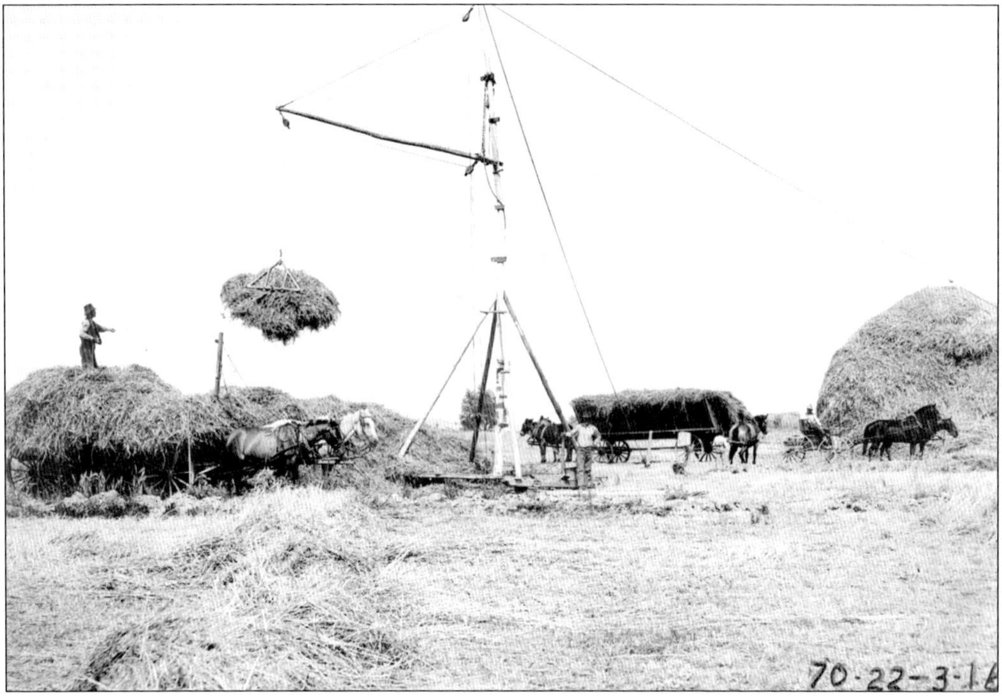

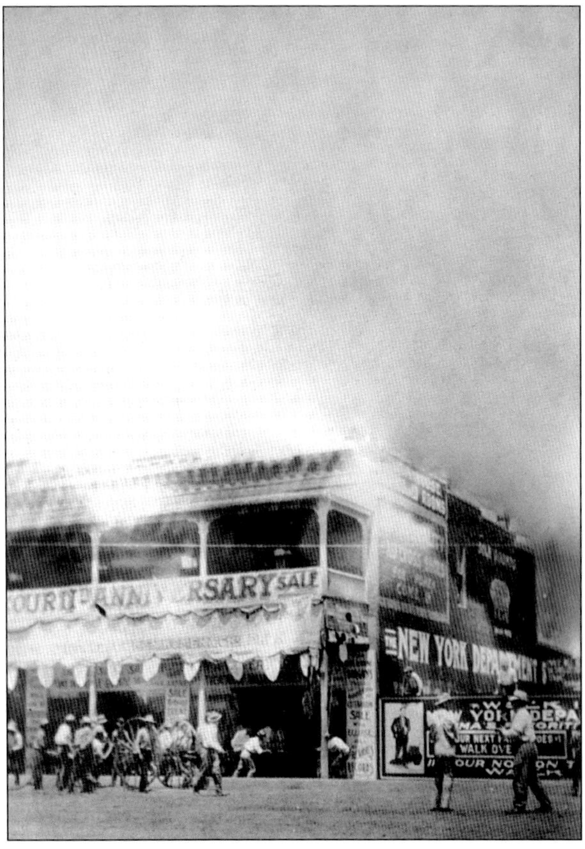

Like mine freighters, area farmers also stayed with horses and wagons long into the automobile age. In this photograph, hay is being loaded onto hay wagons that rival the size of some of the famous freight wagons.

The other great danger to a Yuma businessman was fire. After floods washed away adobe and fires wiped out wood, it became clear that brick was the best material for building in Yuma. Still, brick was no guarantee that a building was safe. In 1923, the Cotter Building, one of the town's finest structures, became engulfed in a raging fire. This photograph shows, with a little help from a touch-up artist, the burning of the New York Department Store.

Five

The Hard Life

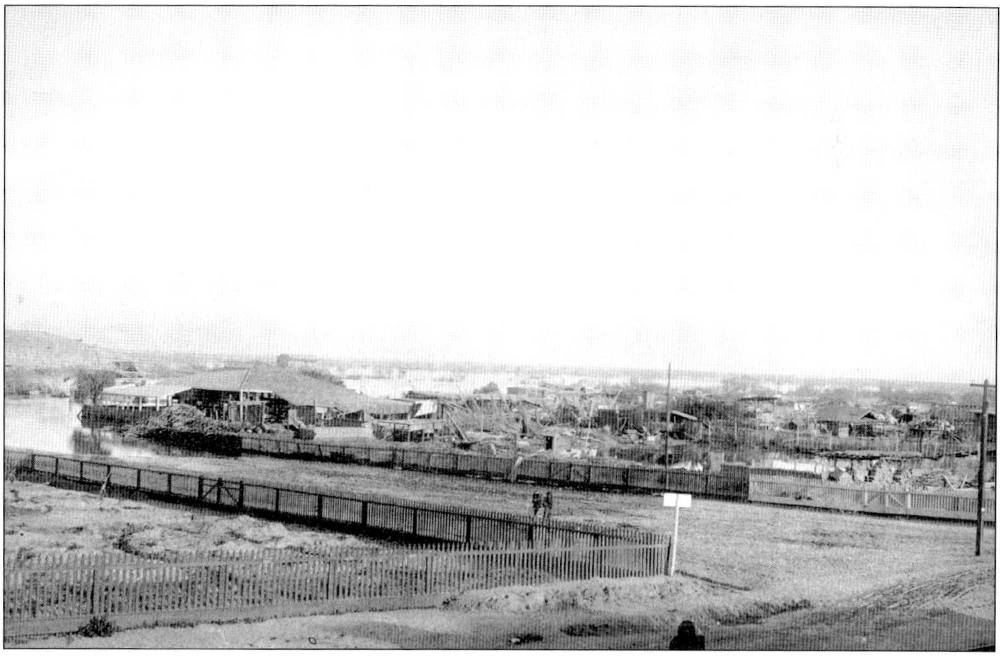

Early Yuma was not most people's idea of heaven. Still, many of the early residents truly did love this place, and they spent many of their evening under the light of an oil lamp, defending their chosen home in letters to loved ones. Editor Dorrington often wrote his sister, Annie Reavis, who had come to La Paz in 1869 with her husband, Isham Reavis. She hated her time in the desert, worrying much of the time that her baby would be stolen by the Apaches. "My dear sister, please put aside your hatred of this land and come for a visit," Dorrington wrote Annie in Nebraska. "It is much less than you believe and much more than you realize. We would have a grand time together." At times, though, the land lived up to its stereotype. There were floods, fires, earthquakes, death by Apache, and death by the mysterious "brain congestion" of summer. In February 1891, the waters of the Gila and Colorado Rivers began rising swiftly. Leading merchants E. F. Sanguinetti and John Gandolfo closed their stores and sent their employees to strengthen the levees around Yuma. As they toiled, the water broke first through the Colorado levee and then the Gila's. Downtown was soon consumed in water.

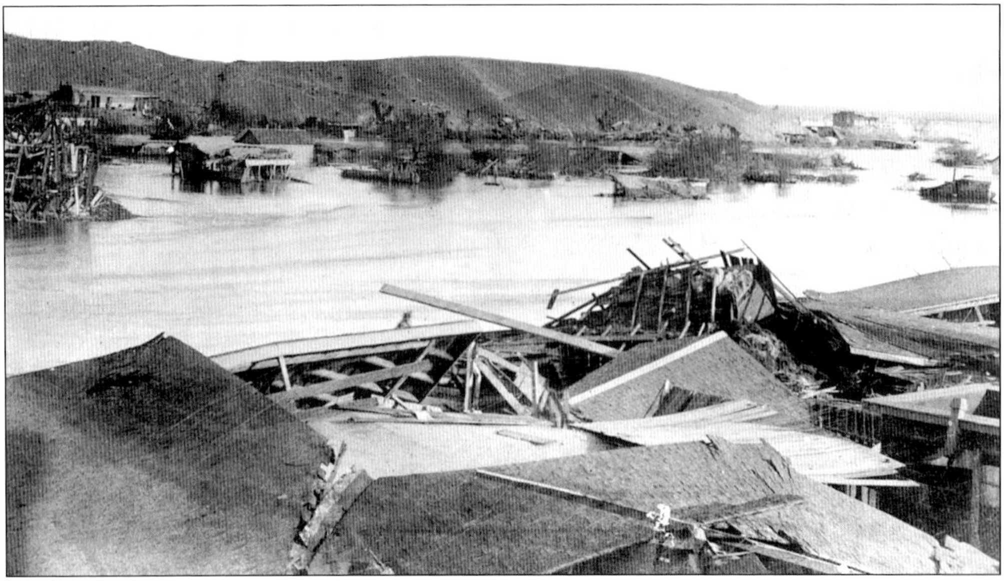

As waters began to rise at the confluence of the rivers, Dorrington asked the famed Quechan runner, Shampooec, to carry a letter to his friend George Norton in the Mohawk Valley in an attempt to gauge the crest of the waters upstream. Dorrington believed from old Quechan stories of previous floods that if the Mohawk Valley was flooding, Yuma was likely doomed. Shampooec left Yuma at 6:00 p.m. on Saturday evening, dashing through boggy lowlands impassable by horse and twice swimming across the swollen river. He came running into Yuma late Monday evening, covering 180 miles in 37 hours. Amazingly, Shampooec apologized to Dorrington for not making the trip quicker. Shampooec returned with news that the Mohawk Valley was flooded. The news, though, was of little good once he reached Yuma. The town was already flooded and, as Dorrington wrote, the town, made mostly of adobe, had already "melted away like sugar." Many more Quechan came to the aid of Yuma residents, even as all their own possessions were washing away. Dorrington used this fact to push once again for money for the tribe, which already had long been shorted on funds promised them by the federal government. "The Indians came to the rescue of Yuma, and did all they could, leaving their homes where many lost all they had," Dorrington wrote in March of that year. "They worked well and some means should be devised by which they will receive their pay."

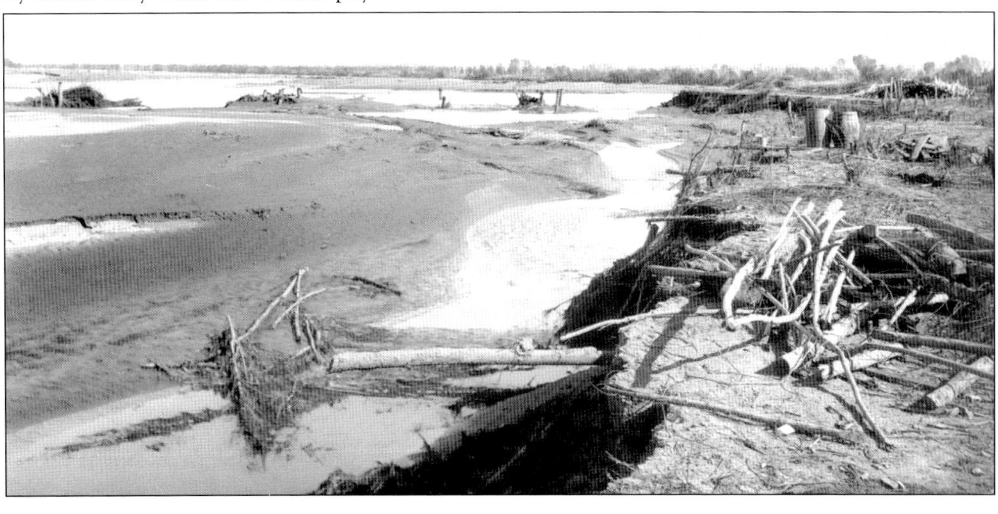

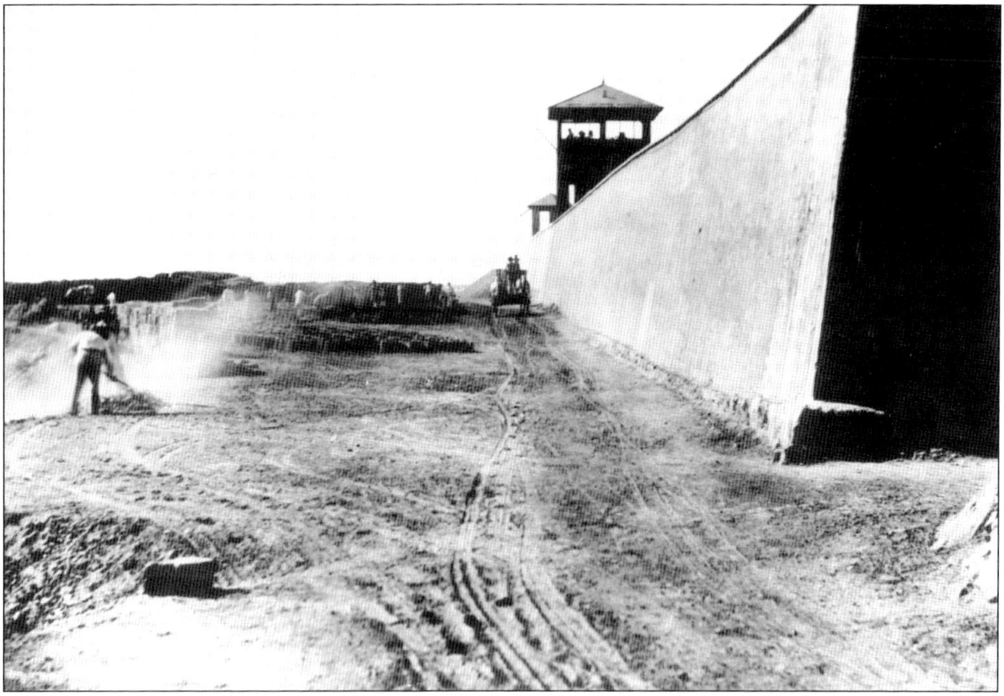

In 1875, the Arizona Territorial Legislature was on the verge of awarding $25,000 to the upstart town of Phoenix for the construction of a prison to lock up the criminal element that was running roughshod over Arizona. But Yuma's representatives, Jose Maria Redondo and R. B. Kelly, jumped in and argued that a site confined by the raging waters of the Gila and Colorado Rivers would be better. They eventually won. The prison, with its massive adobe walls, opened on July 1, 1876, when seven inmates moved into new cells they built themselves. More than 3,000 prisoners would pass through these walls, including 29 women. One of those women, stage robber Pearl Hart, was arguably the most notorious criminal to reside there. While 26 successful escapes by inmates of the prison were made, all but two were on outside work crews. According to information from the Yuma Territorial Prison State Historical Park, now on the prison grounds, despite its infamous reputation as "the hell hole," prison records in fact show the prison was humanely administered and was "a model institution for its time." By 1907, the prison was severely overcrowded and had no room for expansion on prison hill. The convicts constructed a new prison in Florence, Arizona, where the state prison remains today.

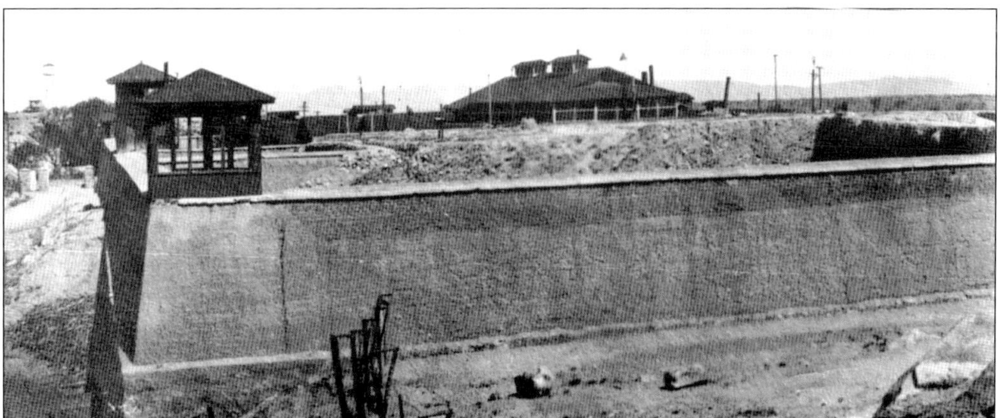

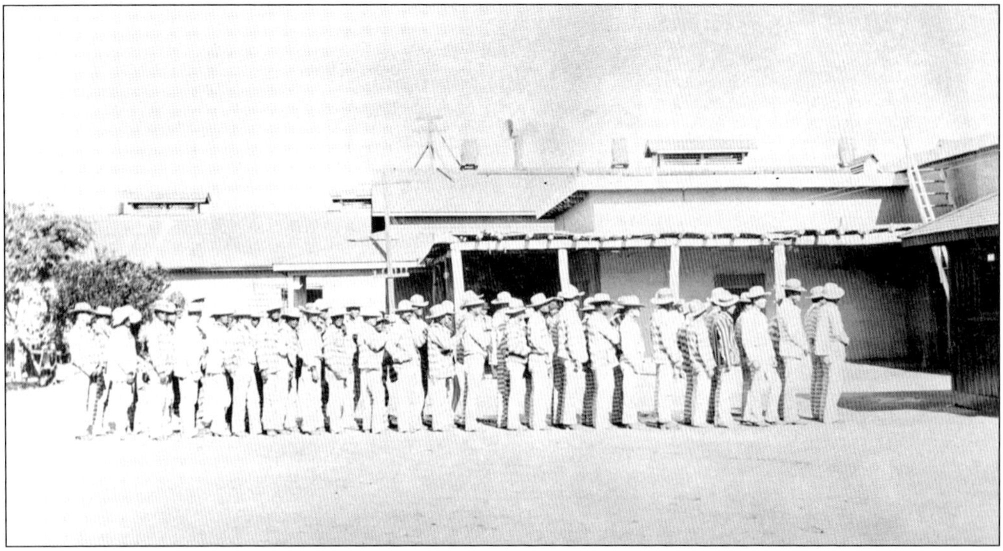

Schooling was available for convicts, and many learned to read and write in prison. The prison housed one of the first "public" libraries in the territory, and the fee charged to visitors for a tour of the institution was used to purchase books. One of the early electrical generating plants in the West furnished power for lights and ran a ventilation system in the cell block. Indeed, the prison and its prisoners were actually the focus of much progressive and Christian support from the community. While early Yuma has a reputation for being a rough-and-tumble town, many of its leading citizens were in fact deeply humanitarian in many of their efforts. Consider this letter to the editor of the *Sentinel* in 1882 from one of the prison inmates, which began the push by Yuma residents to build what became the largest library in the region: "Permit me, through the columns of your valuable paper, to ask the generous and liberal minded to donate to the inmates of (the prison) any books or periodicals that they may have to spare." Still, there was little mercy if inmates rioted. In 1887, seven prisoners attempted an escape by taking the prison superintendent hostage. Within five minutes, four of the inmates had been shot dead by one guard, marksman B. F. Hartlee, but not before one of them had given the superintendent, Thomas Gates, a grisly stab wound to the neck from which he never recovered.

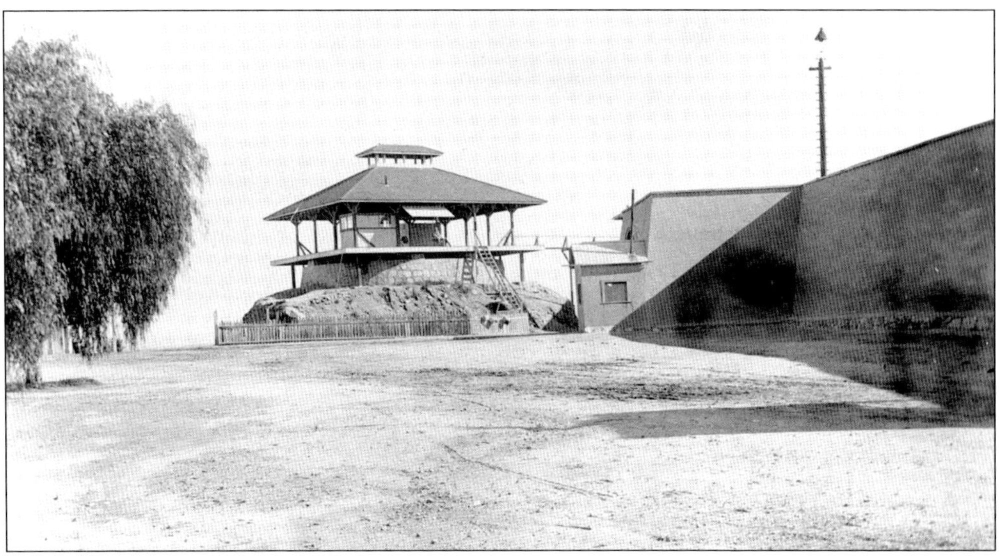

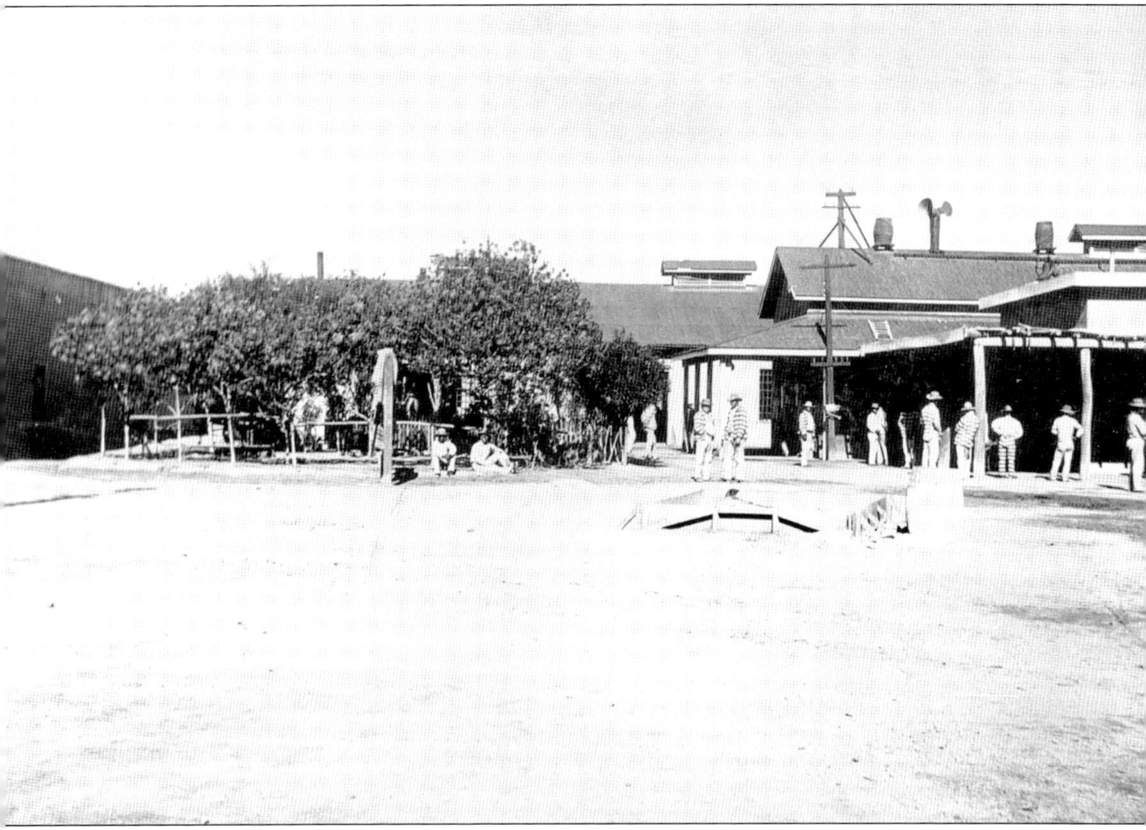

The prisoners even had their own fruit trees, seen here at left. By 1893, the prison also had running water pumped from the Colorado River, flushing toilets, a sewer system, electricity, and forced-air ventilation—amenities few residents of Yuma enjoyed. This explains why, while outsiders called it the Hell Hole, locals called it "the country club on the Colorado."

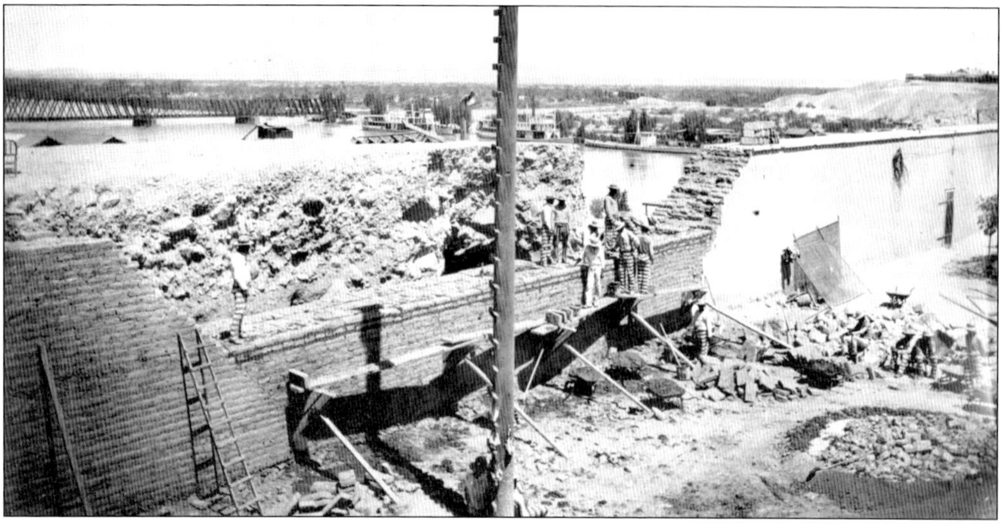

The exterior walls of the prison were constructed with adobe block plastered smooth for appearance and protection against rain. By 1890, when this picture was taken, much of the adobe had begun to deteriorate. Prisoners repaired the walls as they succumbed to the weather. For four years, from 1910 to 1914, the prison buildings were turned into the Yuma Union High School. A little later, the school's sports teams took on the nickname the "Criminals," or the "Crims."

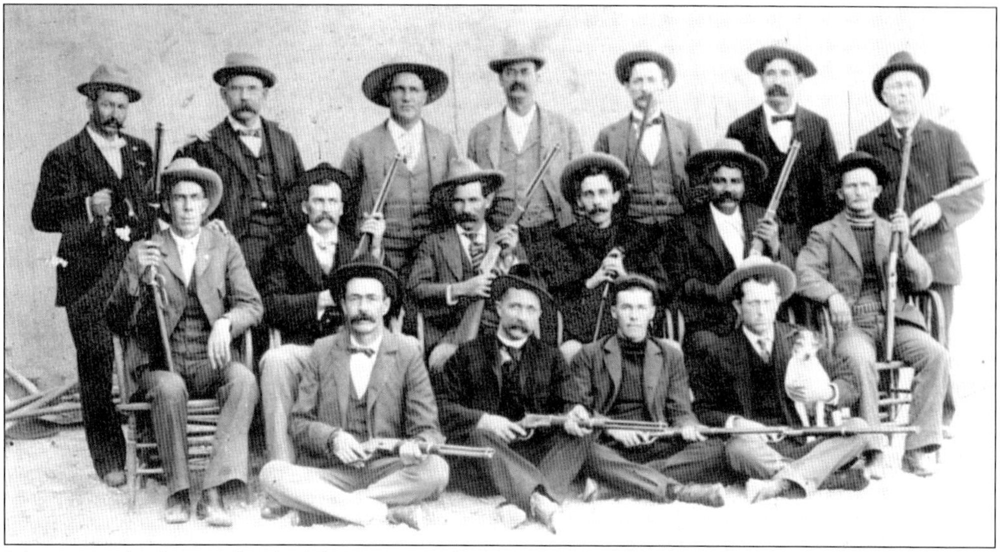

The prison had several colorful superintendents, probably none more than John Behan, who is most remembered as one of the main adversaries of Wyatt Earp and Doc Holliday in Tombstone. The violent Tombstone episode had political overtones. The Earp brothers were Union men, Republicans, and as such drew the support of many of the territory's Republican politicians for their actions in Tombstone. Behan, a Democrat who after a stint in the territorial legislature became the sheriff of Cochise County in 1880, was the man who arrested the Earps for murder after the gunfight at the O.K. Corral. At the time, Republican editor and legislator Dorrington came under intense criticism by Behan and other Democrats for supporting such vigilante behavior as shown by the Earps. In 1888, Behan was named superintendent of the Yuma prison. From the moment he arrived in town, Dorrington began returning the favor, pounding the Democrat lawman with fierce editorials calling for his removal for all sorts of perceived offenses.

The arrival of Pearl Hart (standing behind the girl with the guitar) created scandal in the prison and in Yuma, especially once the prison doctor announced she was with child. It was argued she gained many favors by "playing to the fantasies of lustful men," as one writer put it, and this may have led to her pardon in 1902, about two years short of her five-year sentence for stage robbery.

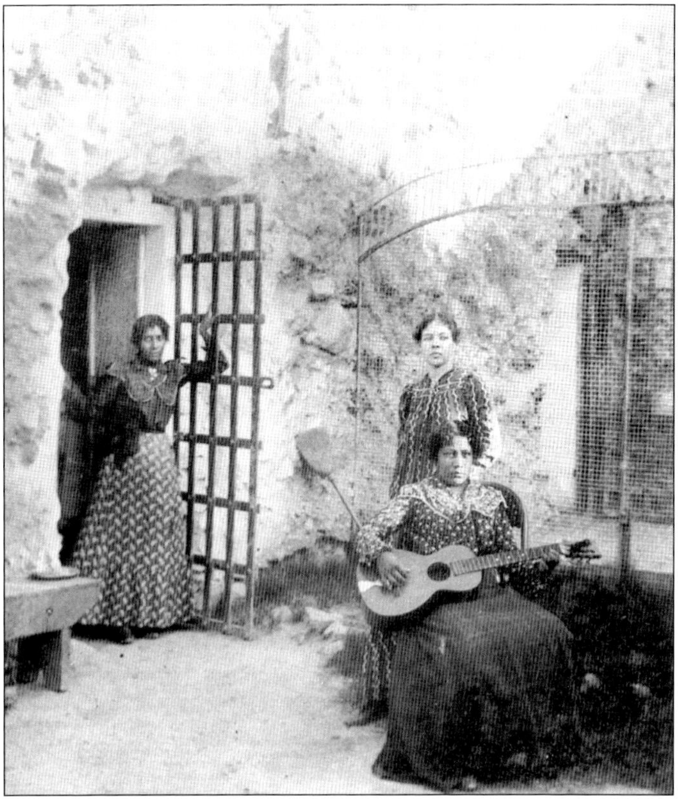

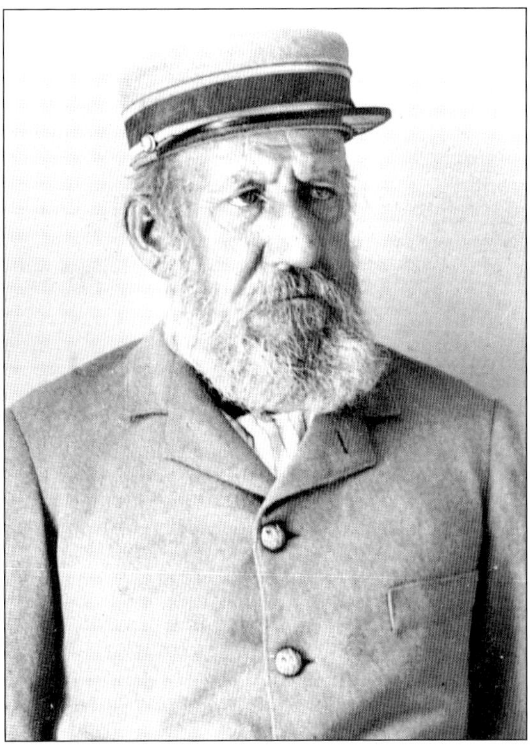

Guard B. F. Hartlee (left) was considered a hero after crushing the prison riot of 1887 with his Winchester. Although Hartlee killed four rioters, it was actually another inmate, Barney Riggs, who picked up a gun and shot the convict Puebla as he was plunging his knife into Superintendent Gates (pictured on page 84).

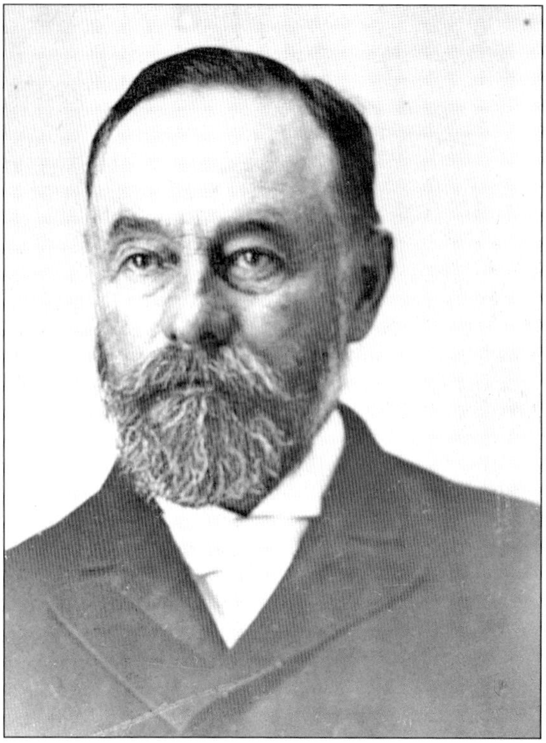

Gates never fully recovered from the knife wounds inflicted by the convict Puebla during the 1887 prison riot. He died an invalid.

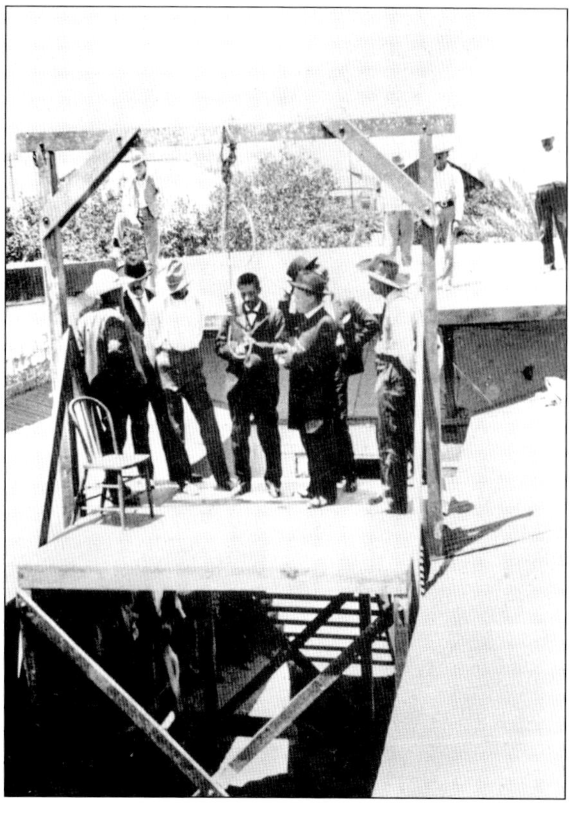

In 1905, two years after violent criminal Martin Ubillos murdered a fellow inmate, he was sentenced to death, which would be carried out in town. Dorrington wrote about the hanging the next week in his newspaper, an event he would tell people later was one of the most difficult to cover in his life. The story began with this elegant lead: "With his lips murmuring, but with a look of horror on his sensual, brutish face, Martin Ubillos was swung into eternity at the end of a rope in the jail yard here last Friday." Interestingly, Yuma again showed its humanity even as it executed a murderer, since nobody in town wanted to pull the lever on Ubillos. Finally, an old cowboy from the northern part of the country had to be brought down to perform the duties. The execution of Ubillos, a grisly spectacle that many citizens thought was made far too public, was the first and last of its kind in the city.

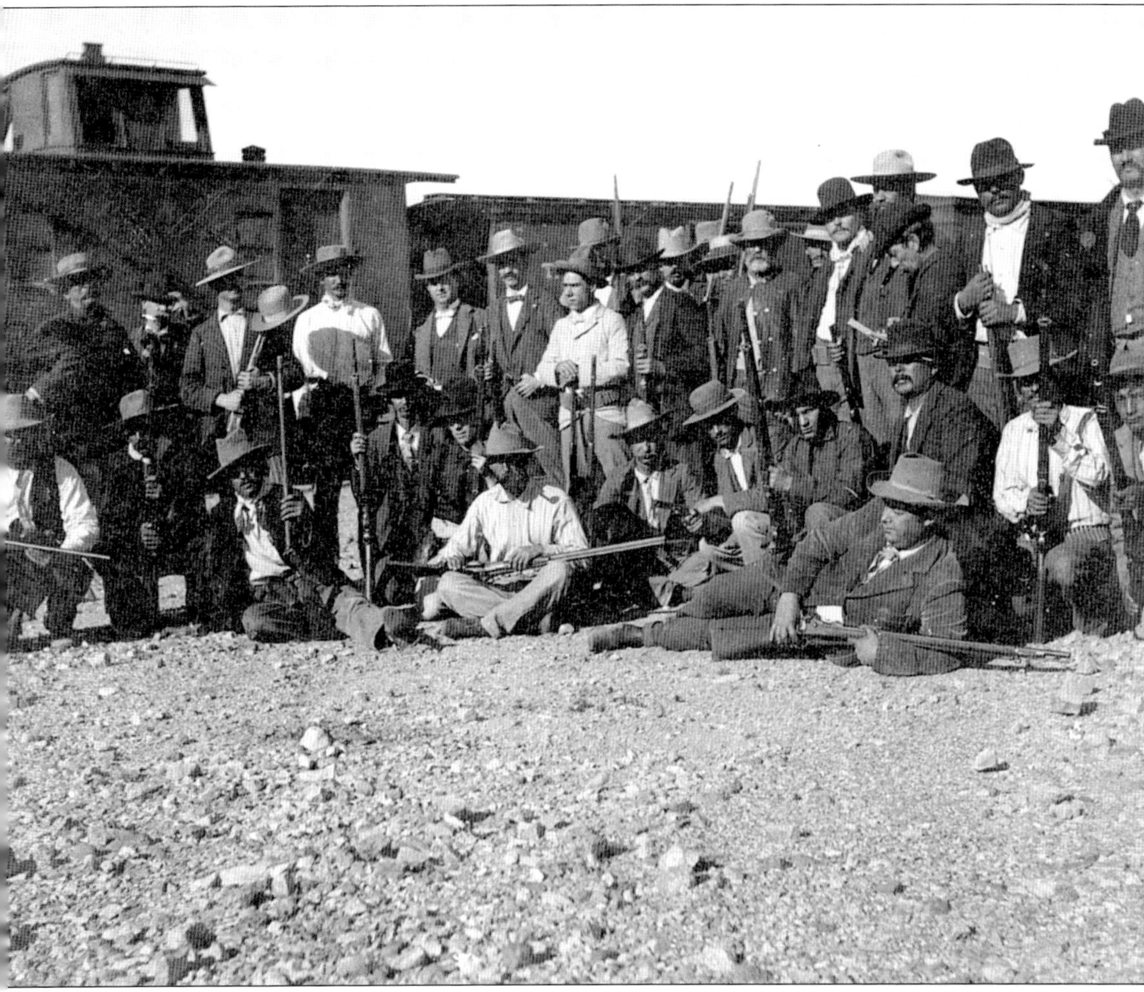

This is the posse that hunted down Thomas Hart, the murderer of Undersheriff Matt DeVane. After Hart's arrest for killing DeVane, he was sentenced to be hanged and was placed in the county jail. Hart escaped the jail with his cellmate and, with a pistol and rifle they stole from the sheriff's office, jumped on a nearby switch engine and forced the engineer and foreman off. The two took the train nearly five miles from town, where they jumped off and headed south toward the Fortuna Mine. The train was sent on to confuse anyone trying to follow. A posse followed on its own train, with half of it breaking off on the path to La Fortuna. For his effort, Hart was shot dead and buried at the spot he fell in the desert.

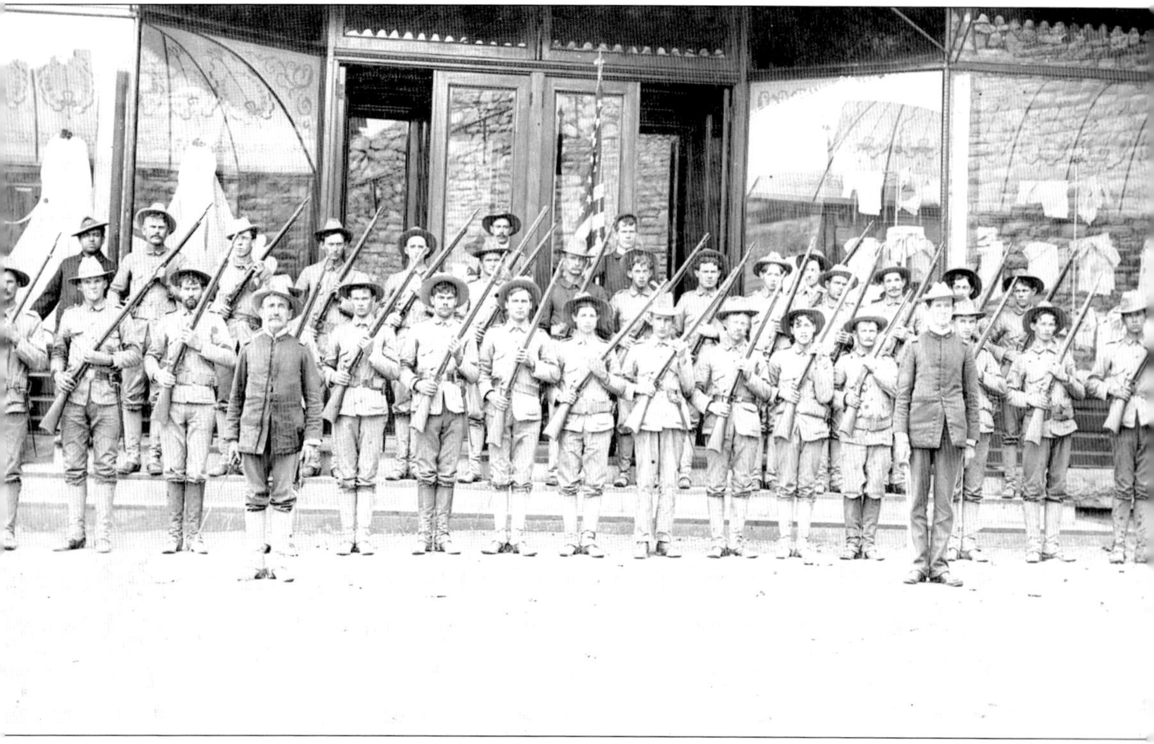

By 1890, one year before this photograph was taken, Arizona National Guard units could be found in all of Arizona's major towns. Eight years later, the Arizona volunteers would gain immortal fame when they joined the First U.S. Volunteer Cavalry to fight during the Spanish-American War. Under the unit's principle organizer, Lt. Col. Theodore Roosevelt, several Arizonans became heroes as part of the "Rough Riders." Six men from Yuma were chosen to go with Roosevelt.

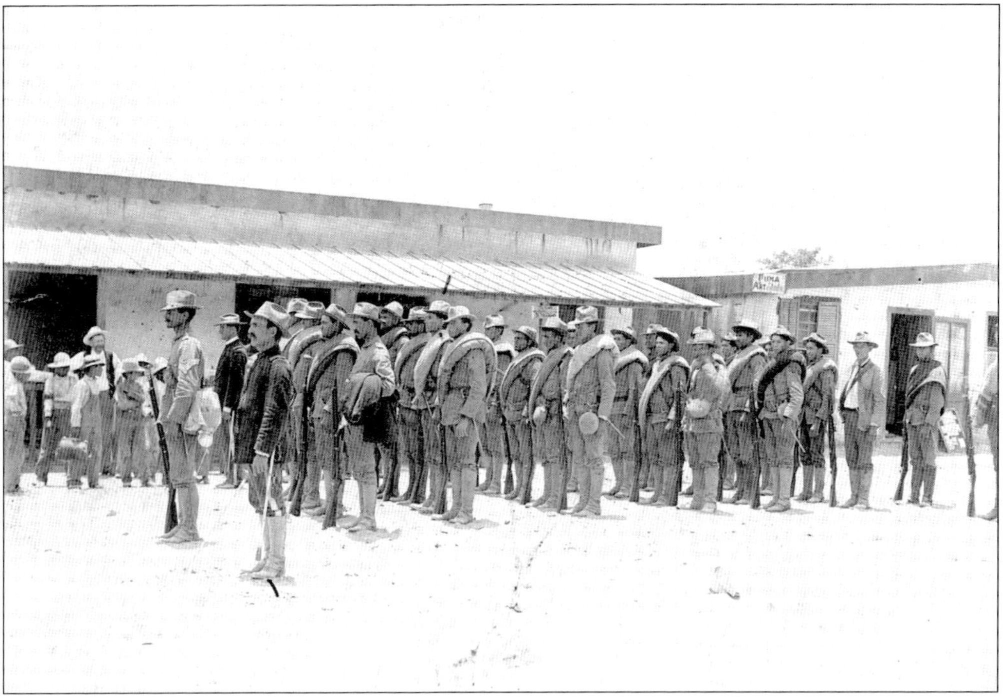

This photograph, taken on October 9, 1903, shows Company H of the Arizona National Guard drilling at the northeast corner of Third Street and Maiden Lane. The soldiers are facing west. The image was a gift from Yuman Pete Ayala to his sister Nellie.

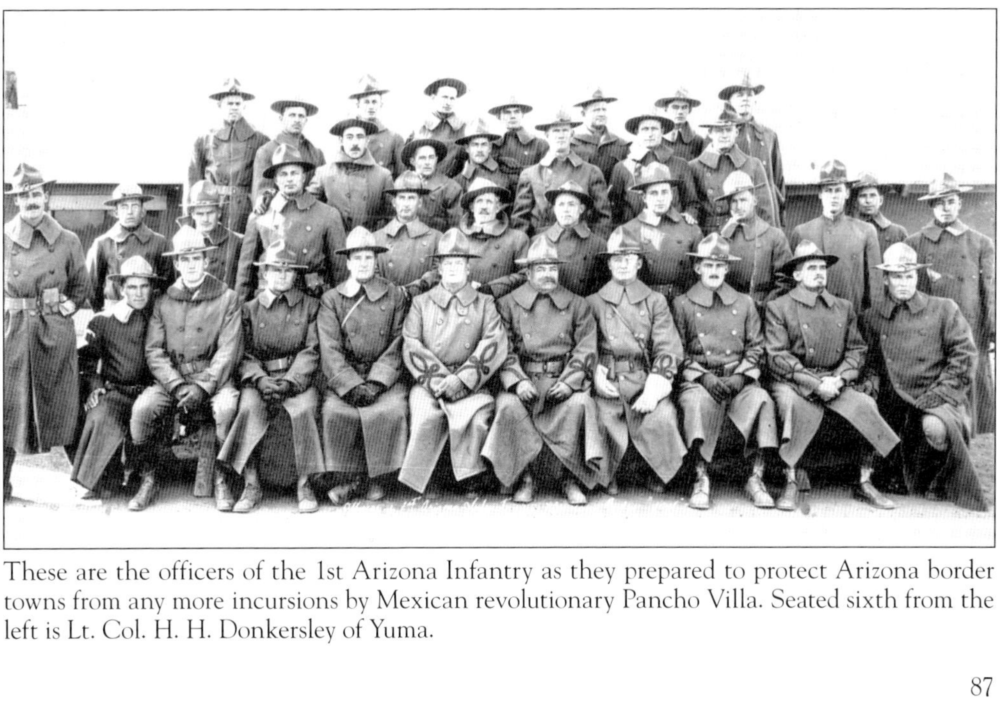

These are the officers of the 1st Arizona Infantry as they prepared to protect Arizona border towns from any more incursions by Mexican revolutionary Pancho Villa. Seated sixth from the left is Lt. Col. H. H. Donkersley of Yuma.

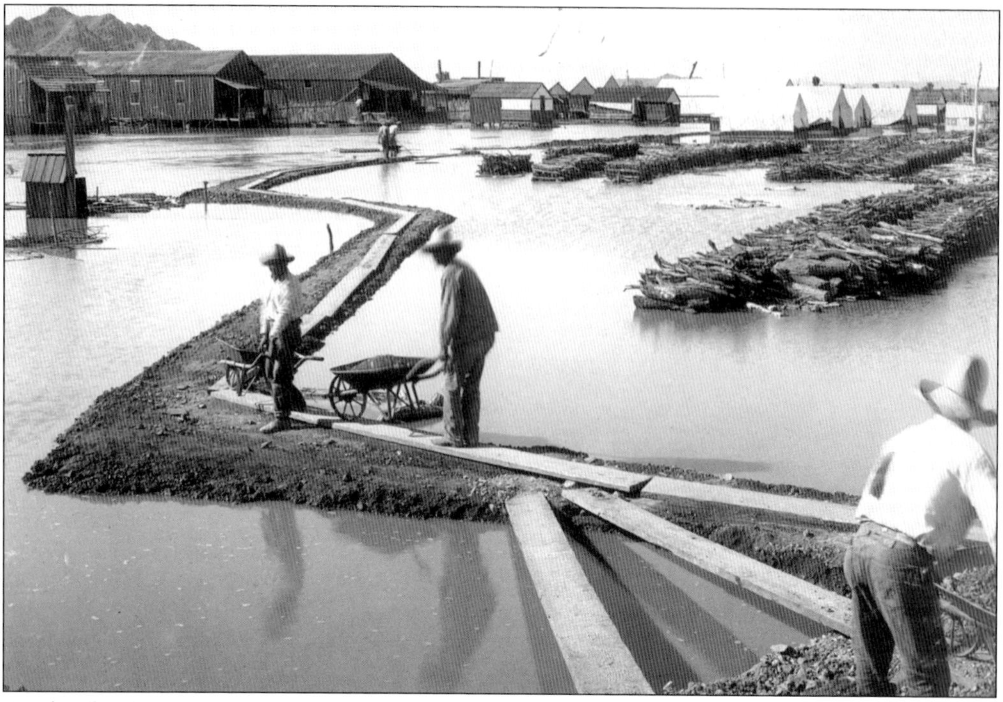

As the floodwaters rose in 1916, residents worked frantically to build dikes to limit floodwater damage to downtown Yuma. They were only moderately successful. Gophers were blamed for undermining the levees that protected the cities. After the 1916 flood, the city council finally prohibited the building of downtown structures with adobe blocks. That didn't matter much, because dams built along the Gila and Colorado Rivers would soon diminish the chances of another great flood.

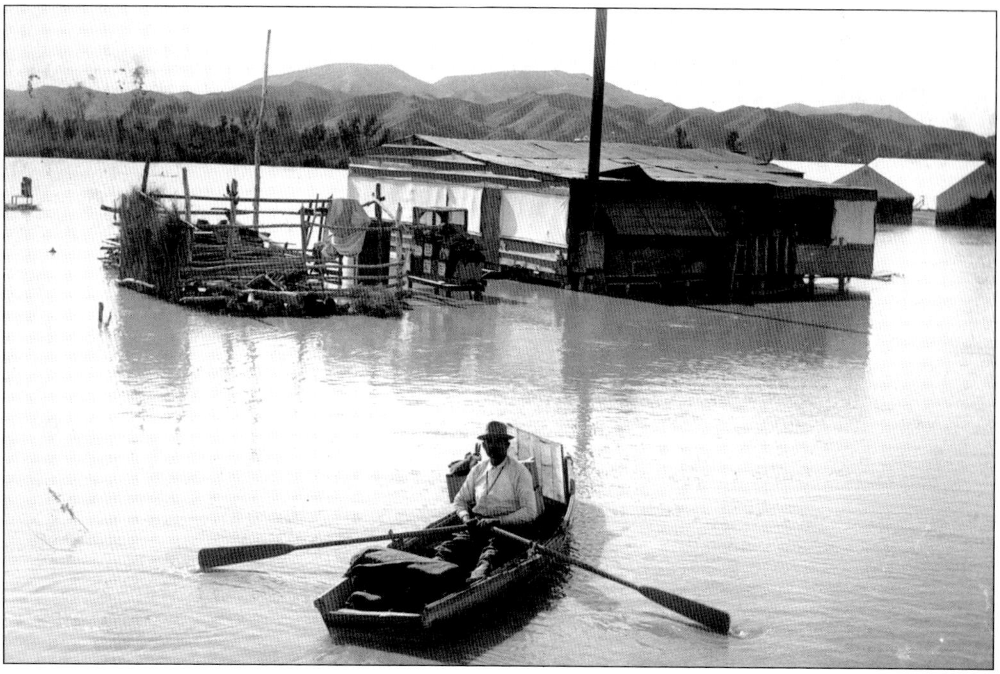

Six

The People

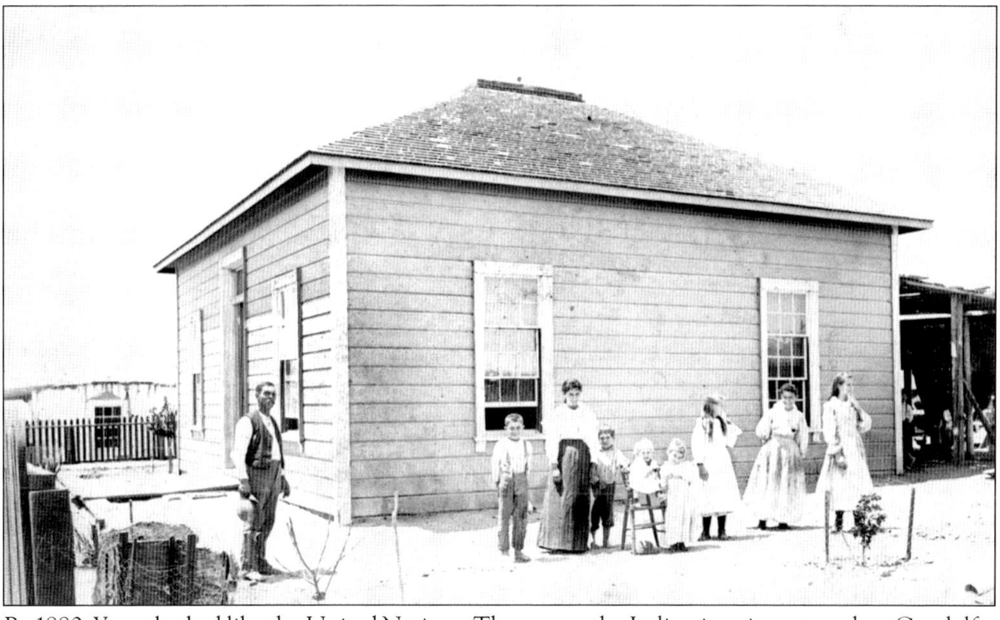

By 1880, Yuma looked like the United Nations. There were the Italian immigrants such as Gandolfo, Ginocchio, and Sanguinetti; Redondo, Armenta, and Valencia from Mexico; Rechemacher and Humboldt from Germany; "Russian George" Angelo; Dorrington, a Methodist, and his dear friend, Abe Frank, a Jew; Sam Kee Laundry; and Fitzgerald and O'Donnell. They all came together with little in common except that they could handle the heat. But like few places on Earth, all these differences meant very little. The people of early Yuma worked together. They had to if they wanted to survive. And within a generation, the families, such as the Townsends and the Alvarados, were intermarried. Viola Townsend Alvarado is at far right in this Townsend family portrait. To the left are Marcia Townsend (Sullivan), Emma Townsend (Stahl), and Edith Townsend (Breedlove). Frank, Harry, and Arthur Townsend are also pictured.

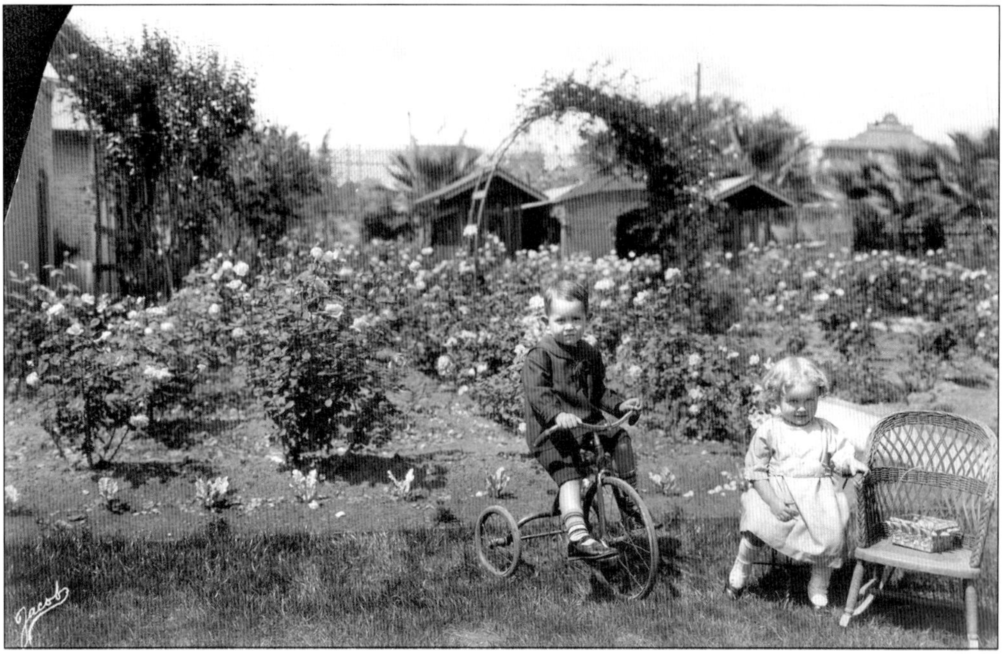

Frances and Rosemarie Sanguinetti were blessed with a beautiful garden in which to play. The home of E. F. Sanguinetti and his wife, Lilah, now serves as the State Historical Society's museum, while some of the garden remains today to shade several small shops and arguably the finest restaurant in Yuma.

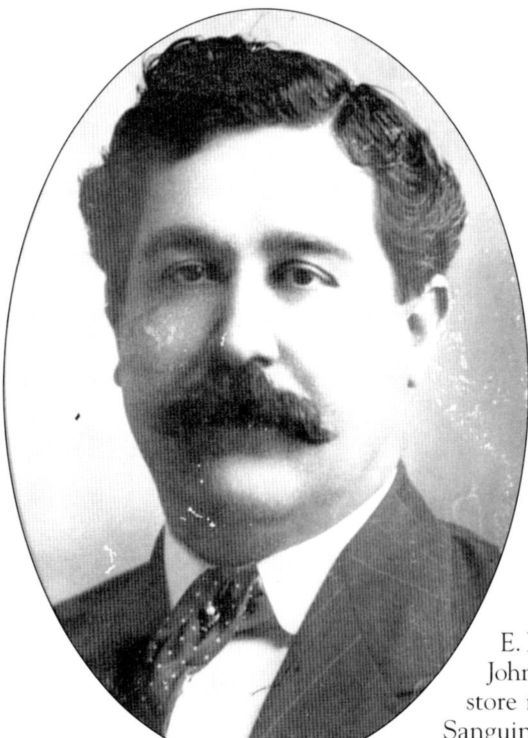

E. F. Sanguinetti and another Italian immigrant, John Gandolfo, together operated the largest general store in the region. Besides getting into banking, Sanguinetti also supplied merchandise to dozens of smaller towns and mining camps in the region.

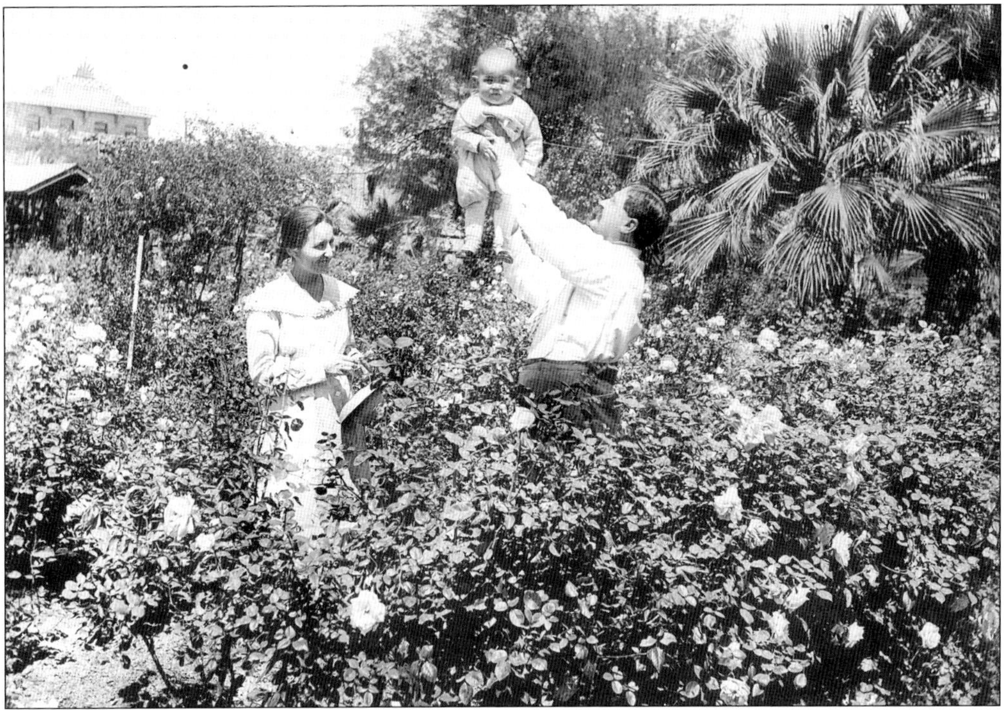

The Sanguinetti's home sat in the swankiest neighborhood in Yuma, but one that is quite modest in comparison to the ritzy addresses in other cities. Others who lived on their block, which used to straddle the Southern Pacific line, were Isaac Polhamus, Capt. Jack Mellon, Henry Fitzgerald, and, later, Joseph Godfrey, Pablo Figueroa, and Judge Abe Frank.

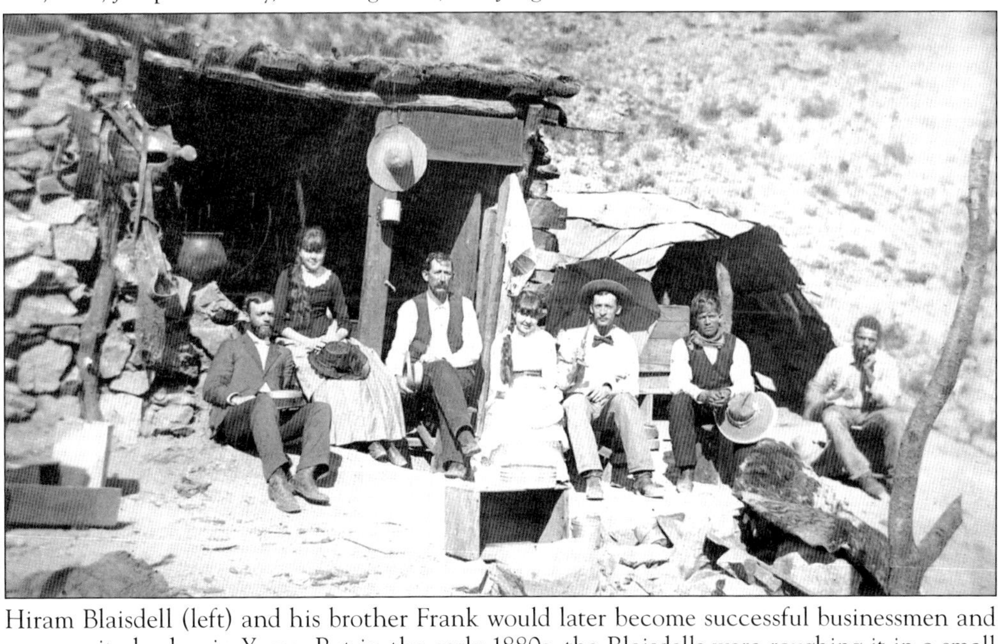

Hiram Blaisdell (left) and his brother Frank would later become successful businessmen and community leaders in Yuma. But in the early 1880s, the Blaisdells were roughing it in a small shack at the Esperanza Mine, which Hiram managed. Also pictured, from left to right, are Winnie Johnson, John Bogan, Mamie Johnson, Richard Wheeler, unidentified, and unidentified.

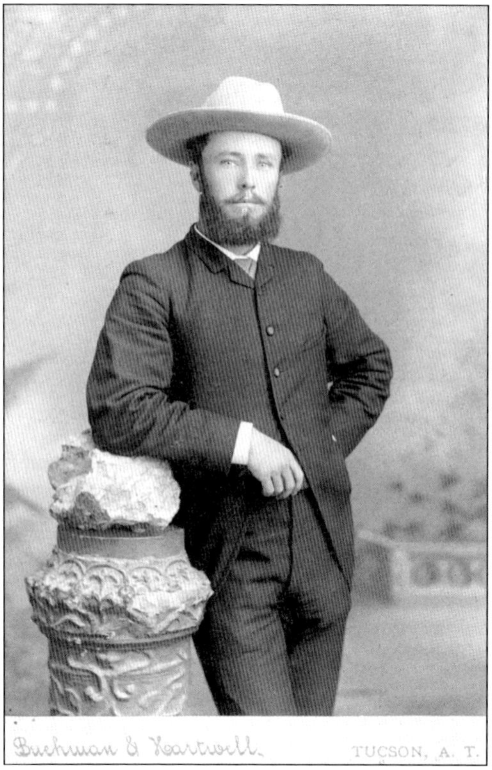

This photograph of Frank Blaisdell, Hiram's brother, likely was taken while the brothers were working the Esperanza Mine. Frank Blaisdell is better known for having started the power company and the telephone company in Yuma.

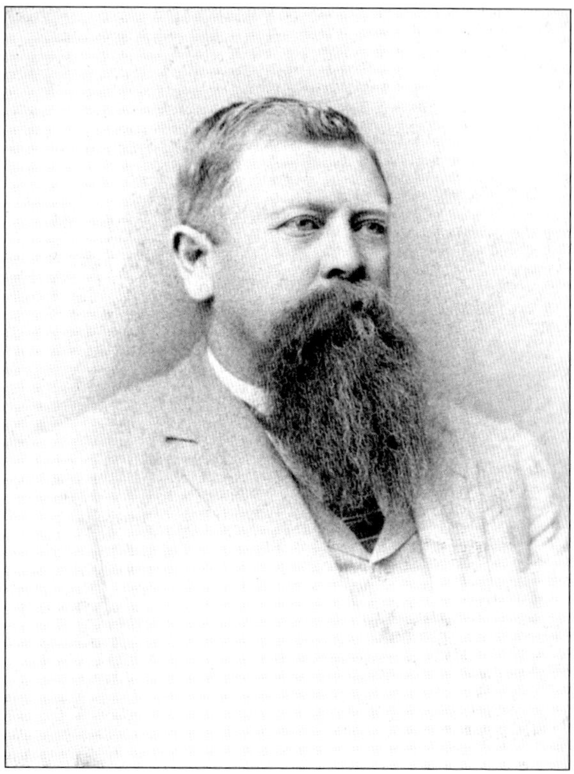

George Norton was an early leader who attempted to irrigate the Mohawk Valley east of Yuma. This is a clip from the *Sentinel* in 1885:

> Hon. George W. Norton, a large owner in and contractor for the construction of the Mohawk Canal, spent two or three days of this week in town. He reports the work is steadily progressing toward completion. There are 12 teams and about 20 men regularly employed excavating and three more teams just arrived from Sacramento, will be at once added.

Along with the Gandolfos and the Sanguinettis, the Modestis were another prominent family of Italian or Corsican descent in Yuma. The Modesti family was also well known outside of Yuma as the family that owned and operated Hotel Modesti at Aqua Caliente, 90 miles east of Yuma along the Gila Trail. The hotel is still standing, but the hot springs there have long since dried up. The family included, from left to right, (in front) Benjamin, the youngest; (first row) Althee Jr., Mr. and Mrs. Modesti; (second row) Angelina, Sylvester, Antoinette, and Ernestina; and (third row) Phinoclade and John.

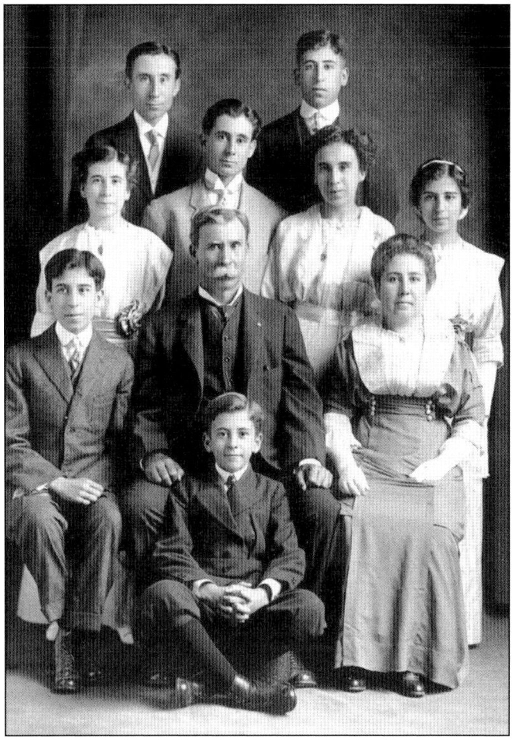

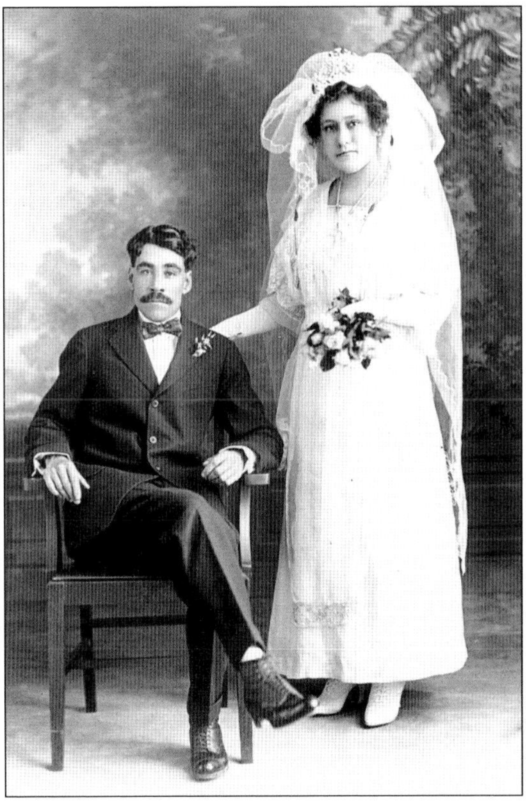

Police officer Chon Lopez and his new bride, Carmen Gomez Lopez, are pictured here. For the most part, law enforcement jobs in Yuma were not as dangerous as similar jobs in Arizona's more notorious towns. It was argued by the city's booster that this was because of the good work of local law enforcement officials such as Lopez.

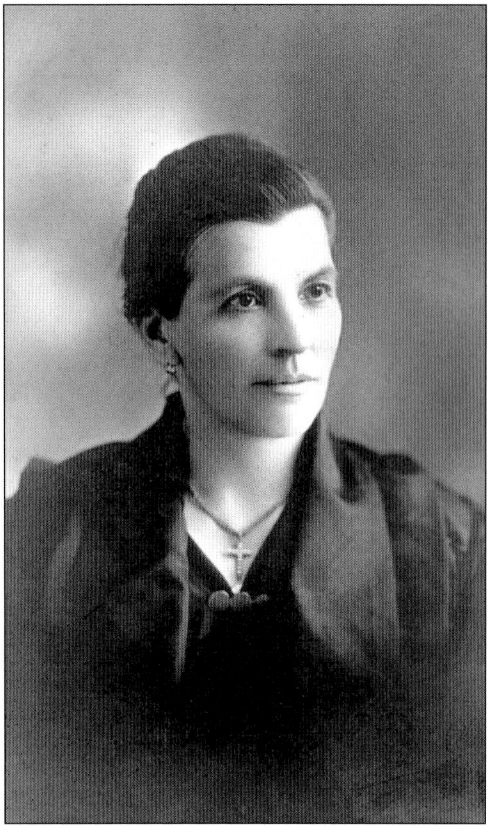

Mrs. John Stoffela, who owned a substantial amount of property around town, was one of Yuma's earliest prominent businesswomen. Yuma's very first businesswoman was Sarah Bowman, better known as "Great Western," who was famous for providing good food and good fun to soldiers at army posts throughout the country. Bowman was buried at Fort Yuma before being moved to the Presidio at San Francisco when the cemetery was moved there.

Several generations of the Avila family came together for this photograph. Pictured, from left to right, are (first row) Palemon Avila (who owned a laundry shop in Yuma), Teofila Avila (the family's matriarch, who was born in 1823 in Sonora, Mexico), Palemon Avila Jr., and Erasto Avila; (second row) Carlos, Adelina, Flavia, and Adela; (third row) Pancho, Joe, unidentified, Henry, and Rudy.

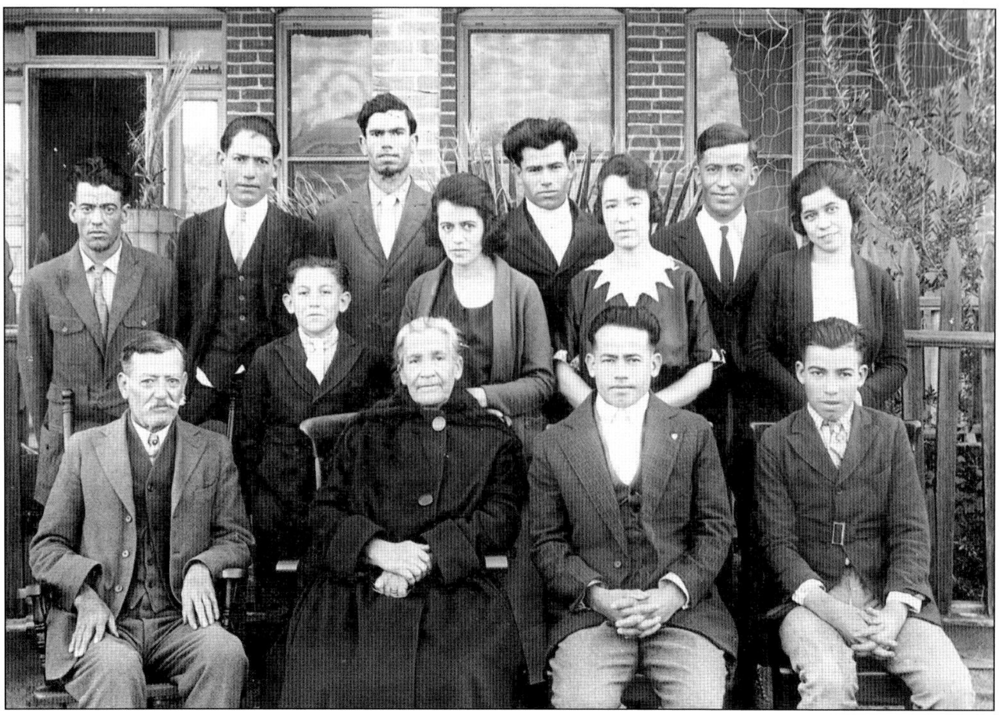

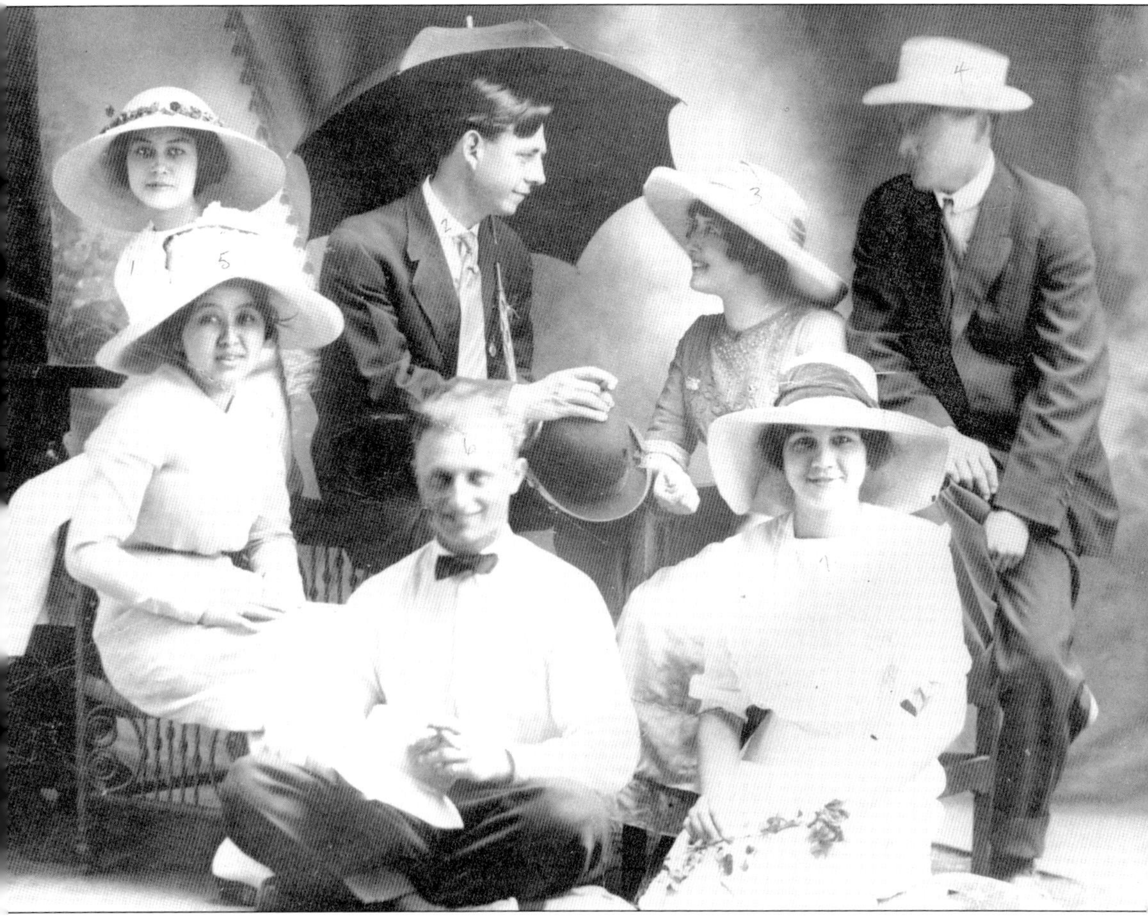

In her introduction to the 1976 Yuma County Historical Society book on early Yuma, Rosalie Robles Crowe described three stages of development for a community: the survival years, the establishment of institution years, and the frosting years. This photograph most definitely finds Yuma in the frosting years, which Crowe described as, basically, the time when residents could start thinking about fun and enlightenment. Pictured are two daughters of Frank Hodges, Frances and Margaret, along with James Hodges, Charles Garcia, Edwin Hansberger, and Aureola Noriega. Notable again is the close relationship between Latinos and Anglos in Yuma.

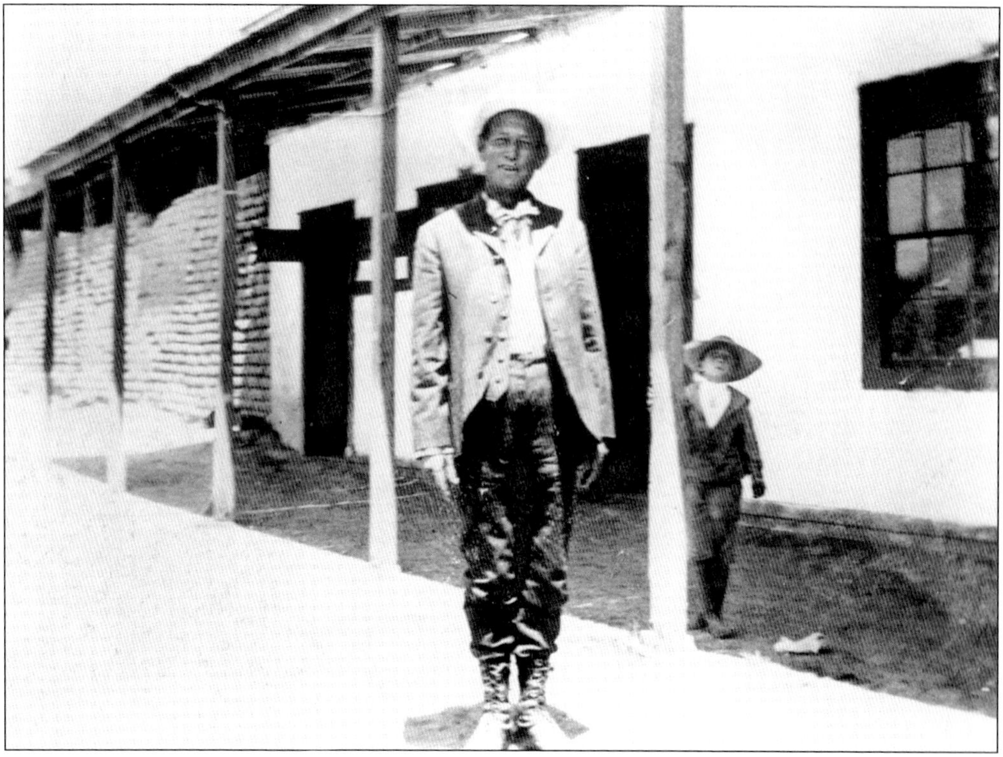

When nobody in Yuma wanted to serve as hangman at Martin Ubillos's hanging, this man was brought down from northern Yuma County to do the job. He had a large audience thanks to the invitations sent out to citizens, which read, "The Sheriff of Yuma County, Arizona, announces that on Friday, June 16, 1905, at the hour of 11 o'clock a.m., Martin Ubillos will be executed in the jail yard in this city, for the murder of Simon Aldrete. You are respectfully invited to witness the execution."

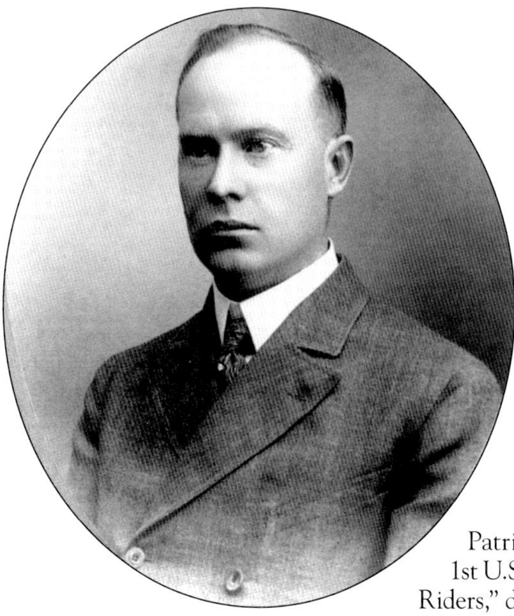

Patrick Sullivan served as a trooper in the famed 1st U.S. Volunteer Cavalry, Teddy Roosevelt's "Rough Riders," during the Spanish-American War.

Seven

COMMUNITY LIFE

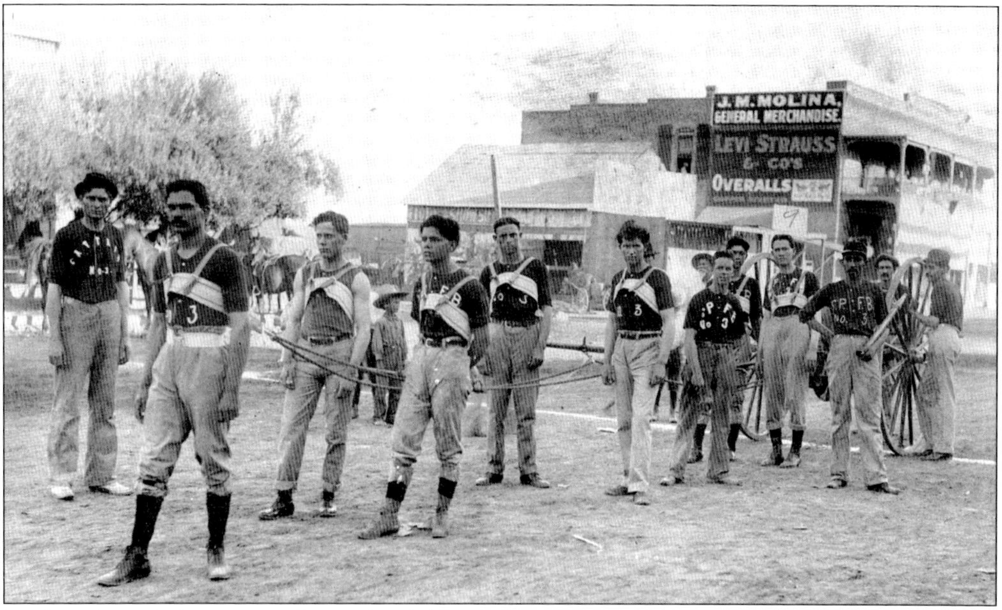

In Yuma's early days, as with much of the West, it was every man for himself. In time, that Law of the Jungle became increasingly unproductive and not enjoyable, as communities and institutions formed and parades, dances, and events brought people get together to have some fun. At times, they didn't have fun, as seemed to be the case when editor Dorrington wrote this of his community in 1898:

> The "regular" doctors are fighting the "irregular doctors," the "reputable papers" are demeaning the "disreputable newspapers," the gold bugs are trying to kill the silver bugs; the bulls are booming the price of wheat, while bears are trying to mow it down; one religious denomination is after the other, while the devil is after them both; the employer is out to crush the employee, while he is seeking to bleed his employer; people in India are starving, while America is reveling in over-production with thousands of people in enforced idleness, while the wealthy are squandering their millions in riotous living, raging fever for gold is everywhere epidemic and everybody wants to go to the Klondike. What's the matter with the fool people anyway?

When the world gets too crazy, there's always the volunteer fire department to renew the faith in humanity and community. In this case, it was the Southern Pacific Fire Brigade, Hose Company No. 3 of the Yuma Volunteer Fire Department, another favorite of the Yuma parade circuit.

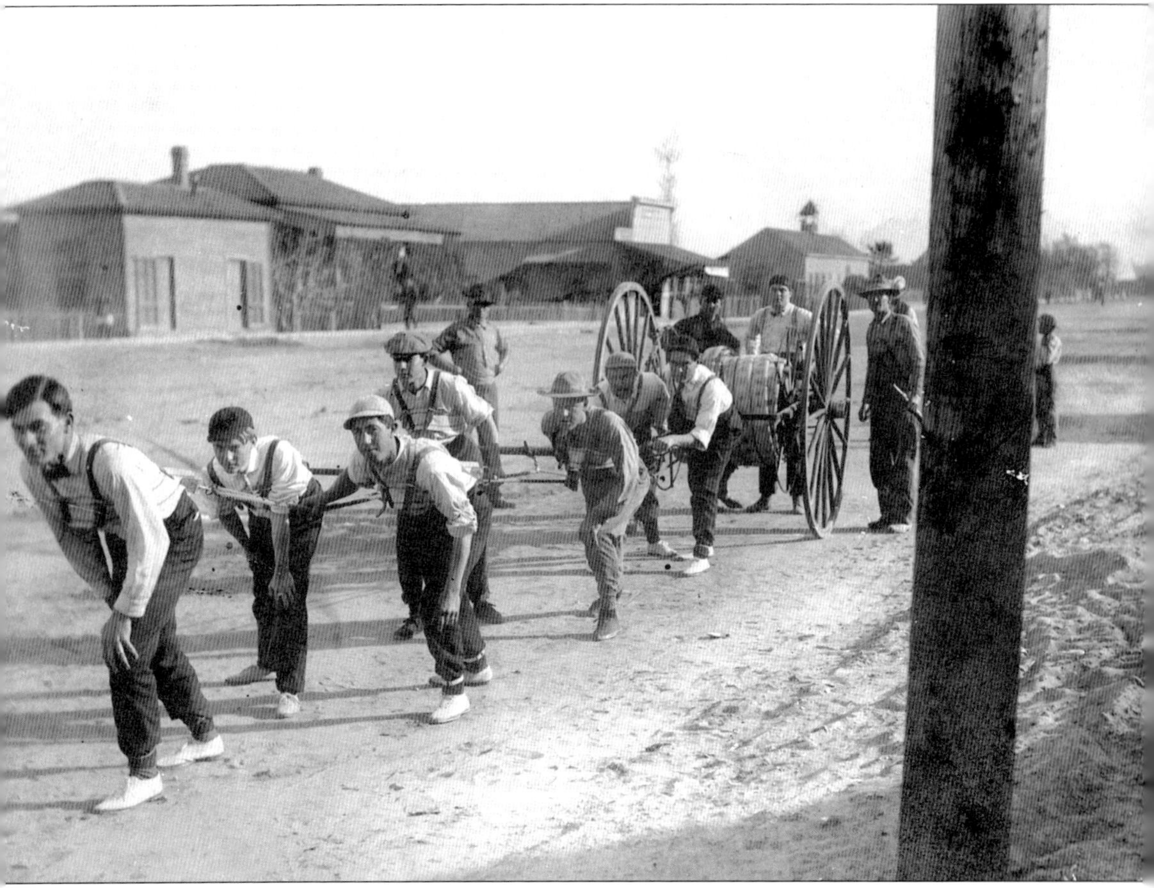

Identified in this photograph of Yuma's first fire department is Charles Yoakum, who is standing back by the water barrel on the hose cart. Pulling the hose cart full of water was no easy job. When the fire bell would ring, volunteer firemen rushed to the station, strapped themselves into the hose-cart harness, and began running. Sometimes only a few firefighters would start pulling before being joined by firefighters as they made their way to the fire. If the hose cart had too far to go, the firemen would sometimes be so exhausted that other citizens would have to begin the job of fighting the fire for them. Notice also that the firemen are wearing light leather or canvas shoes built for speed, a rarity among the heavy work boots common in the early West.

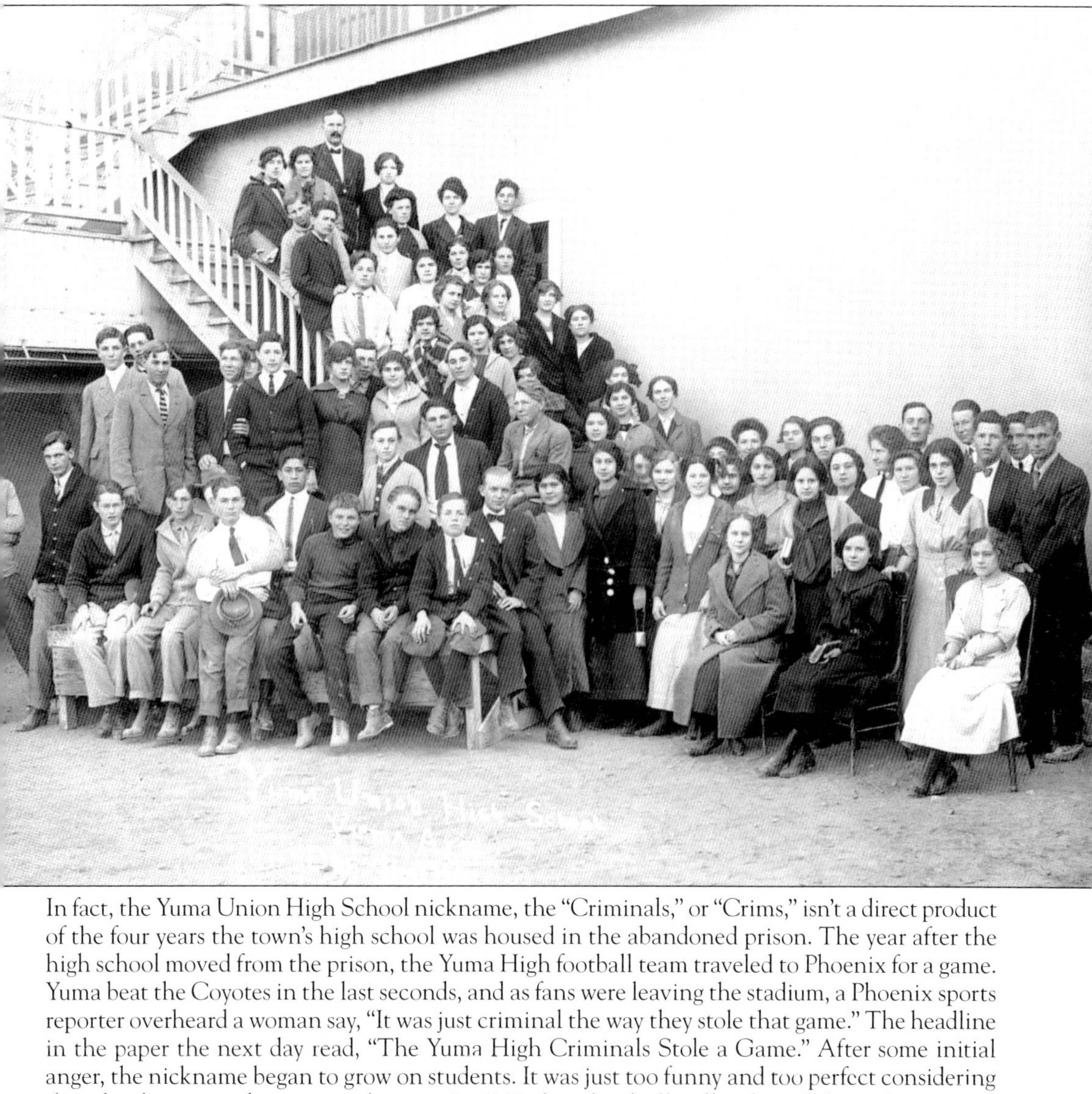

In fact, the Yuma Union High School nickname, the "Criminals," or "Crims," isn't a direct product of the four years the town's high school was housed in the abandoned prison. The year after the high school moved from the prison, the Yuma High football team traveled to Phoenix for a game. Yuma beat the Coyotes in the last seconds, and as fans were leaving the stadium, a Phoenix sports reporter overheard a woman say, "It was just criminal the way they stole that game." The headline in the paper the next day read, "The Yuma High Criminals Stole a Game." After some initial anger, the nickname began to grow on students. It was just too funny and too perfect considering the school's time at the territorial prison. In 1917, the school officially adopted the nickname and Yuma High became "the home of the Criminals." This photograph from 1913 shows the student body looking nothing like a bunch of criminals. Remember, too, that the prison was still one of the more modern facilities in the town when it was used as the school. And unlike the real criminals, the Yuma Crims were released during the summer months.

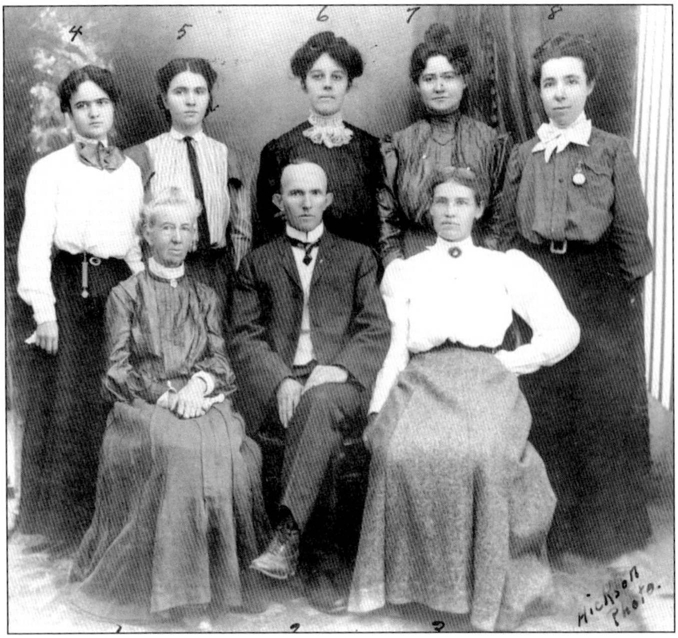

For nearly 50 years, Mary Elizabeth Post (first row, left) was the guiding light of Yuma's schools. More than just a schoolteacher or administrator, she was a political force who constantly pushed to better the educational experience of Yuma's youth of all races. For a decade, school board candidates were broken down into two groups—those who support Mary and those who don't. Ruth Leedy Gordon wrote a fascinating biography about Post, *Portrait of a Teacher*, available in the Sanguinetti House bookstore.

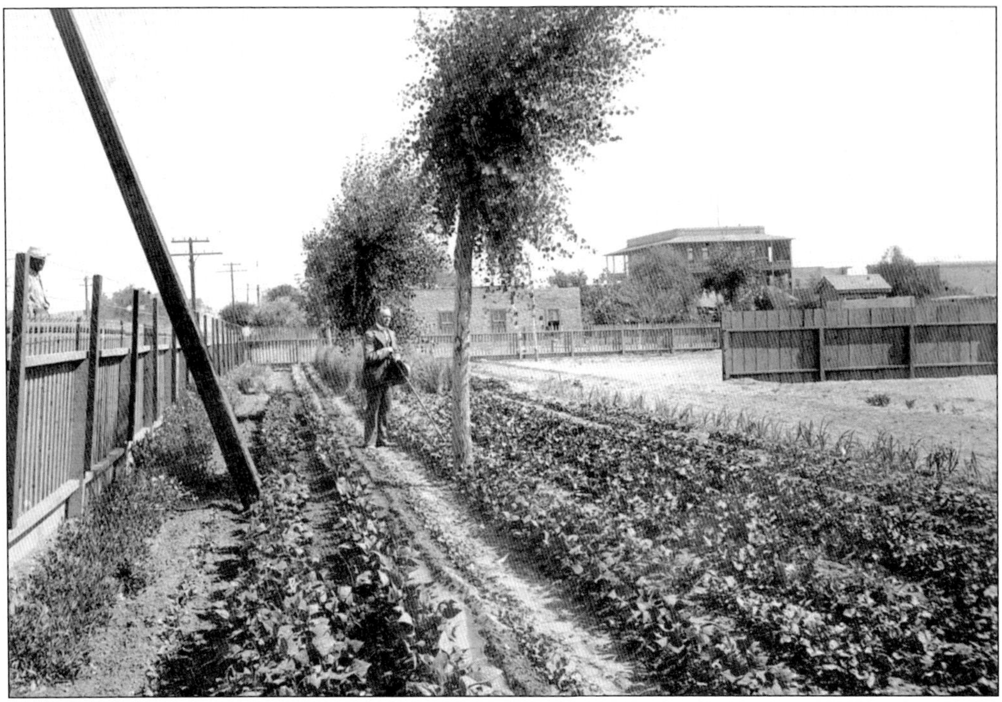

When Henry Miller served as principal of the public school around the turn of the century, he also served as chief gardener of the school garden, which provided a wealth of fresh vegetables for the schoolchildren. It was said that after leaving Yuma, Miller went to explore Tiburon Island in the Gulf of California where he was killed and then, the story goes, eaten by cannibals.

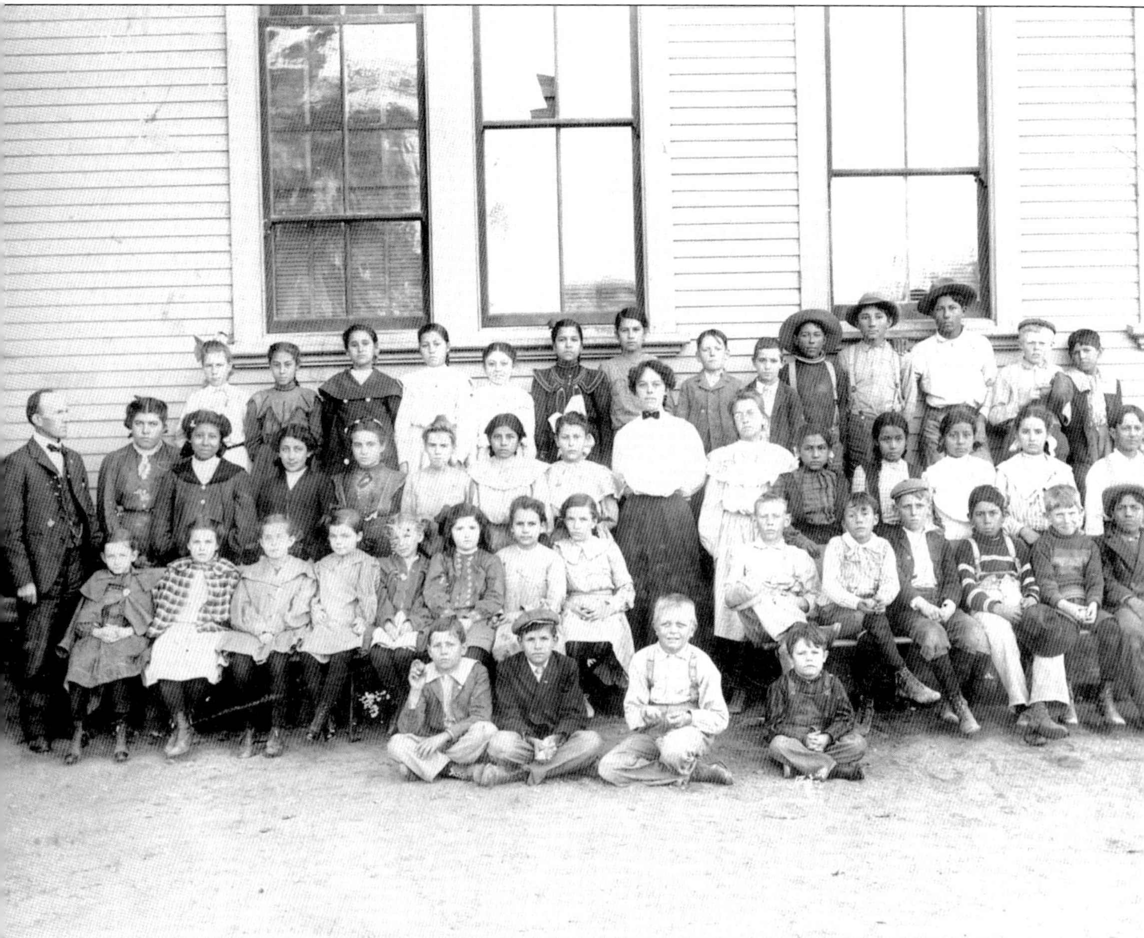

A principal point of contention during school board elections was whether female teachers were capable of providing enough discipline in the classroom. Mary Elizabeth Post, who was bilingual, argued that female teachers could be just as strong, and much more caring, than their male counterparts. According to Gordon's book, Post's principal foe in this argument was the "supercultured Easterner, Colonel Dorrington, who many of the more cultured English-speaking people looked to . . . to counter the coarse influence of the many raw frontiersmen." According to Post's own memoirs, she finally got editor Dorrington on her side when she agreed to support him in saving the mesquite tree in front of his house from road widening. "The tree's twisted body—bearing witness to long struggles with the wind and weather—as contrasted to its feathery fronds, appealed to the colonel's poetic side, and that tree became his great pet." With Post's help, Dorrington was able to save the tree. Gordon writes, "In this fight the long enmity between Miss Post and Col. Dorrington was finally blotted out." And from that time on, female schoolteachers became the norm in Yuma. Post is in the Arizona Women's Hall of Fame.

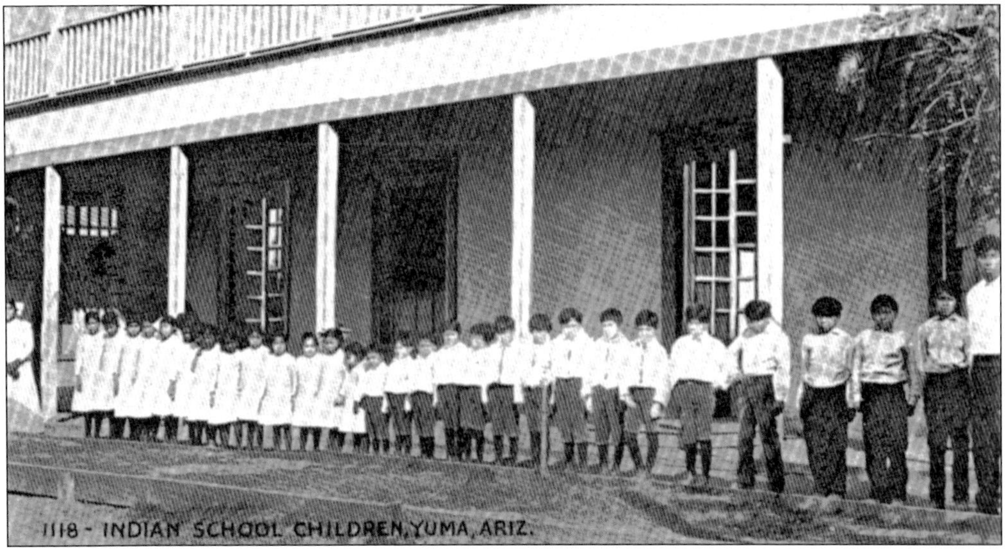

The Yuma Indian School is not held in fond memory by most in the Quechan community. Like similar schools, the goal of the institution was to teach Indian children how to fit into the Anglo world. That often meant washing away the core values of the tribe. The memoirs of nuns who taught at the school speak of constant difficulties, some of which were as mundane as school dress codes:

> Among other things which bothered the Sisters was the Indians' custom of going unclothed or dressed in "Adam's fashion" as the Sisters described it. The summer heat did not encourage the Indians to wear clothing and they considered their long hair as covering enough. Those who did accept some of the bright, new clothing the Sisters gave them did not put it on, however, unless they saw the Sisters coming.

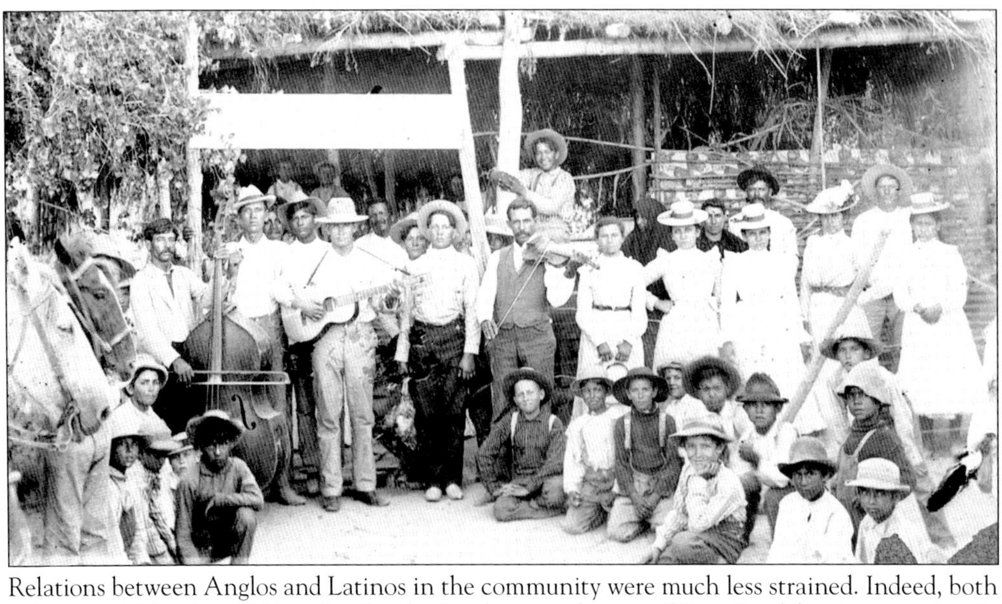

Relations between Anglos and Latinos in the community were much less strained. Indeed, both cultures quickly adopted bits of each other's culture, and many of Yuma's celebrations were a mix of American and Mexican traditions.

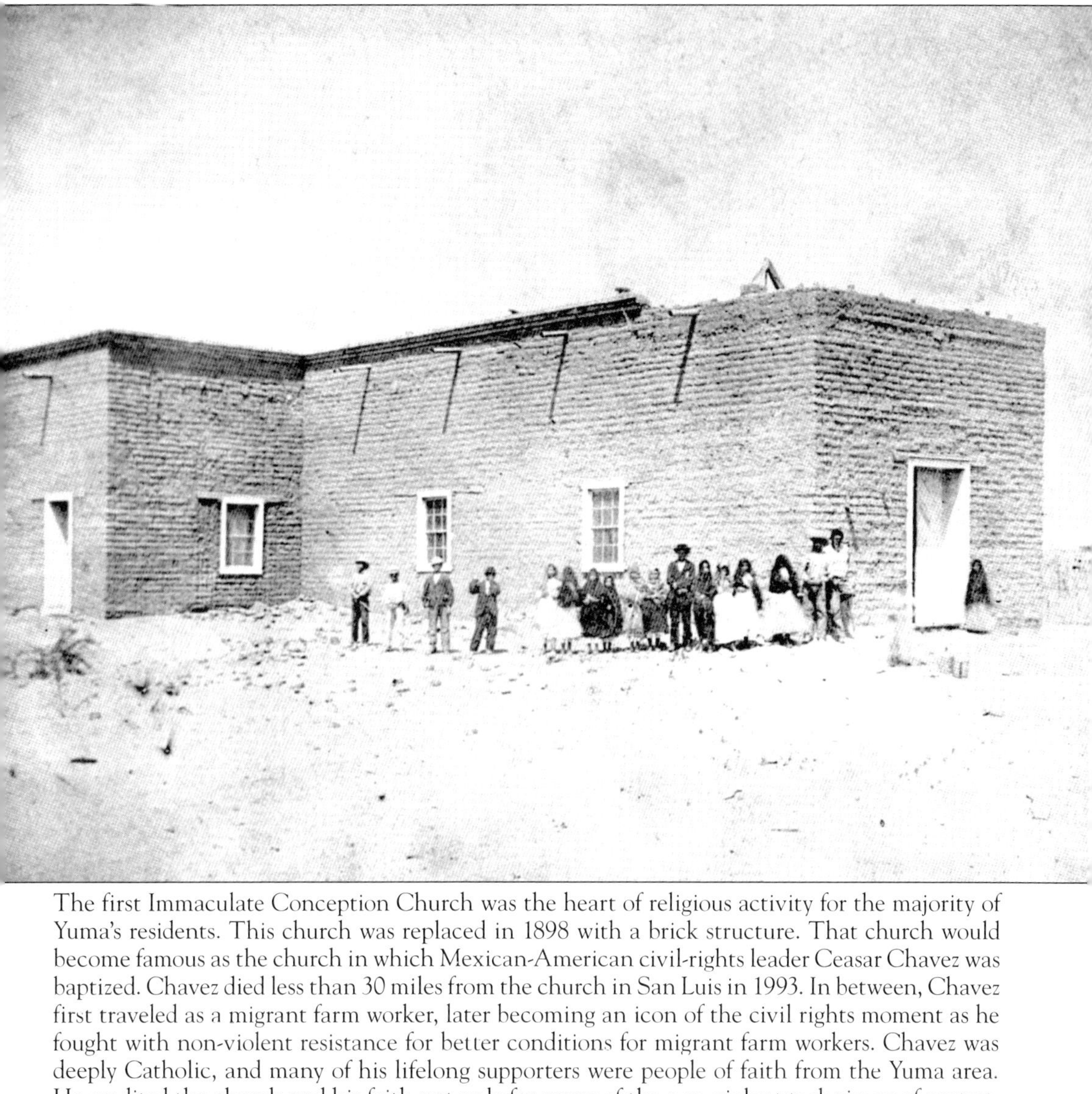

The first Immaculate Conception Church was the heart of religious activity for the majority of Yuma's residents. This church was replaced in 1898 with a brick structure. That church would become famous as the church in which Mexican-American civil-rights leader Ceasar Chavez was baptized. Chavez died less than 30 miles from the church in San Luis in 1993. In between, Chavez first traveled as a migrant farm worker, later becoming an icon of the civil rights moment as he fought with non-violent resistance for better conditions for migrant farm workers. Chavez was deeply Catholic, and many of his lifelong supporters were people of faith from the Yuma area. He credited the church and his faith not only for many of the non-violent techniques of protest, but for maintaining him when he was faced, often, with deep hostility.

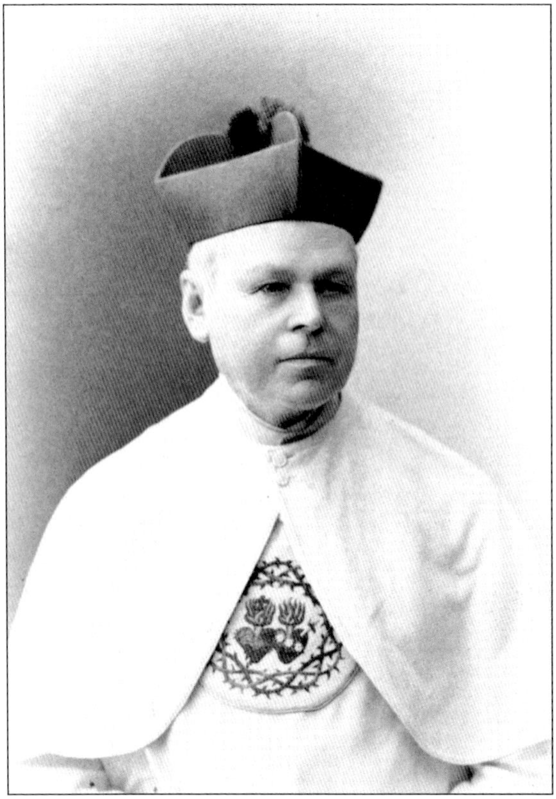

J. B. Salpointe served as a visiting pastor at the Yuma mission in 1866 and 1867, an appointment that would start a long relationship between Salpointe and the Catholic community of Yuma. After his time in Yuma, Salpointe was placed in charge of the priesthood in all of Arizona, a job that had him crisscrossing the territory as he escorted priests out of Santa Fe to their churches in the territory. This was extraordinarily dangerous work that constantly forced him to travel through Apache lands. During one trip, Salpointe could find no one willing to take him and his priests between Las Cruces and Tucson— the *jornada del muerto* (the journey of death)—because of the certainty of Apache attack. "The priests offered a good sum of money for horses and a guide but nobody would risk his life for the sake of any money," Salpointe wrote of one trip in the late 1860s. In 1885, Salpointe was named the Archbishop of Santa Fe, giving him authority over a wide swath of the Southwest, including Arizona.

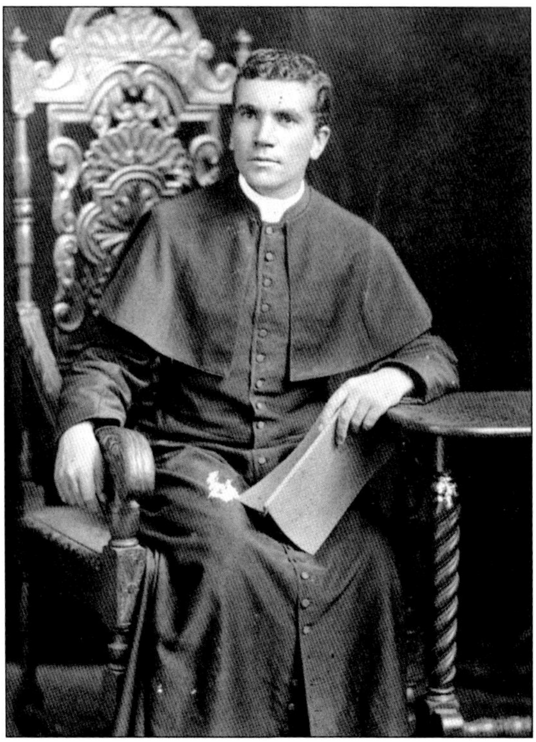

Father Vandermaesen served as pastor for Immaculate Conception from 1903 to 1909.

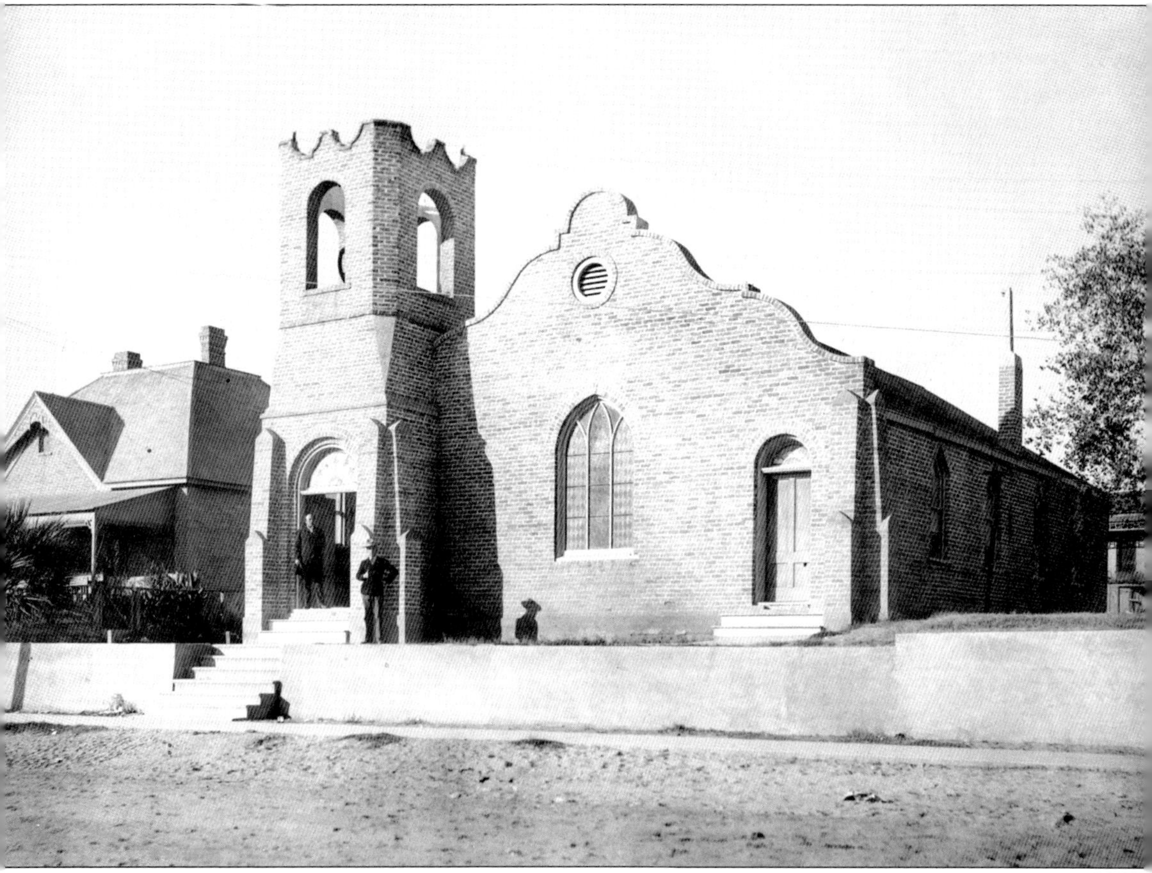

The brick facade hides the original frame structure of the Yuma Methodist Church, which, at the time it was built, was the only Protestant church between Gila Bend and Beaumont, California. In 1887, the leaders of the Methodist Church in America were notified that Yuma was still without a Protestant church. They soon sent a missionary to organize a church and a board of trustees. A fund-raising effort was started. Besides expected support from Mary Post and John Dorrington, both of old Eastern Methodist stock, several Catholic business leaders in town helped the effort. Another supporter, and member of the board of trustees, was Capt. Jack Mellon, known as "Handsome Jack" and for his ability to cuss in Quechan, Cocopah, Spanish, and English. At the church's dedication service, after several speeches, the presiding elder asked Captain Mellon to speak. Mary Post related the moment in her memoirs: "After a painful pause, and a snicker here and there, finally Capt. Mellon spoke up in a distressed tone and said, 'Oh hell, let it go at that.' " The crowd paid little attention to the slip, Post wrote, "because everyone was use to the slips of the good captain's tongue anyway."

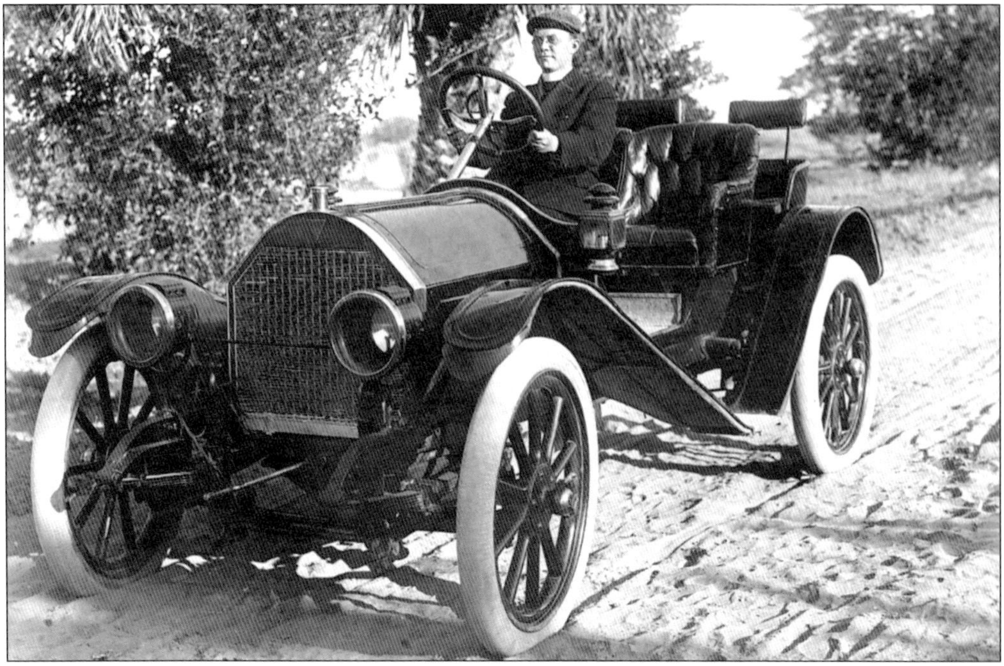

Before 1910, priests and doctors and others who made house calls, or who needed to travel to mining camps or work camps such as this one, typically traveled in a horse-drawn buggy. Most buggies in Yuma, as one can imagine, were built with a roof like the one pictured here. On the other hand, convertible automobiles were popular with Yuma residents because of the increased air flow. The automobile in this 1914 photograph is an Oldsmobile owned by the Stoffelas. In the driver's seat is Father Rouselle, who apparently was lent the automobile by his parishioners to make calls. The horse and buggy remained, however, for years after automobiles arrived in Yuma. Notice the road beneath the Oldsmobile. After a good rain, most of the region's roads were impassable by automobile.

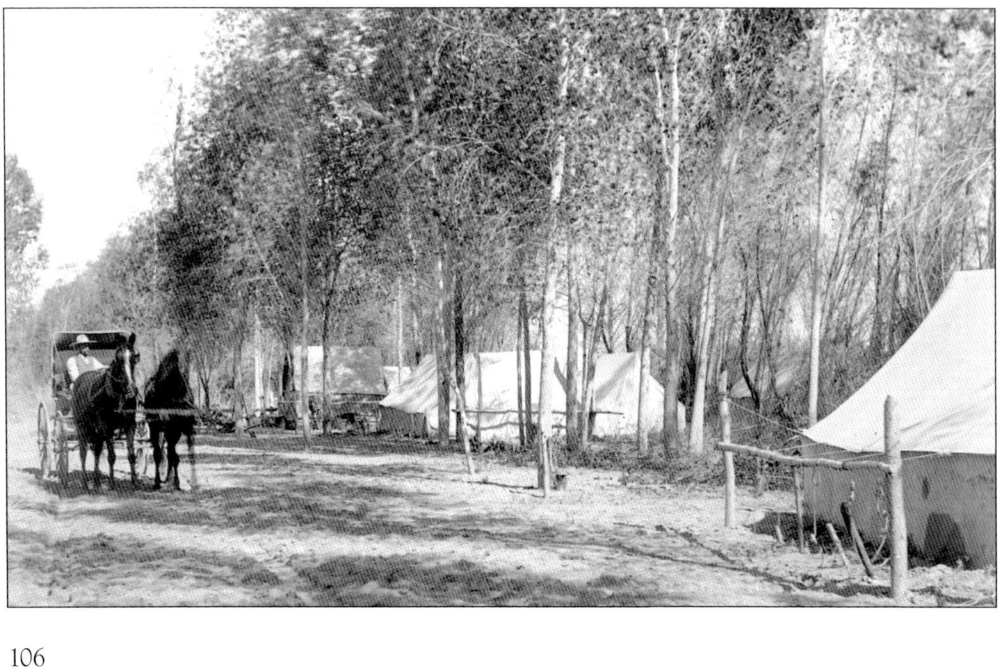

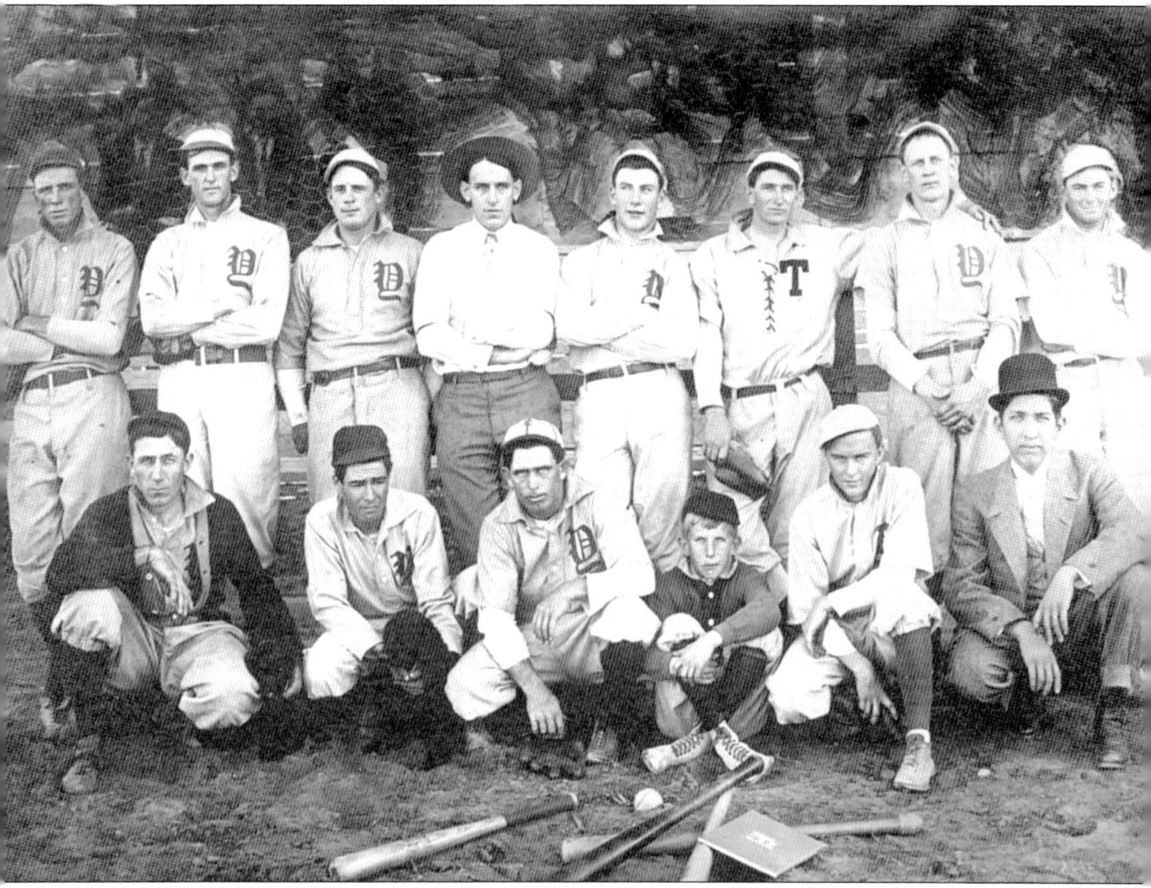

The early-town teams of Yuma again show a racial harmony not seen in other parts of the country. In Yuma's case, Latino players and Anglo players worked in harmony on the baseball field. Oddly enough, that general harmony concerning racial issues in Yuma, and Arizona in general, is one reason Major League spring training first came to the desert. When Jackie Robinson debuted with the Dodgers in 1947, he was not allowed to play in Florida, which didn't allow games with mixed races. Both the Giants and the Indians were close behind with black players. Instead of going to Florida, they decided to move Spring Training to Arizona to take advantage of what one writer described as "lessened racial tensions." That paved the way for the Baltimore Orioles' move to Yuma in 1954. The San Diego Padres came to city in 1969. Both teams have since left. But with Yuma's long tradition of supporting baseball, the hope is that spring-training baseball will soon return to the city.

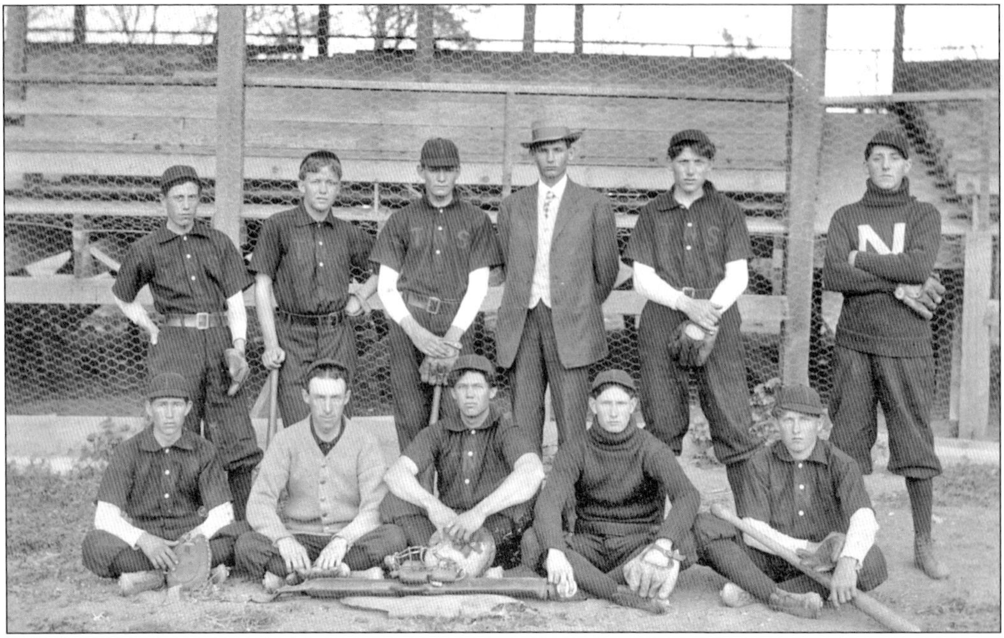

The Yuma town teams were made up with several young men with long family ties to the town. And sometimes a ringer was brought in from California. Pictured here, from left to right, are (first row) unidentified, Fred Ayer, John Sykes, Art Miller and Johnny Miller; and (second row) Jess Clifford, Wiley Hanson, Earl Standage, Halbert Miller, Maurice Blome, and Johnny Lynch.

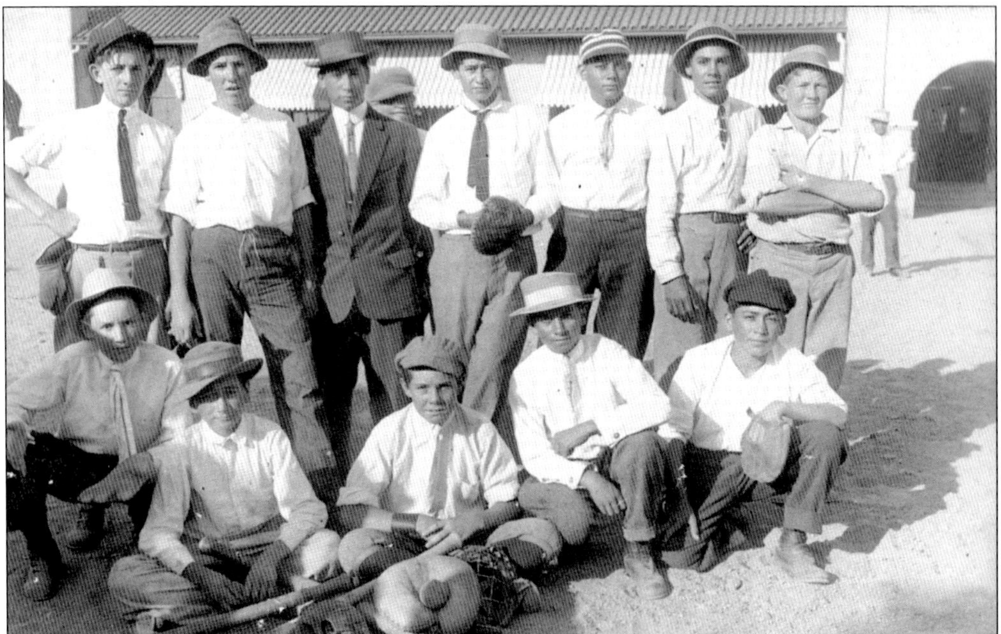

For much of the 1910s, there was always a Hodges boy on the local baseball team. Pictured here, from left to right, are (first row) Henry Hodges, Tom Hodges, Royal Stahl Jr., Eddie Hodges, and Abe Ochoa, and (second row) Earl Lee, unidentified, Robert Wilson, Robert Tapia, Paul Figueroa, Clyde Jones, and Frank Ferguson.

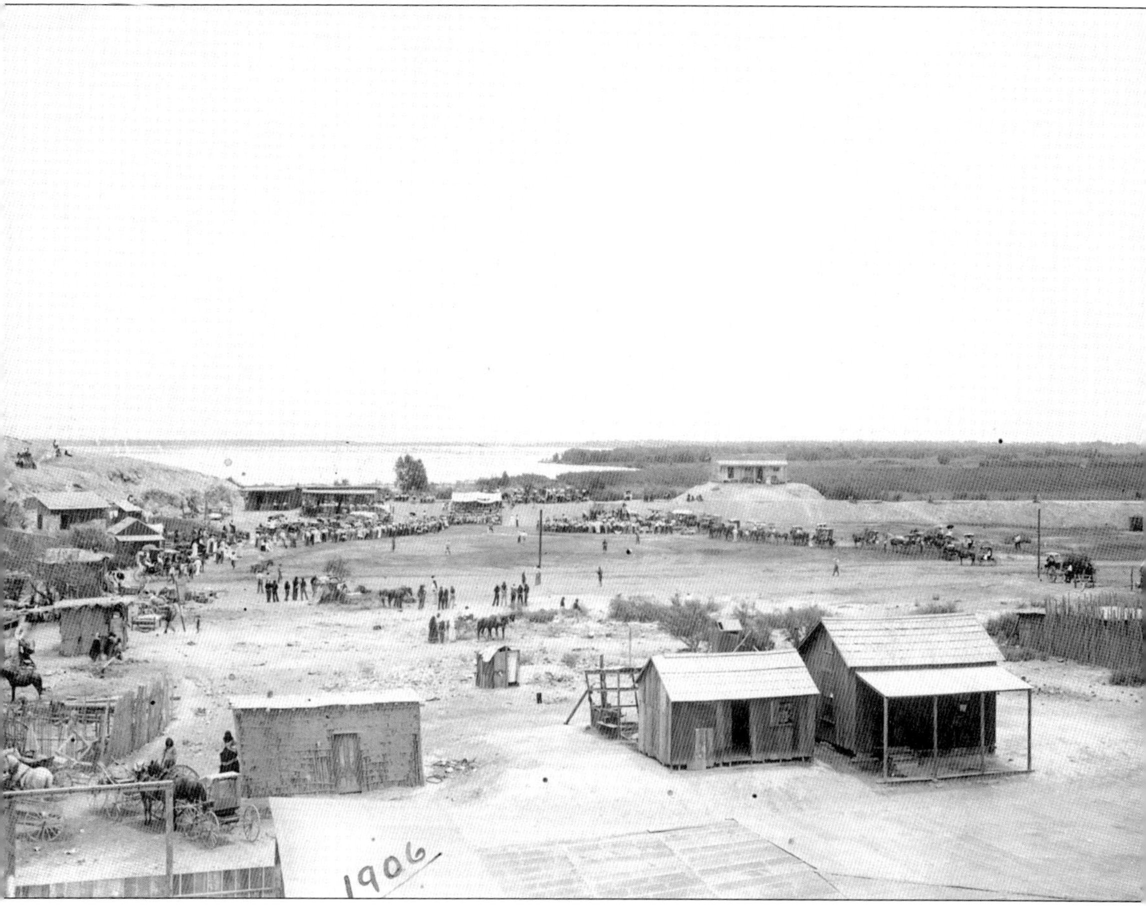

In 1909, Yuma's town council voted to give the Yuma Baseball Association $15 a month for upkeep of trees and other landscape around the town ball field. From this 1906 photograph, it can be seen why council members felt the ballpark could use some sprucing up. Home plate is in the distance by the tent with the white awning, the levee serves as a backstop, and at close look it can be detected that the game drew several hundred spectators. Even with the intense heat of summer, baseball was still a very popular sport to play and watch in Yuma. Beyond baseball, the image gives an idea of the destruction that would be caused when the levees break.

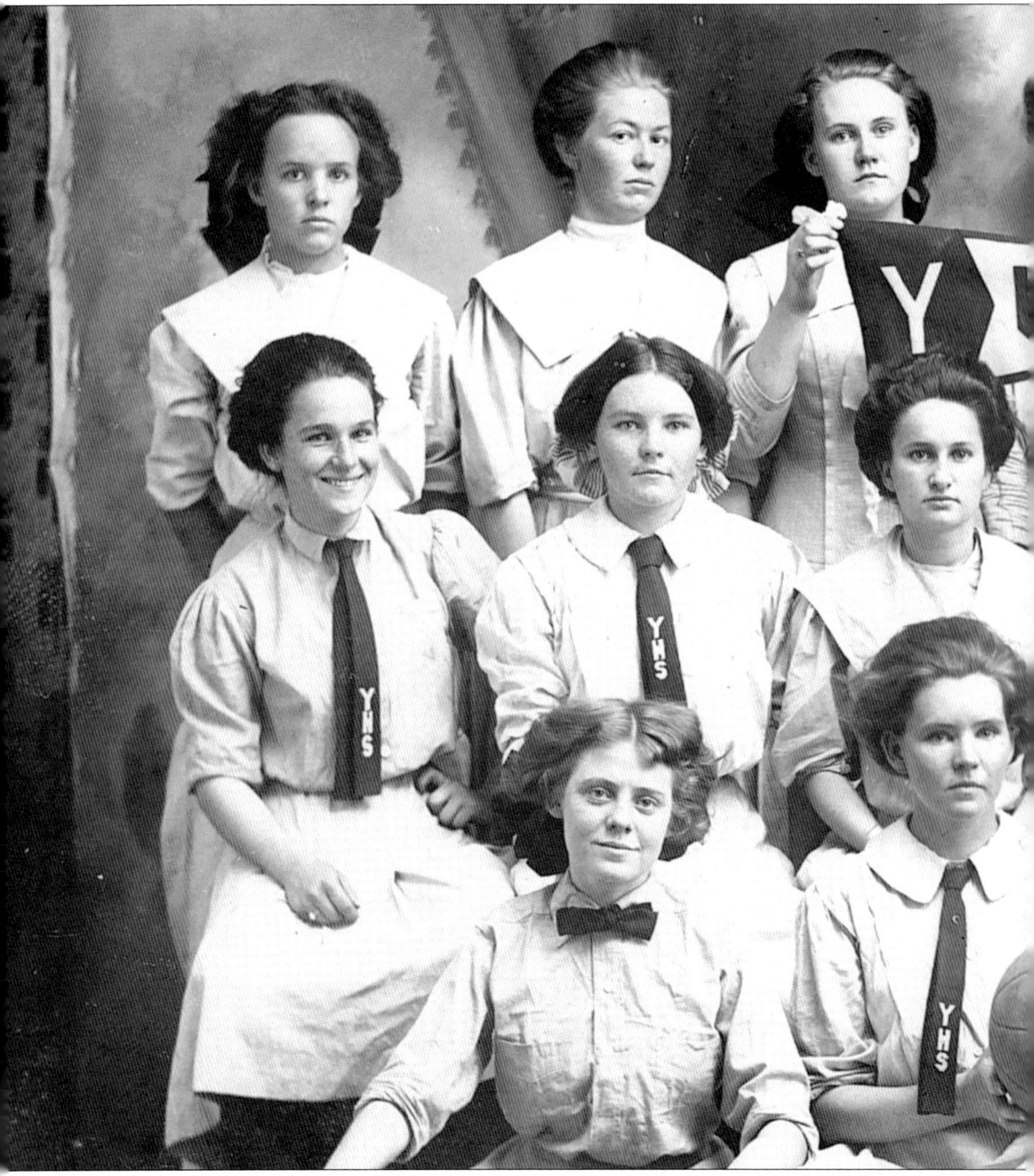

That Yuma High had such a successful women's basketball program only 19 years after the creation of the game is a testament to the strong female leadership in the community and in the schools. It speaks volumes of the work of women such as Mary Post and Fanny Reese Pugh, who, when she was named secretary of the Yuma Chamber of Commerce, was believed to be the first woman to hold that position in the country. Pugh later was elected president of the Arizona Federation of Women's Clubs. The Women's Club was so powerful in Yuma that they were successful in getting the hours shortened for female clerks by pressuring area businessmen. Yuma women were meeting to discuss ways to bring about universal suffrage. At the meetings, though, Post and Pugh were

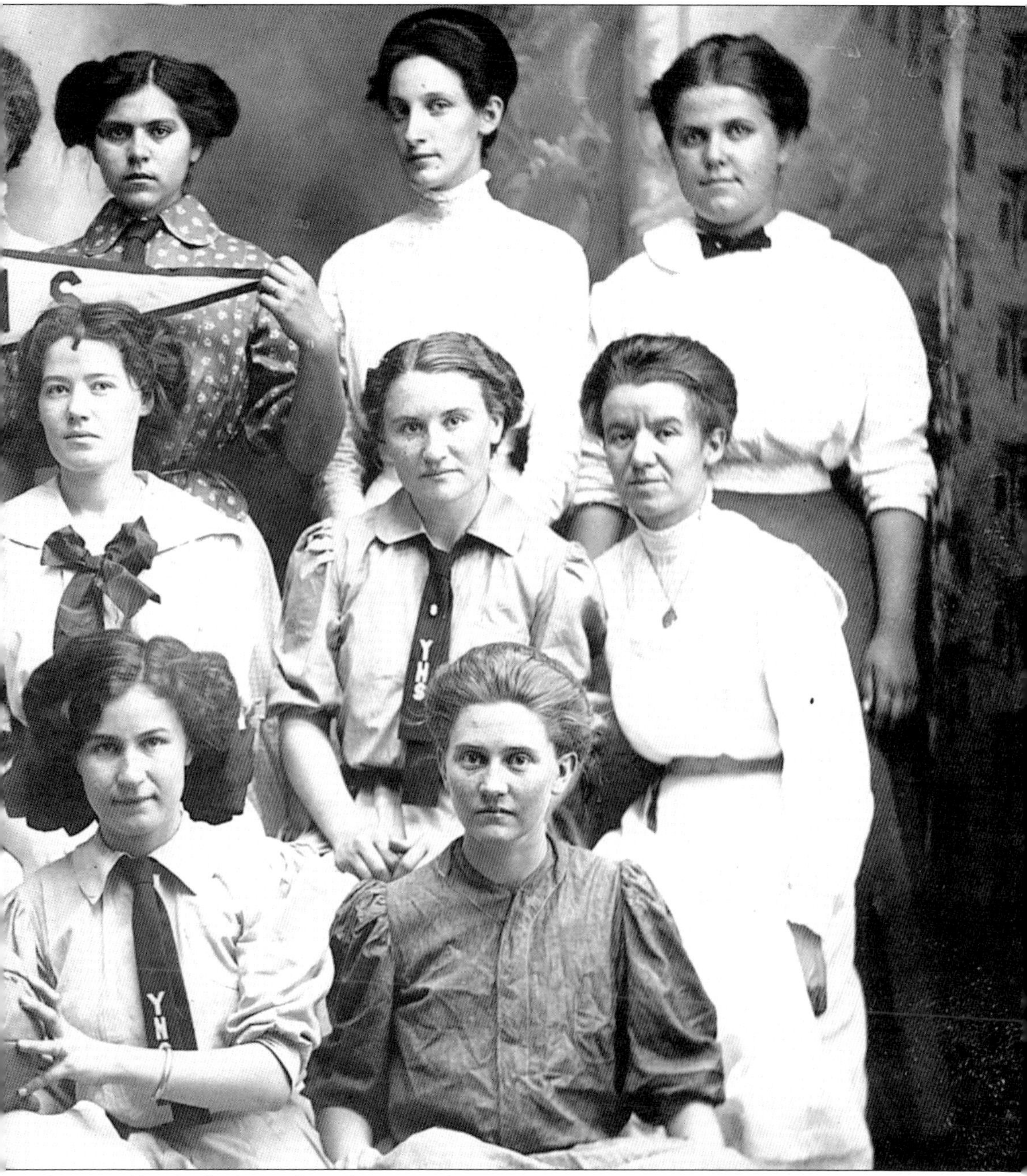

frustrated by the high number of women who were against women voting. Their argument was that "women belong in the home," according to Post. Nonetheless, women were granted equal suffrage by an amendment to the constitution of the new state of Arizona. As far as the game was concerned, the Yuma women's team played under some of the odd early rules of the game. For example, in 1910, the year of this photograph, dribbling was outlawed and double-teaming was considered a foul. As for women throughout the early history of Yuma, the uniforms for girls, long in the legs and arms for modesty, were uncomfortable and excessively warm. Worse yet, there were no timeouts in the game.

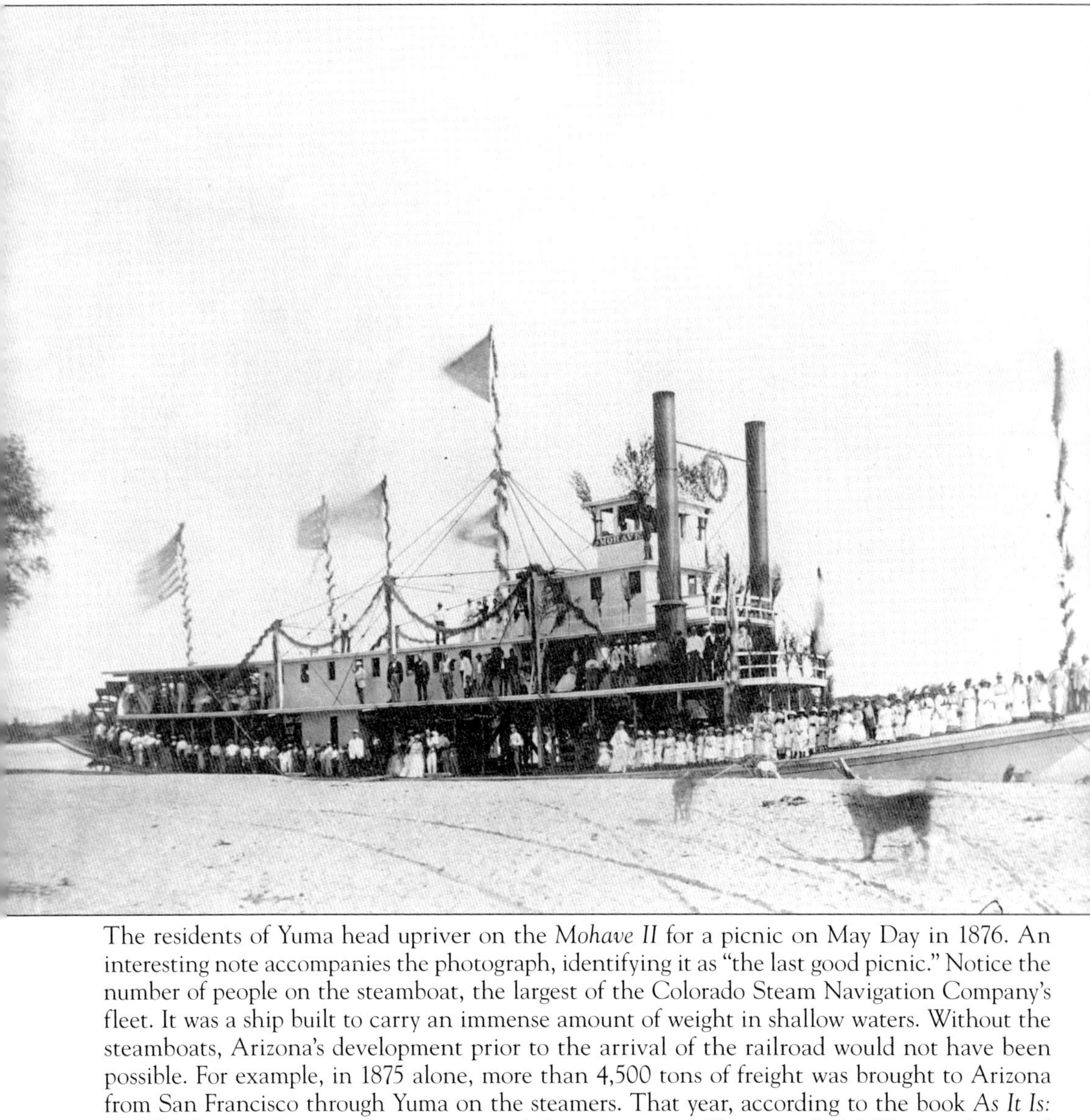

The residents of Yuma head upriver on the *Mohave II* for a picnic on May Day in 1876. An interesting note accompanies the photograph, identifying it as "the last good picnic." Notice the number of people on the steamboat, the largest of the Colorado Steam Navigation Company's fleet. It was a ship built to carry an immense amount of weight in shallow waters. Without the steamboats, Arizona's development prior to the arrival of the railroad would not have been possible. For example, in 1875 alone, more than 4,500 tons of freight was brought to Arizona from San Francisco through Yuma on the steamers. That year, according to the book *As It Is: Or, The Coming Country*, the steamers took from Arizona at Yuma nearly 1,000 tons of mineral ore, 60 tons of wool, 6,170 tons of hides, and 1,400 tons of pelts.

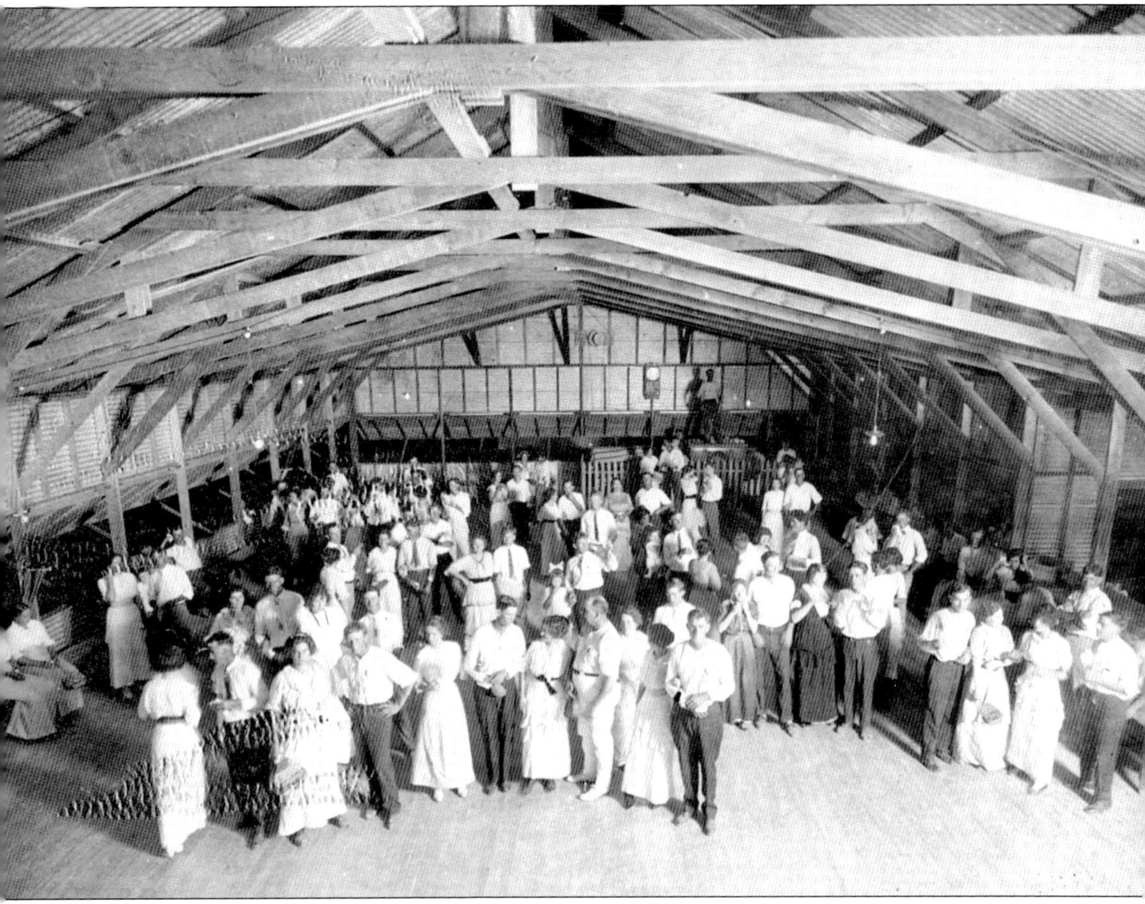

This is a rare indoor photograph, likely taken with the help of a powerful light positioned to the right of the photographer. Nichols Hall was a favorite spot for barn dances like this one in 1910.

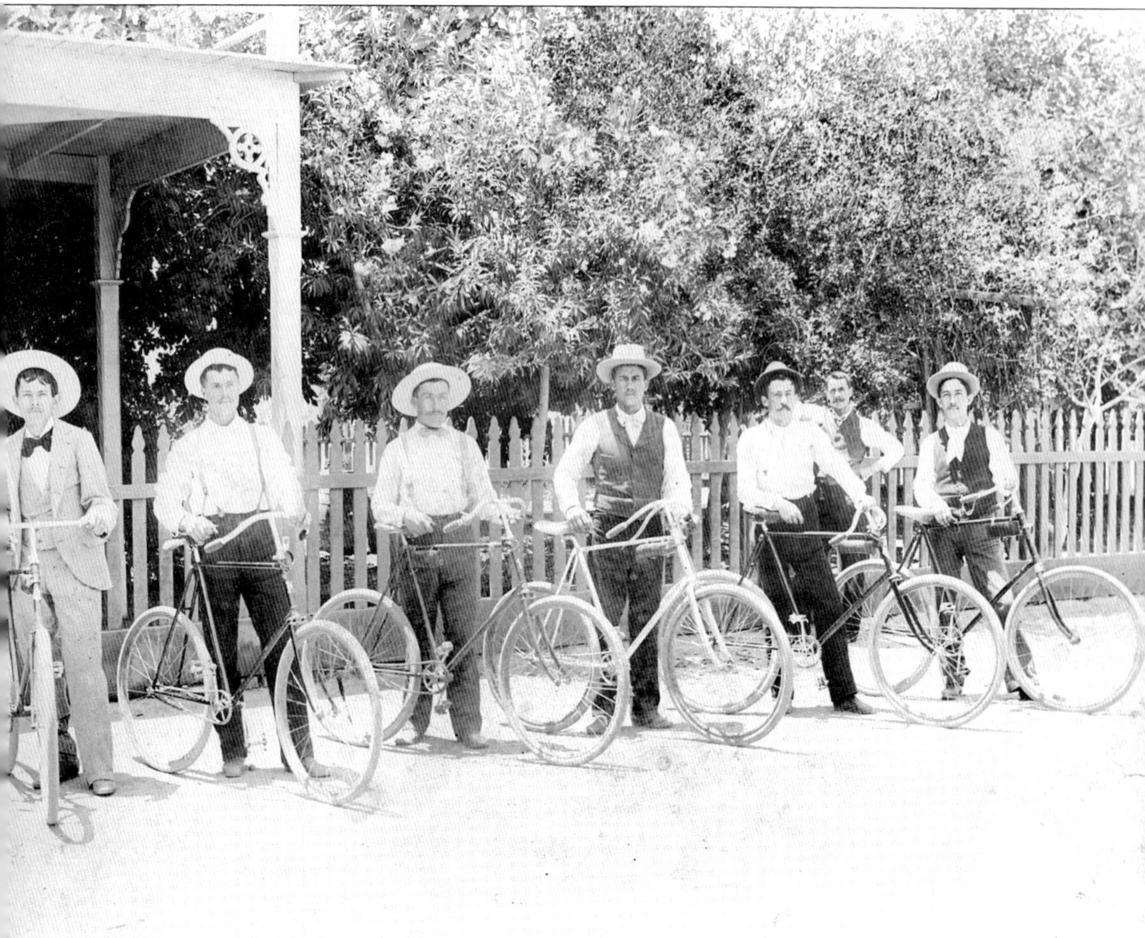

While most of the first generation of Yuma pioneers wouldn't be caught dead on such a contraption, riding bicycles became a popular pastime for their children. Here six young Yumans are dressed for a weekend ride in June 1896. This image was taken in front of Dorrington's house. The group posed for several photographs that day, two of which (one from the Pancrazis and one from the DeCorses) ended up in the historical society's collection. The riders, from left to right, are Charlie Reese, Albert Townsend, Henry DeCorse, Sixto Salazar, Angel Pancrazi, and Andrew Pancrazi.

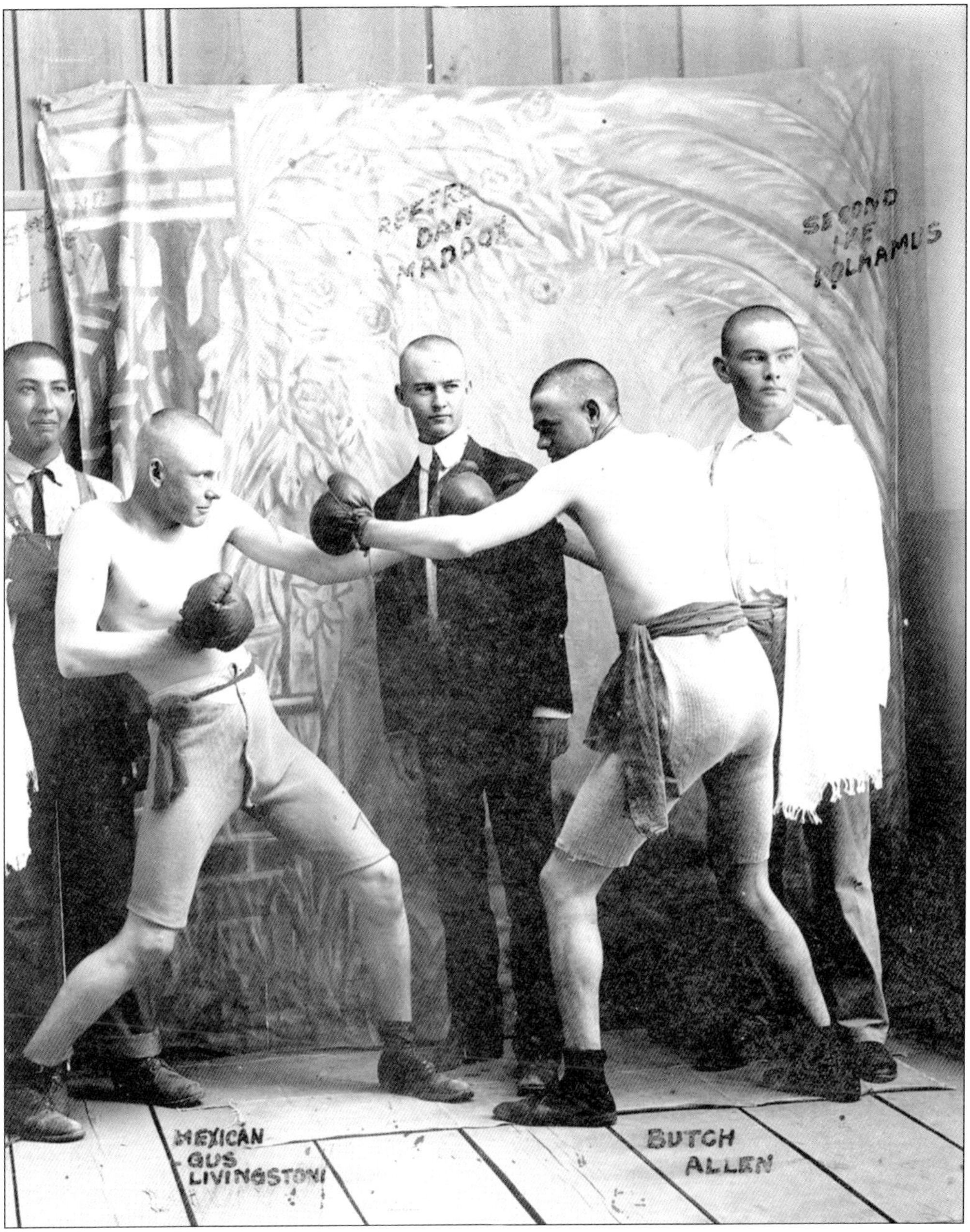

Yuma's youth around the turn of the century seemed up for most any form of sport or entertainment, including boxing. It's not clear if this fight actually went off or if it was just staged for the photograph. The two fighters are Gus Livingston (left) and Butch Allen. Helping the referee are one of the Levy boys (left) and Isaac Polhamus's son, Ike (far right). Dan Maddox, looking dashing in suit and tie, was the referee. Imagine Gus Livingston's father, or Ike Polhamus's father, engaging in such an event. Quite simply, the generation after the pioneer generation of Yuma was able to have a lot more fun than their parents. They grew up in what Brinckerhoff and Crowe called "the frosting years" of Yuma, the stage of a community's life when, as Crowe wrote, "A community worries not about life itself but about the quality of life available to all its citizens."

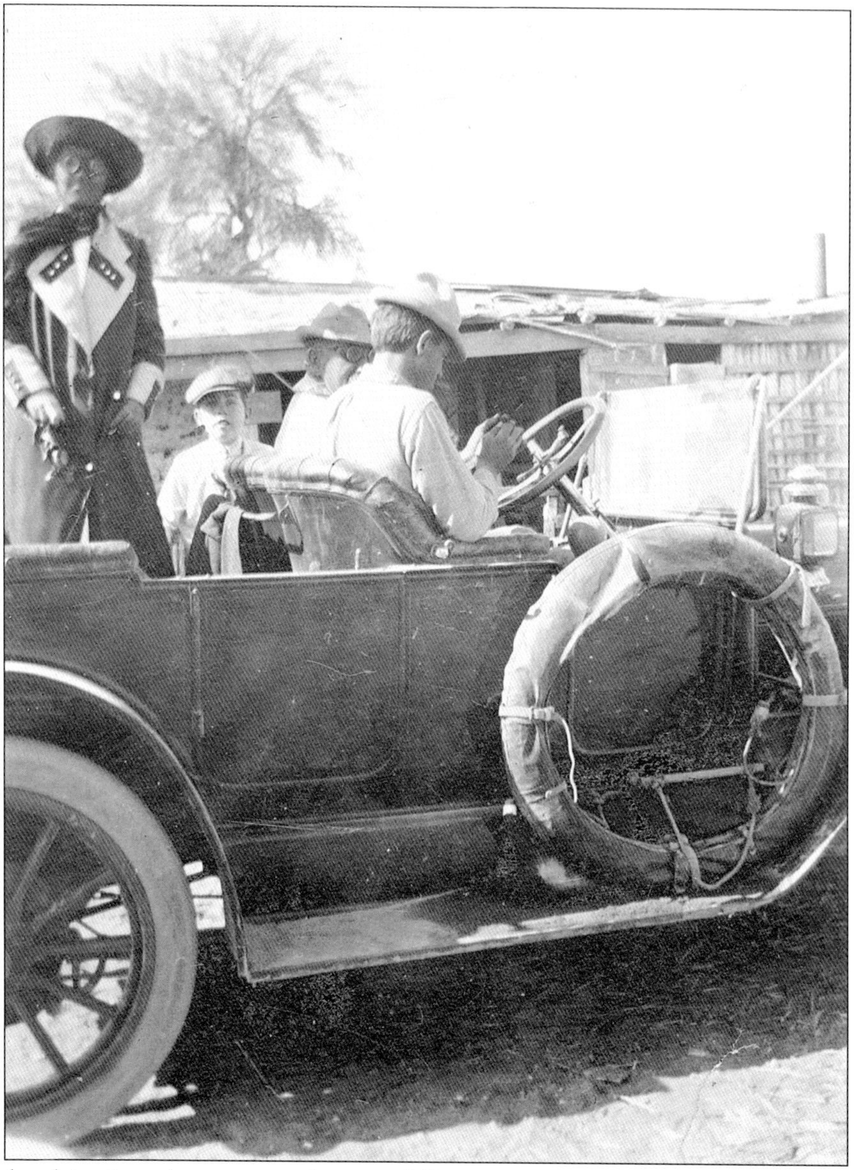

A Sunday drive into the countryside around Yuma was more of an adventure than in most American towns. To the west were the great sand dunes, to the east and north were some of the roughest mountains in the country, and to the south was Mexico. The roads in 1911, when this photograph was taken, were either sand, loose dirt, or broken granite. The travelers on this day look as they though they made a trip to one of the mining camps. Notice the extra tire tied to the side of the car. The back seat also likely is carrying gallons of water for both the engine and the riders. And just getting up and down hills outside town could be a huge and frightening challenge. Mary Post described the problem in Gordon's book:

> No attempt had been made to flatten the sand hills—the narrow road followed the contours of the hills, which were, in some instances, quite steep. So, in driving over the planks one could not drive too slowly down a grade, as fairly good momentum was required to make it up the next grade. . . . Successfully driving over that road was quite a feat.

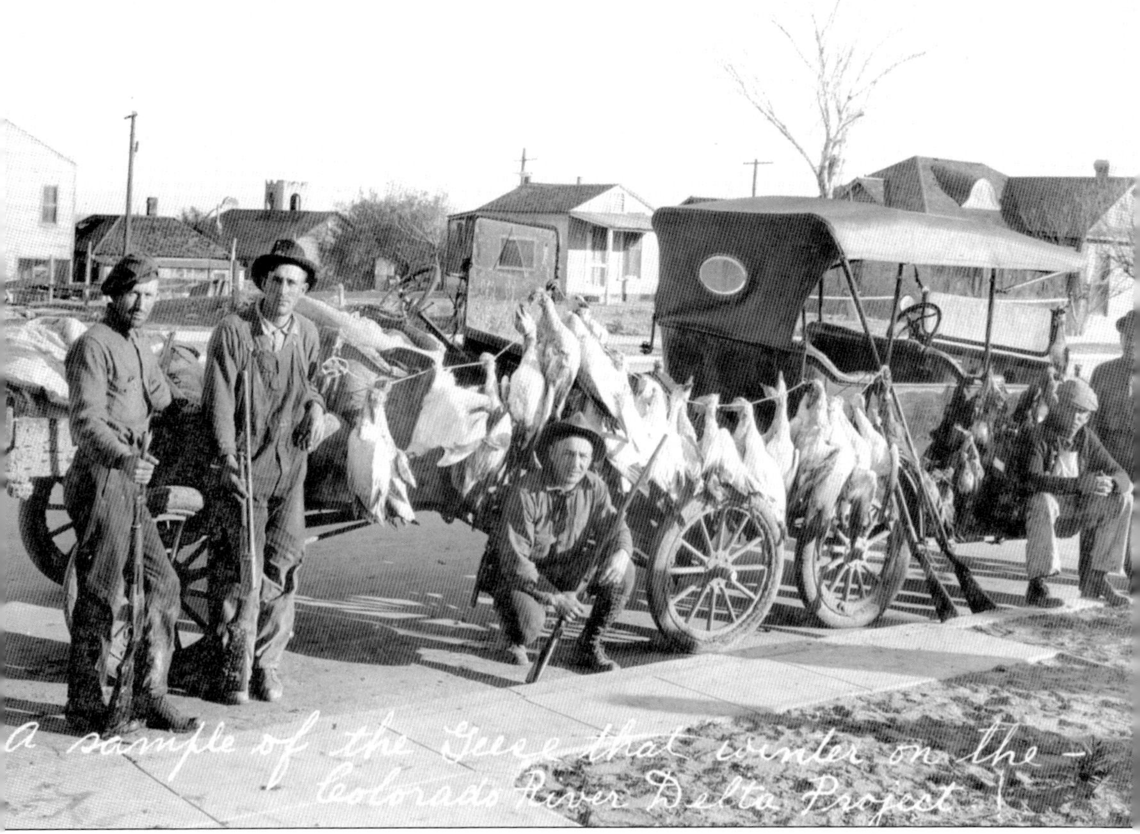

This image is a chamber of commerce dream that shows the bounty of geese found in the waters of the Colorado River Delta Project. Throughout Yuma County, hunters had myriad opportunities, something visitors don't expect from the desert. In the mountains, mule deer and desert bighorn sheep were plentiful. The biggest hunting opportunities came, though, with the creation of Laguna Dam and the series of lakes and canals that now cover the valley. Dove and quail became plentiful and irrigation brought water to tens of thousands of acres. Before all the irrigation canals, and before any Anglos, small-game hunting made up a large part of the Quechan diet. Indeed, all the Yuma tribes up and down the Colorado River used game and fish from the river valley to live.

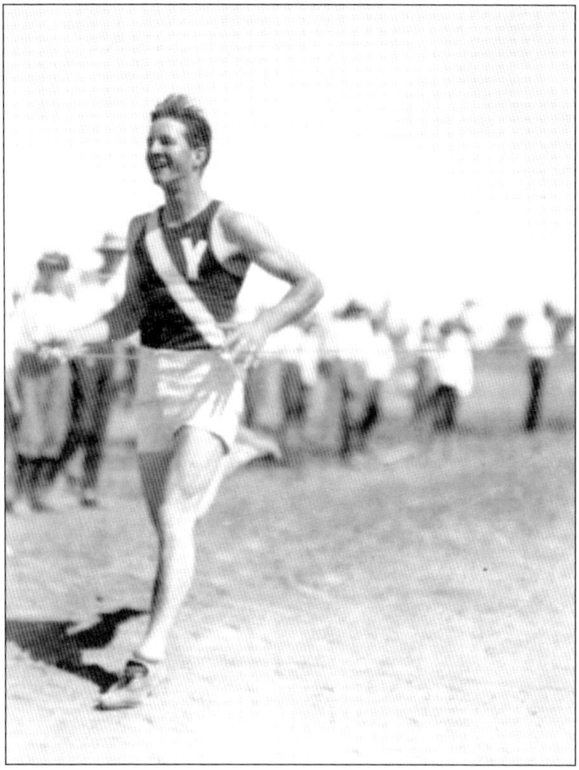

Carl Dean Haughtelin was a star athlete at Yuma High. Haughtelin's mother, Kathryn, was twice a delegate from Arizona to the Republican National Convention.

Reflecting the Mexican heritage of the community, Yuma held a celebration of *Los Pastores* (The Shepherds) at Christmas. Dolores Redondo Figueroa, seated in the center, was the director of the 1915 production. Also pictured, from left to right, are (first row) Rudolph Avila, Emilia Ghiotto, Ruby Ochoa (Hodges), Lenore Garcia (Giron), Charles Garcia, Mrs. Figueroa, Celia Valderas, Theresa Figueroa (Lorona), and Genobebo Ubert; (second row) Angelita Monroy, Flavia Avila, Adelina Valderas, Frances Martinez, unidentified, Joe Redondo, Maria Monroy, Angelina Redondo, Jesus Anaya, Sofia Lorona, Manuel Bernal, and Manuel Monroy.

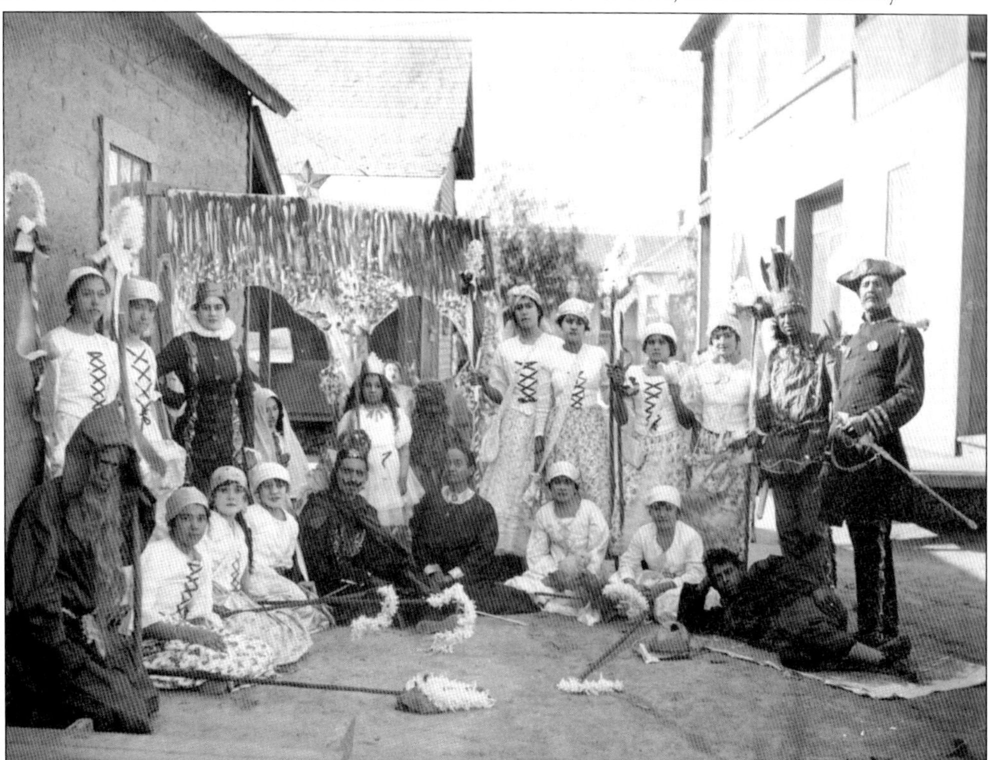

Eight

The New Yuma

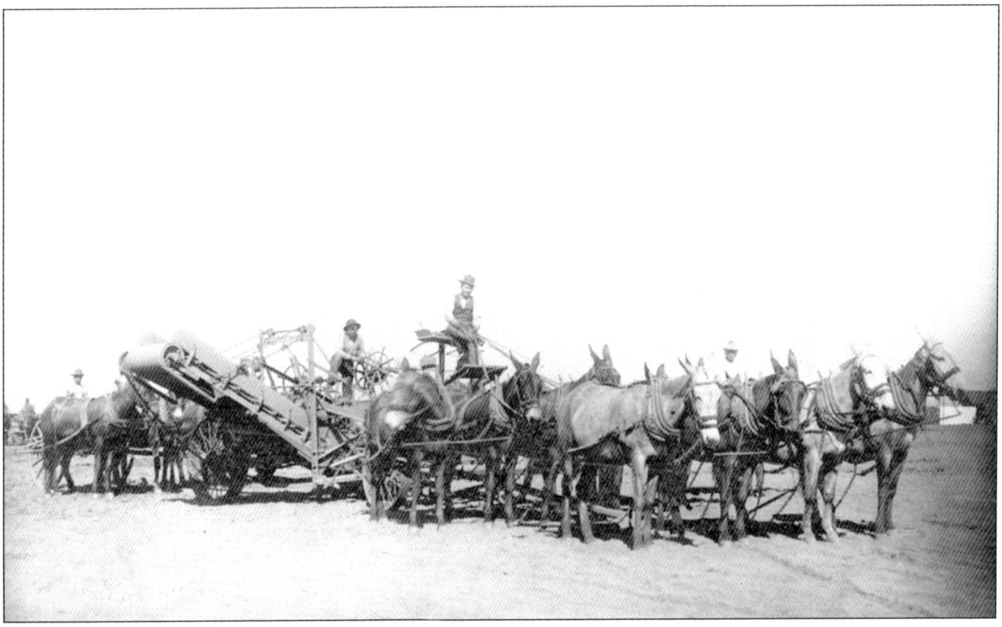

Even though the second generation of the town is at play, Yuma at the turn of the century was still an isolated and limited community. And as more roads and train tracks cut north and south through Arizona, and as automobiles improved, the city was no longer a critical supplier of the region. Luckily, and with a lot of pushing from the city's leaders, new opportunities began to arise in the 20th century. The Laguna Dam was likely a saving grace for the city. With the grand project, the once-feared water of the Colorado now could be directed anywhere it was needed. Farming became the lifeblood of the city. As the Colorado was being tamed and redirected, new machines came available to allow farming on much larger scale. The last yoke holding Yuma was the oppressive summer heat. But that would be dealt with in the future, some 40 years later, when the home air conditioner turned Yuma into a boomtown once again.

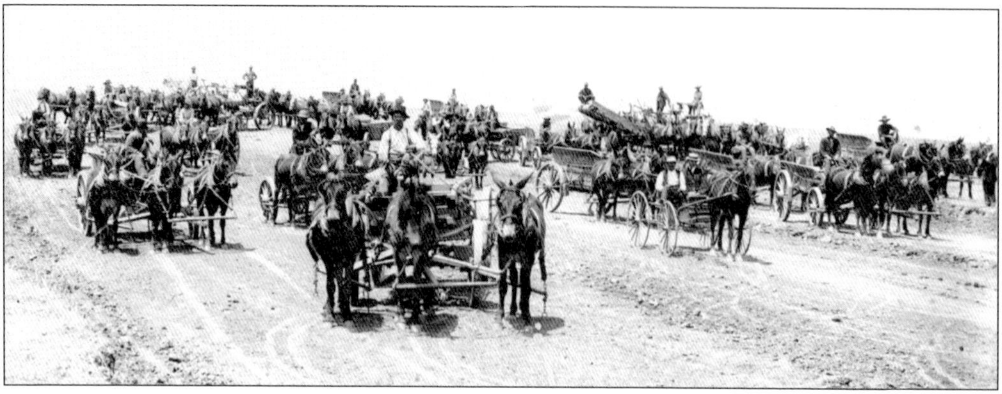

One of the largest private attempts at a canal off of the Colorado was the Ludy Canal, built by J. E. Ludy, which began construction in 1900. Ludy told the *Sentinel* his ditch would have "water for the millions." Such canals were giant undertakings, as this photograph depicts, bringing dozens of jobs to the community. And each time a canal was built, a small community called a dredging camp would follow the work. These towns were very much like the rowdy mining towns. Indeed, the employees were often out-of-work miners. Sometimes trouble ensued. This item from the *Arizona Republican* describes one such incident:

> The trouble occurred in 1902 at the dredger camp on the Ludy Canal, about five miles below the city, on Sunday morning. The exact particulars are hard to get, but it seems that a man named John Kelly fatally shot another man named Womack.
>
> Womack and his wife had separated and Mrs. Womack secured employment at the camp as a cook. Womack did not take kindly to this arrangement made by his wife and followed her to the camp during the absence of Mr. Ludy. He raised a disturbance with his wife and others took in hand the quarrel. Kelly interested himself to the extent of fatally shooting Womack and after the deed he went to Yuma and surrendered to the authorities.
>
> Kelly created a disturbance at the same camp less than a year ago and cleared out the camp with a shotgun. He was arrested and fined on that occasion. Both the dead man and his slayer are said to be quarrelsome.

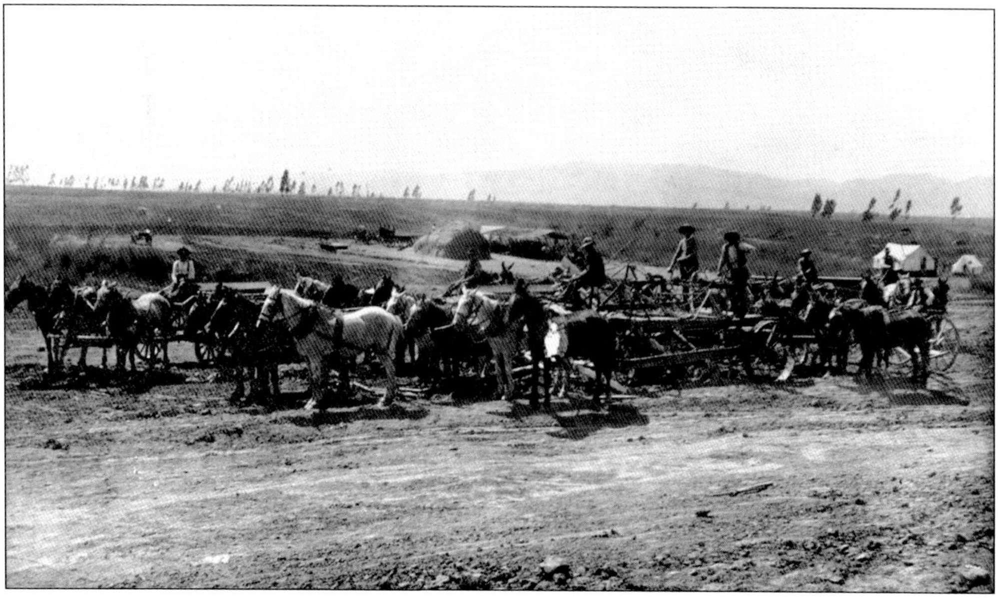

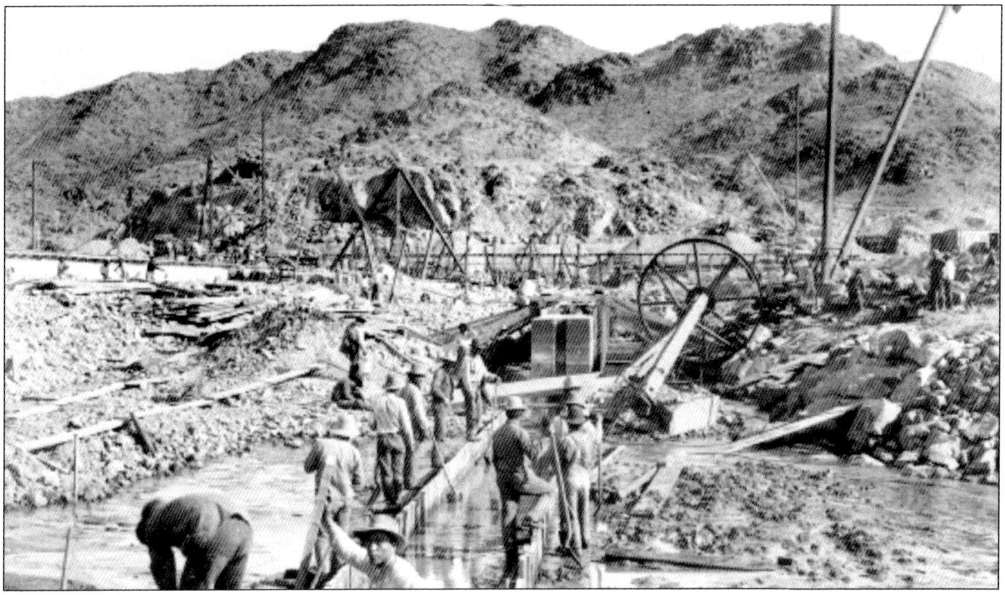

The Ludy Canal eventually became part of the Yuma Project of the U.S. Reclamation Service, which began with the construction of the Laguna Dam 13 miles upriver from Yuma. It was, even on a national scale, a massive undertaking. The dam was nearly a mile long and 200 feet wide. Just after the turn of the century, engineers and surveyors were sent to the river to find the best location for a dam. But it was as though the Colorado River, like a young bronco, wanted nothing to do with being tamed. In 1904, then several times in 1905, the river flooded, wiping out work on the river and threatening to destroy wide swaths of the Imperial Valley on the California side. Beyond flooding, the Colorado also brought with it millions of tons of silt, which quickly clogged up canals. The above image shows the driving of sheet piling for a foundation for the lower wall on the Arizona side of the project. This photograph was taken March 2, 1906. The below image shows the small-gauge track and train used to haul heavy equipment and materials to the dam site.

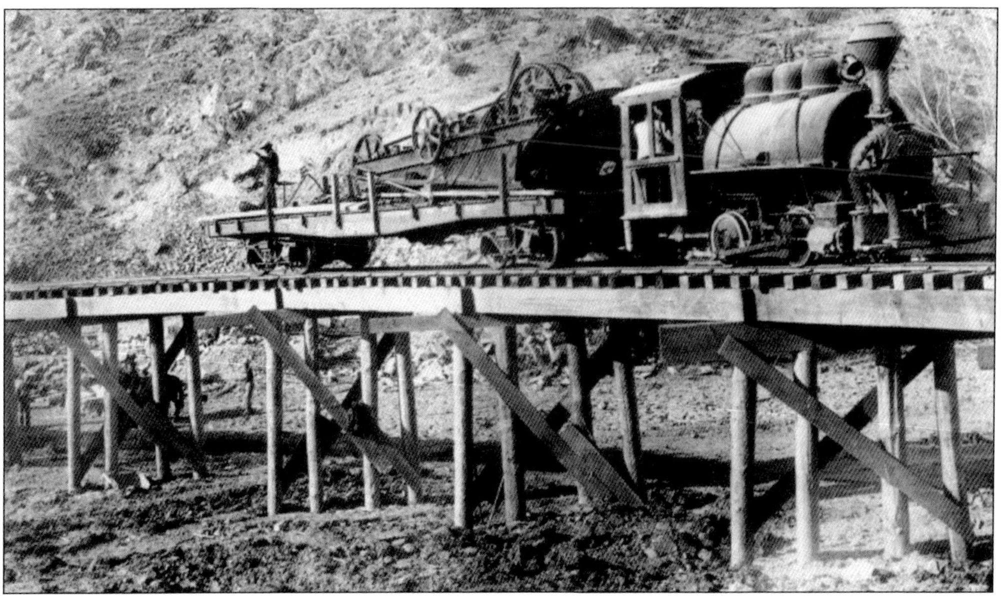

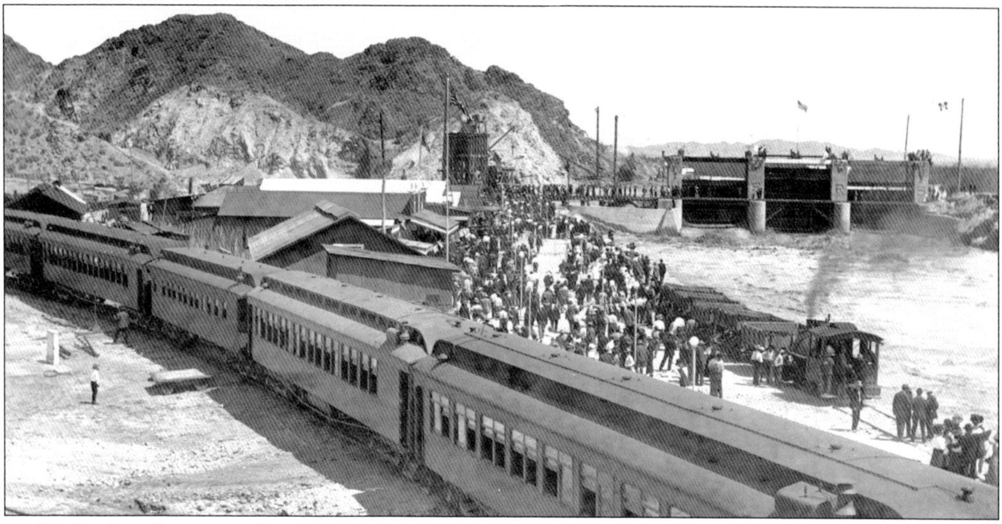

It's likely there has never been a time in Yuma's history so exciting as the months leading up to the completion of the Laguna Dam. It was a project that promised thousands of acres of rich farmland, hundreds of new jobs, and millions of dollars pumped into the economy. It was not surprising then that much of Yuma took the train up to the dam site for the celebration of its opening in 1909. It was not surprising either that much of the town turned out for the subsequent parade and a town barbeque boosters argued "could be the biggest ever in the West." Throughout the day, the reclamation service engineers were treated like movie stars. The acclaim was deserved. Consider this excerpt from a reclamation service report to the board of engineers:

> The problem before the engineers was to build a structure founded on the alluvial deposit of the valley that would control the river and at the same time divert water to canals at each end of the structure in such a manner that it would be possible to eliminate a good deal of the silt before the water was allowed to pass to the canals. Nothing of the kind has been built in the country. . . . This resulted in a design fashioned after that of the Okla Weir, across the Jumna, in India, and following the lines of another weir across the Nile below Cairo.

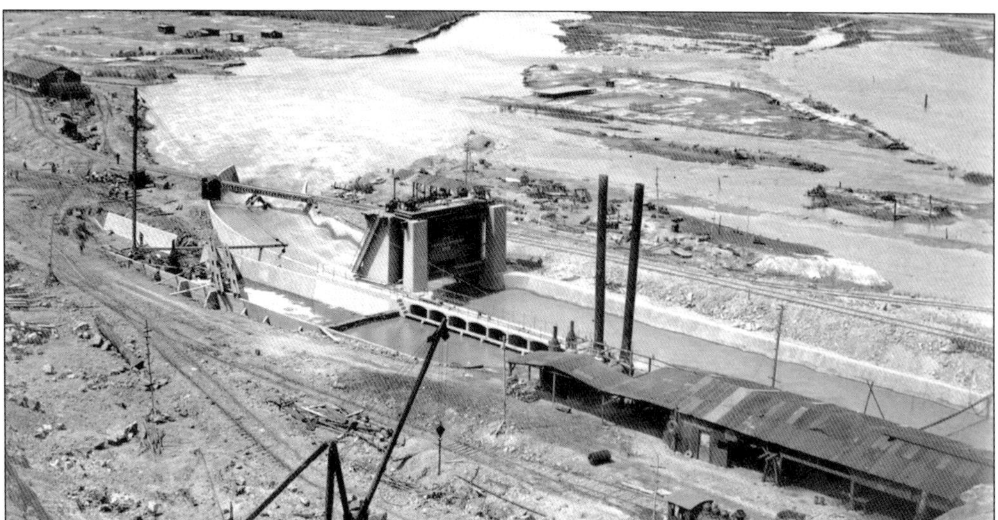

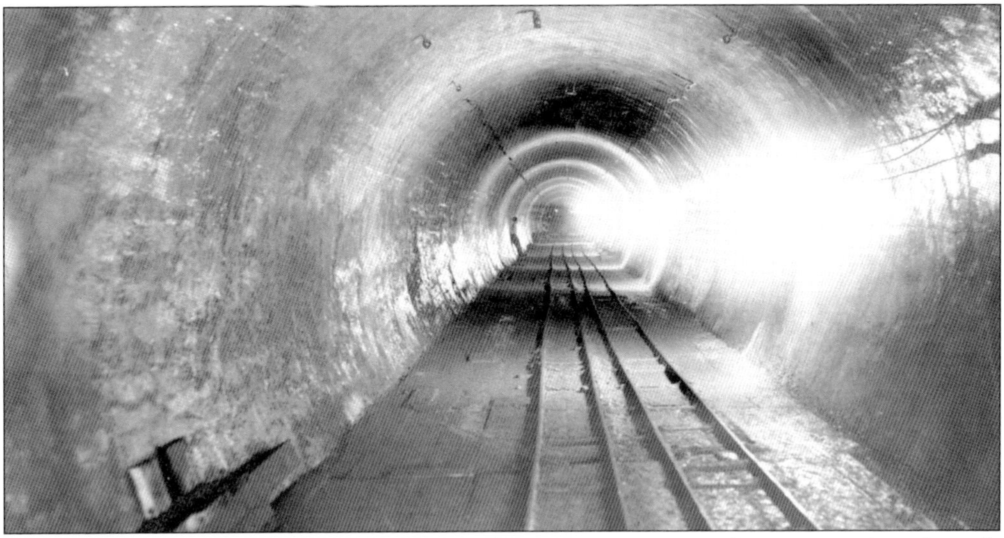

The second phase of the Yuma Project was another engineering marvel—a giant siphon through which water was drawn from the California side of the river and released into the Arizona side—that was a strange but necessary way to get an abundance of nearly silt-free water to the Arizona side. The siphon, pictured here, was 965 feet long and about 40 feet below the river. It was basically a small Chunnel. Prior to it being filled, residents were allowed into the tunnel for a tour. "For the first time in history human beings went from Yuma . . . to the California side of the Colorado River through a 900-foot tunnel 40 feet beneath the river bed," a reporter wrote. On June 28, 1912, Yumans watched as the first water flowed up through the siphon, which, with the Laguna Dam, cost a total of $7 million. "Miss Anna C. Egan," the *Sentinel* reported, "Superintendent of the Fort Yuma Indian School, pressed the button connecting the big motor at exactly 8:25 this morning," and the water rushed "madly into the big Siphon for the first time."

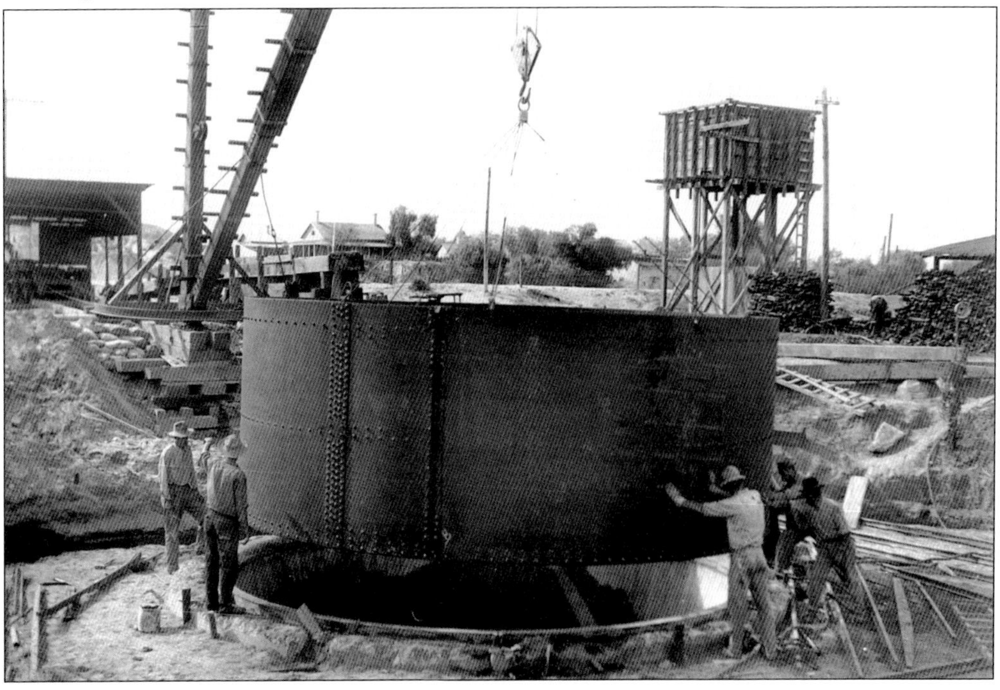

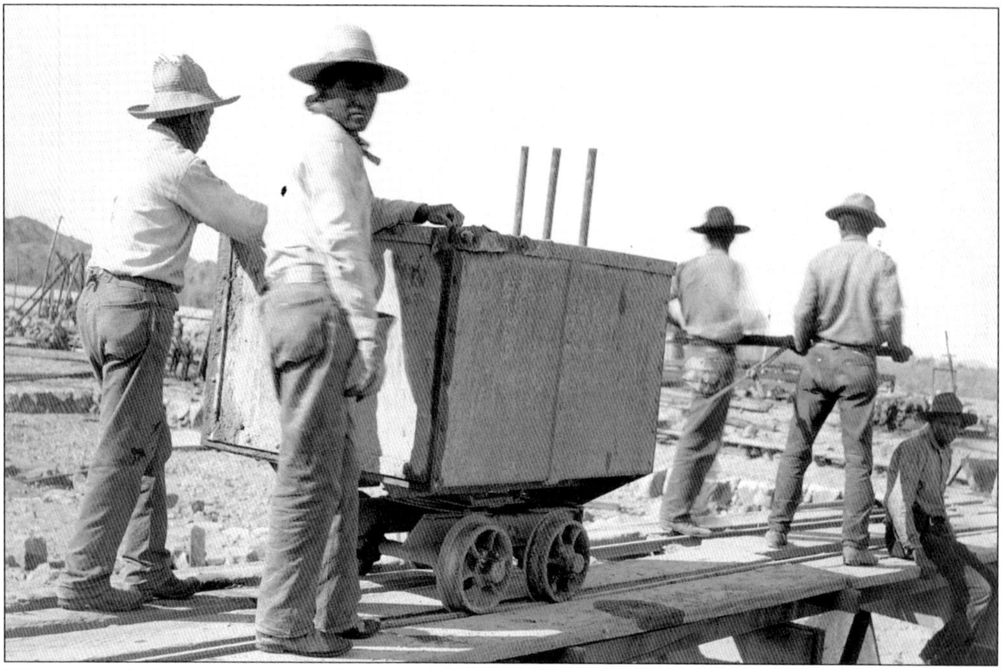

The *Sentinel* editor wrote the following at the completion of the Yuma Project:

> The greatest event in Yuma's history and one of the greatest achievements in mechanical engineering history was consummated at nine o'clock this morning when the water from Laguna Dam coursed its way into the open gate at the Yuma project siphon, down the shaft . . . under the river and out on the Arizona side where it will flow to the 100,000 acres of the richest land in the world, in the Yuma Valley.

It was the impending completion of the Yuma Project that lead the *Sentinel*'s editor and owner of 30 years to lay down his pen. His work was done, he wrote. He was now of a past era. Yuma's future was bright and in safe hands, and it was time to pass the reins. Ah, but even the reins had passed. It was now the age of the automobile.

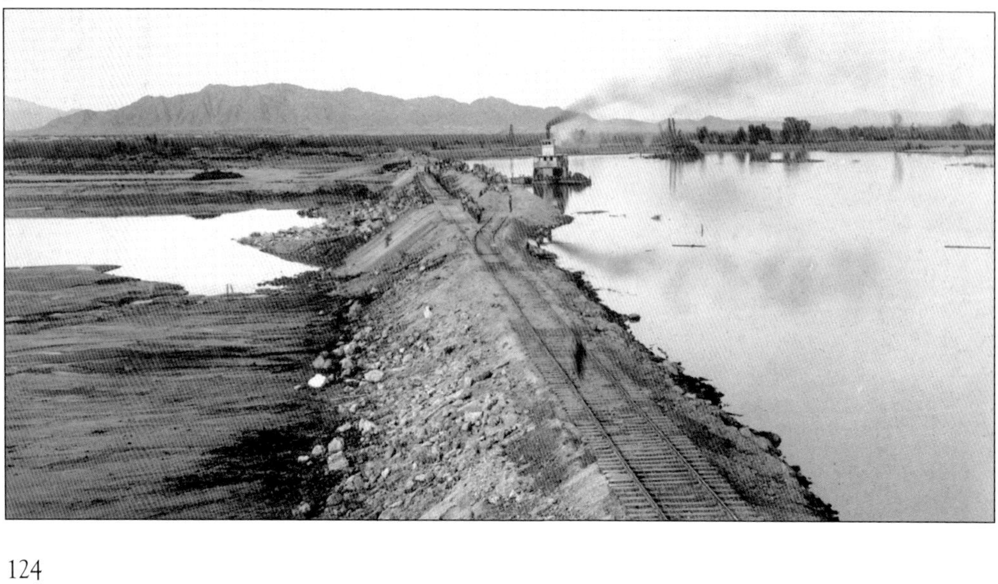

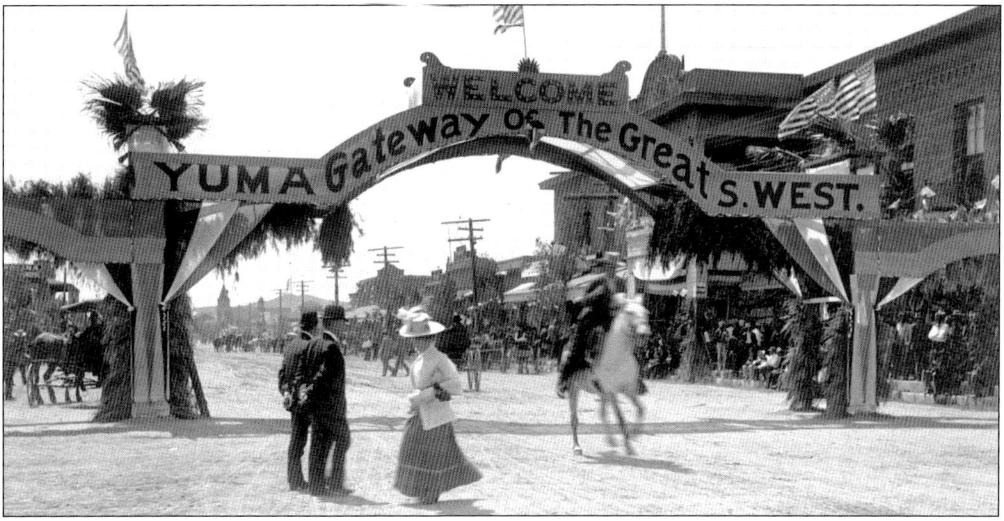

With the excitement surrounding the coming of the Laguna Dam and water to the Yuma Valley, the town celebrations became serious affairs and were as much advertisements for the burgeoning city as entertainment for residents. The most common theme for floats and banners was "The New Yuma" or, for the Laguna Dam celebration of 1909, "Yuma, Gateway to the Great S. West" (the sign makers, running out of room on the sign, abbreviated "South"). The excitement about the coming dam, and coming water, seemed to permeate all aspects of Yuma life. For example, members of the various women's clubs began galvanizing around progressive issues, arguing that this new great city should be a beacon of progressive thought in the West. They marched for women's voting rights and, under the flag of the Women's Christian Temperance Union (WCTU), marched for Prohibition. "Yuma boomed—or, at least, lived in the expectation of a booming—during those exciting years when the dam was under construction," Gordon wrote in Post's biography. A new school was built "without even one squabble," she wrote, echoing Post's memoirs. "During a burst of civic pride, a spacious new court house was built . . . just about as big as the State Capitol Building at Phoenix."

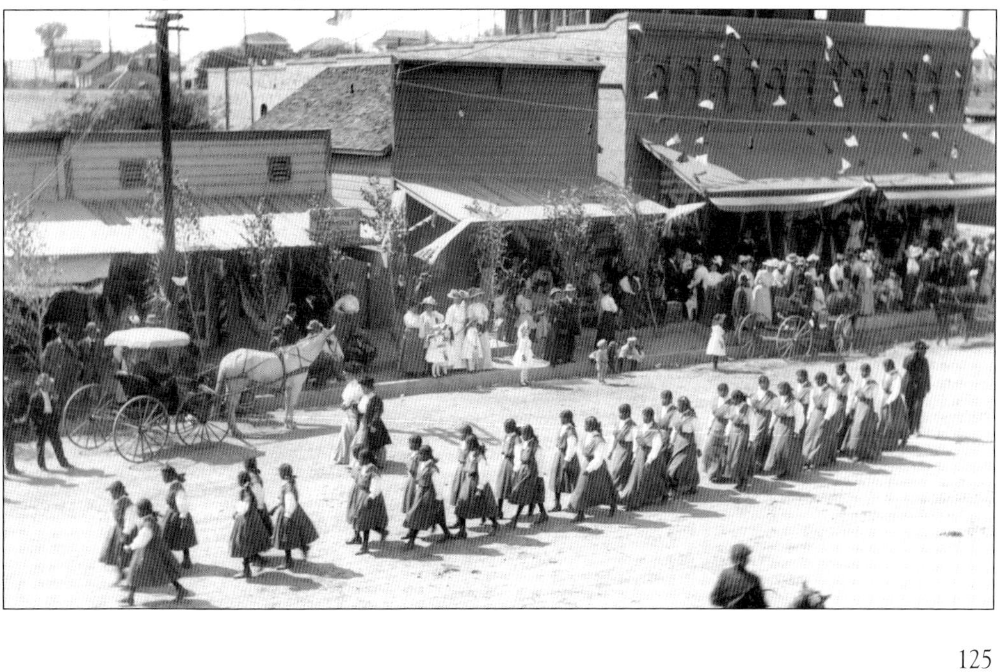

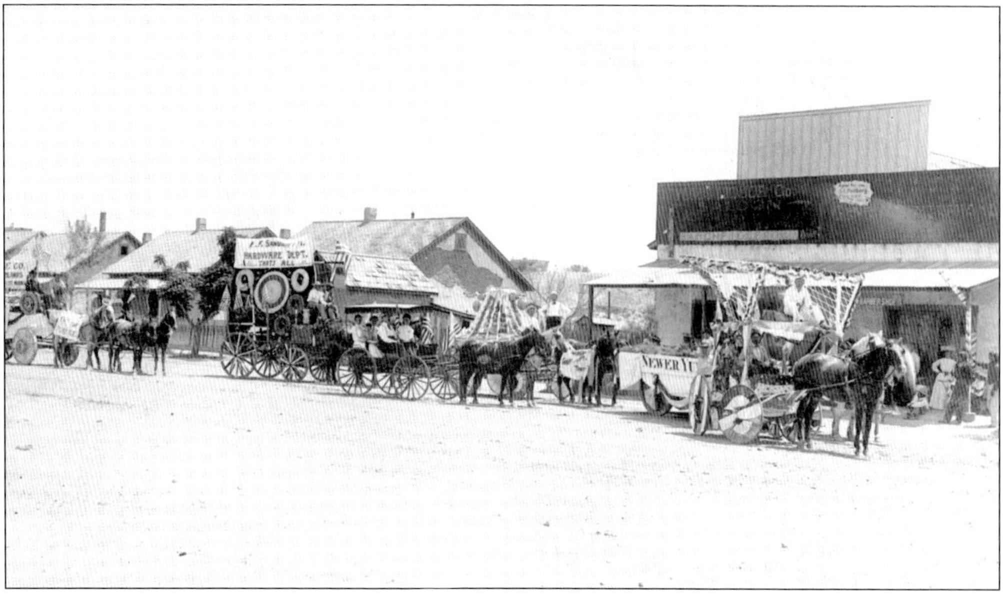

E. F. Sanguinetti loved parades and usually provided several float entries. In 1905, Sanguinetti's junior fire department marched with their hose cart, but, according to a sign on the hose cart, apparently was banned from the voting for best float because, one would guess, it didn't constitute a float. Following the fire boys was Sanguinetti's "Newer Yuma" float, pictured here, which was followed by a float advertising his hardware store. The float sponsored by the Yuma Ice Company is also visible. Note that everyone is wearing white shirts. It was not uncommon at the time to see a man, like the "Newer Yuma" float driver, dressed in all white in the style of Mark Twain.

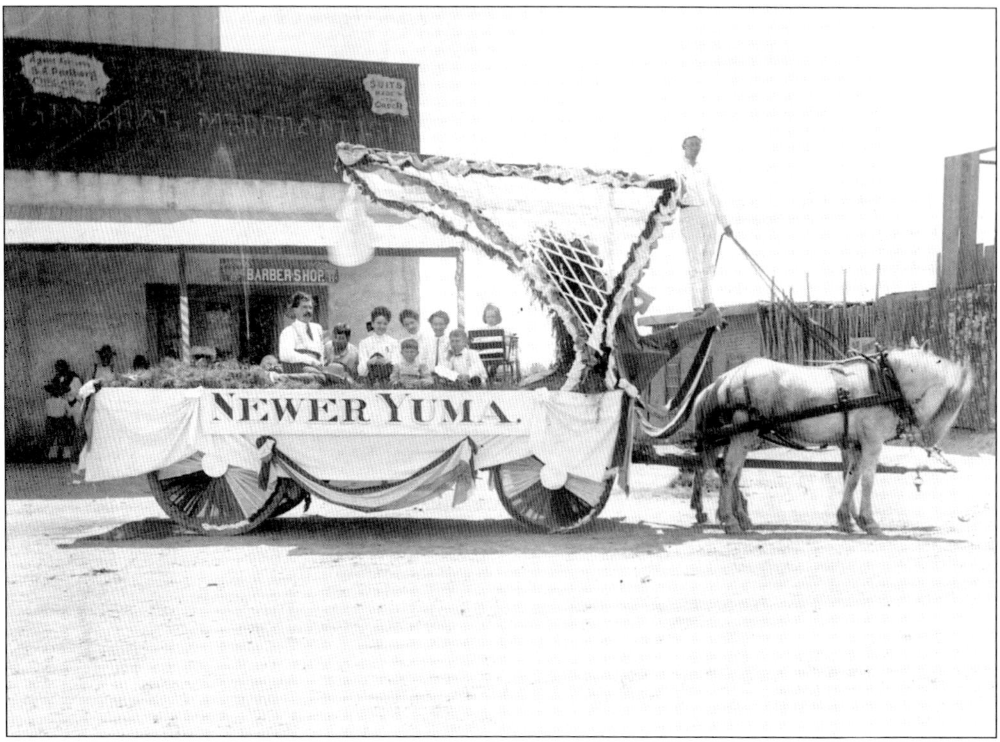

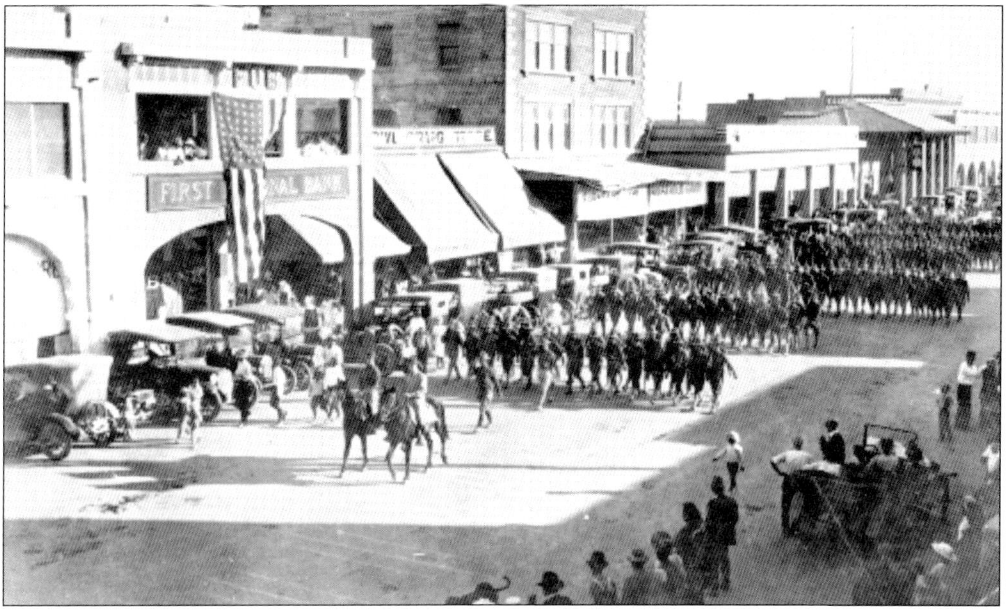

As water began flowing into the Yuma Valley from the Yuma Project siphon, the people of Yuma had little time to celebrate. Within a year, fear replaced joy as concerns about a potential war with Mexico or the chance that the United States could get drawn into a war in Europe grew. Two years later, Mexican revolutionary Pancho Villa, angry that the United States had not supported his push for the Mexican presidency, raided Columbus, New Mexico, which sparked the Punitive Expedition into Mexico by Gen. "Black Jack" Pershing. A year later, many of those same troops would be sent to Europe to fight in World War I.

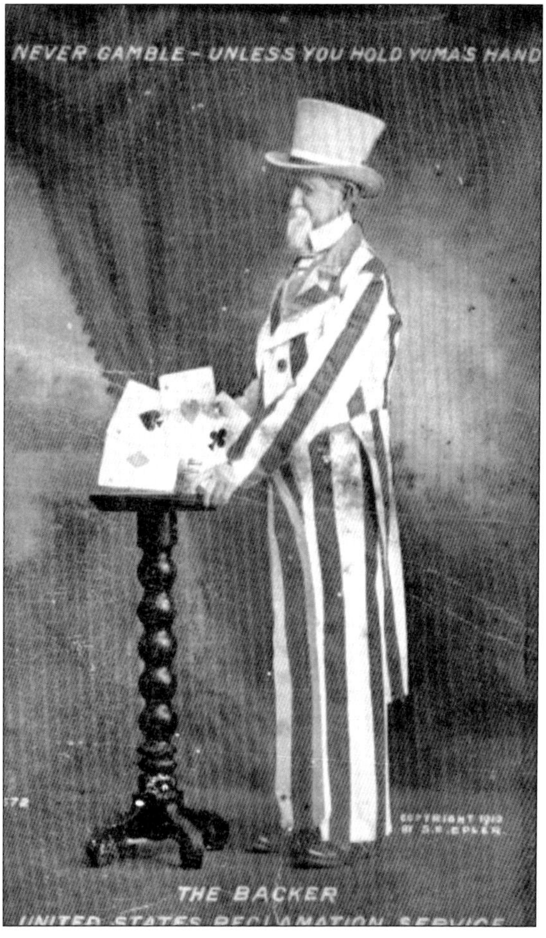

Still the civic pride of Yuma could not be squelched; it just took on a more patriotic tone.